PERFORMING BLACKNESS ON ENGLISH STAGES, 1500–1800

Performing Blackness on English Stages, 1500–1800 examines early modern English actors' impersonations of black Africans. Those black-face performances established dynamic theatrical conventions that were repeated from play to play, plot to plot, congealing over time and contributing to English audiences' construction of racial difference. Vaughan discusses non-canonical plays, grouping of scenes, and characters that highlight the most important conventions – appearance, linguistic tropes, speech patterns, plot situations, the use of asides and soliloquies, and other dramatic techniques – that shaped the ways black characters were "read" by white English audiences. In plays attended by thousands of English men and women from the sixteenth century to the end of the eighteenth, including *Titus Andronicus*, *Othello*, and *Oroonoko*, blackface was a polyphonic signifier that disseminated distorted and contradictory, yet compelling, images of black Africans during the period in which England became increasingly involved in the African slave trade.

VIRGINIA MASON VAUGHAN is Professor of English at Clark University in Worcester, Massachusetts, where she has served as Head of the English Department and Director of the Higgins School of Humanities. She has published three books on Shakespeare's *Othello*: the Garland annotated bibliography (with Margaret Lael Mikesell, 1990), an anthology, *Othello: New Perspectives* (with Kent Cartwright, 1991), and a monograph, *Othello: A Contextual History* (Cambridge, 1994). She also co-edited *Playing the Globe: Genre and Geography in English Renaissance Drama* with John Gillies (1998). With her husband, historian Alden T. Vaughan, she authored *Shakespeare's Caliban: A Cultural History* (Cambridge, 1992), and edited the Arden edition of *The Tempest* (Third Series, 1999).

PERFORMING BLACKNESS ON ENGLISH STAGES, 1500–1800

VIRGINIA MASON VAUGHAN

CAMBRIDGE
UNIVERSITY PRESS

CAMBRIDGE UNIVERSITY PRESS
Cambridge, New York, Melbourne, Madrid, Cape Town, Singapore, São Paulo, Delhi

Cambridge University Press
The Edinburgh Building, Cambridge CB2 8RU, UK

Published in the United States of America by Cambridge University Press, New York

www.cambridge.org
Information on this title: www.cambridge.org/9780521845847

First published 2005
Reprinted 2006
This digitally printed version 2008

A catalogue record for this publication is available from the British Library

ISBN 978-0-521-84584-7 hardback
ISBN 978-0-521-10226-1 paperback

For Alden and the kids,
the warp and woof of my life

Contents

Illustrations

Preface

Scholarship is not crafted, I tell my students, by faceless, nameless people: every work of literary criticism issues from individuals with histories that influence their work. It seems appropriate, then, to explain a little of my personal history to the prospective reader, for I am sure that it has helped to shape this book.

It is probably clear from the text that I write from the perspective of a white American female. I grew up in the 1960s in an aura of middle-class white privilege, and the biggest crises of my adolescence were occasioned by differences with my southern mother over a few superficial social contacts with students of color in my church youth group and in my high school. My early convictions about racial inequality were intense, but to this day I cannot be certain whether they emanated from a genuine sense of injustice, adolescent rebellion against parental authority, or both. Whatever their origin, the convictions remain, as do the problems of racism in the society in which I live and work.

My efforts to understand those problems lurk behind much of my published work. In the cultural history of Caliban I wrote with Alden T. Vaughan, as in my work on Shakespeare's *Othello* and several other essays I have written about early modern English culture, I have tried to understand more fully how our color-conscious world came into being and how white privilege became so deeply entrenched. Discrimination based on gender, language, class, or sexual preference is also unjust, but my experiences as an American have made me particularly aware of racial discrimination based largely on shades of skin pigmentation. The black–white color divide is the underlying context of this book.

An extended discussion of the origins of English racism is beyond the purview of this book. My emphasis instead is on performance, on what audiences saw when they attended stage plays that featured black Moors. This study is but one piece in the puzzle as to how early sixteenth-century inchoate notions about black Africans developed into rigid conceptions of racial difference and a global system of racial slavery by the late seventeenth century. The performances I describe here were a contributing factor to the formation of English racial attitudes, overlapping and colluding with a host of social and economic pressures that shaped the growth of England's slave economy. At the same time, the theatre was a crucial reflection of this process. It was open to a broad cross section of London's burgeoning population; its performances were attended by thousands of people, many of whom could not read or write; and those performances, for the most part, were reinforced through frequent repetition. On London's stages, blackness was "acted out" in ways that profoundly affected images of blacks in English culture. The performances of plays that have come down to us in theatrical scripts circulated in a visual medium quite different from other written texts such as sermons and pamphlets, but they were nevertheless extremely influential. If we want to understand the formation of racial attitudes in this period, the blackface performances that took place on London's stages are certainly an important window.

As my concluding chapter attests, I recognize that the dynamics of blackface performance remain highly controversial. Yet I believe that we must not be afraid to examine the theatrical impersonations that helped to shape English racial views and the ramifications of white actors wearing blackface. I hope all would agree that in our discussion of race there is room for men and women who seek the goal of equal opportunity and share a vision of a color-blind future to differ on their interpretation of the past.

It is customary to conclude a preface with the pronouncement that any mistakes in the book are the author's own, but in this instance, I would like to add that my views – the product of many years of reading and thinking about racial issues in early modern England and its European neighbors – are not set in stone. I offer them as a contribution to what I hope will be a continuing dialogue.

Unless otherwise noted, quotations from Shakespeare's plays are taken from *The Norton Shakespeare*, ed. Stephen Greenblatt, et al. (New York, 1997) and are cited by act, scene, and line numbers within the text. Quotations from the Bible are from the *Geneva Bible: A Facsimile of the 1560 Edition* (Madison: University of Wisconsin Press, 1969). I have retained the spelling as I have found it in my primary texts, although I do substitute "the" for the early modern thorn and make other minor adjustments for the reader's convenience.

Acknowledgments

No book is written in a vacuum, and one incurs many debts along the way. In 2001 I was the lucky recipient of a Mellon Fellowship to the Folger Shakespeare Library, which enabled me to start this project. Without that precious time to read and think, this book would never have been born. As always, I am deeply indebted to the Folger Library staff, particularly Gail Kern Paster, Georgianna Ziegler, Richard Kuhta, Barbara Mowat, Rachel Doggett, Betsy Walsh, and all of the Reading Room staff.

As the project progressed, my ideas were tested by perceptive and critical audiences who graciously listened to my preliminary findings and shared their responses. I owe special thanks to hosts Kathleen Lynch of the Folger Institute, Rachana Sachdev of Susquehanna University, James Hirsh of Georgia State University, and Ralph Alan Cohen of the Blackfriars Theatre in Staunton, Virginia, as well as to the Departmental Colloquium at Clark University, the Columbia University Shakespeare Seminar, and the 2003 Northeast British Studies Conference. In addition, my thinking has been shaped by many ideas gleaned from conversations over tea and coffee with friends at the Folger, at my academic home of Clark University, and, perhaps most importantly, over the dinner table with Alden Vaughan.

The biggest debt is to those who have actually read portions of the manuscript. Linda McJannet and Fern Johnson provided perceptive readings of the first three chapters; James Bulman and John Ford read an entire draft and provided valuable criticism. Alden Vaughan critiqued early and late versions, a labor of love for which I will always be grateful. Outside readers from Cambridge University Press were also helpful, as were suggestions from my editor, Sarah Stanton. I am sure the final product is infinitely better as a result, and I feel incredibly fortunate to have good friends (including a husband) who are careful readers and astute critics.

My work on this project was expedited in countless ways by the support I received from Clark University. The Reference Staff at Clark's Robert Hutchings Goddard Library have assisted with interlibrary loan requests with their usual combination of competence and good cheer. I am especially grateful to Andrea and Peter Klein, whose belief in Clark and its mission led to the endowment of the Klein Distinguished Professorship, which it was my privilege to hold from 2000 to 2004. Funds from this endowment enabled me to hire a wonderful graduate student, Natalie Mühlberger, as a research assistant; her attention to detail has saved me many embarrassments. My Department Chair, Professor SunHee Gertz, has been supportive of this project from its inception. I am also grateful to my colleague Gino DiIorio of the Theatre Arts Department, whose enthusiasm for Shakespeare-acted-out has been inspirational.

In the final stages of my work, I began the quest for appropriate illustrative material. Specific acknowledgments are included in the list of illustrations, but I would like to pay particular thanks to Luke Dennis of the Harvard Theatre Collection as well as to the Photography Department at the Folger Library.

The greatest debt is to Alden and the "kids," the family to whom this book is dedicated.

CHAPTER I

Preliminaries

I

Pierre Delacroix, the central character of Spike Lee's satirical film *Bamboo-zled*, wants to create a television show so offensive that he and his arrogant white boss will be fired. He develops a pilot for *Mantan: The New Millennium Minstrel Show*, expecting that audiences will riot when they see two African-American males blacked up as "coon" figures tap-dancing in a watermelon patch. To his surprise, audiences black and white love *Mantan*. Wearing blackface make-up suddenly becomes hip: the camera pans over a packed house of noisy blackfaced fans, gladly proclaiming themselves to be "niggers." As Pierre's father, the comedian Junebug, opines, "Everybody white want to be black. Everybody want to be black; they all act, sound black."[1]

Lee's racial satire shows white fantasies scripted onto black bodies. Delacroix's collection of "Negrobilia"[2] – old money boxes and other artifacts employing images from the minstrel-show tradition – points to a long history of the material appropriation of blackface images. Shakespearean scholars are certainly aware that the role of Othello was originally performed by a white actor in black make-up, even though the general public is now used to actors of African heritage in the title role. When *Holiday Inn* is shown on television, new generations are exposed to outdated conventions as they watch Bing Crosby don blackface for the Lincoln's birthday musical number. Reruns of *The Al Jolson Story* are also reminders that blackface was once a staple of American entertainment. When blackface is mentioned, however, the form that readily comes to most people's minds is the nineteenth-century minstrel show, and several recent studies of this genre

---

[1] Spike Lee, Director, *Bamboozled*, USA, New Line Productions, 2000.
[2] Hugh Quarshie coined this term to describe his own collection in *Second Thoughts about Othello*, Occasional Paper no. 7 (Chipping Camden: International Shakespeare Association, 1999), p. 3.

explain how this obsolete form of entertainment reflected the complicated social and political conditions of the period.[3]

Nineteenth-century minstrel shows did not invent blackface impersonation. Nor did Shakespeare. The performance practice of "blacking up" thrived in religious pageants of the middle ages as a simple way of discriminating evil from good. Cycle and morality plays set up oppositions between black and white, damnation and salvation, evil and good. Until the latter half of the sixteenth century when the cycle plays were repressed, generations of Englishmen and women enjoyed the yearly ritual of watching good angels pitted against bad angels at the feast of Corpus Christi and other festivals. The sixteenth century's shift to modernity was marked by a transition, however, from the religious identifications of the middle ages to a "racially defined discourse of human identity and personhood,"[4] and that shift was reflected in blackface performances on the English stage. Take Shakespeare's Aaron. When the blackfaced Moor of *Titus Andronicus* gleefully proclaims, "Aaron will have his soul black like his face,"[5] he taps into a premodern religious sign system that identified the bearer as a damned soul, capable of all manner of deviltry. But Aaron's statement also evokes geographical and physical resonances that were beginning to racialize the older religious signification of blackness; as a black Moor among the whitefaced Goths who attack Rome, Aaron suggests a range of what Keir Elam terms "secondary meanings" that relate blackness "to the social, moral and ideological values operative in the community of which performers and spectators are part."[6] Blackface had become more than a simple analogy – blackface equals damnation – and taken on multiple meanings, participating in several readily recognized codes at once. By the time Shakespeare wrote *Titus Andronicus*, blackface functioned as a polyphonic signifier that reflected changing social contexts and helped to create expectations and attitudes about black people.

In the chapters that follow, I present some snapshots of plays, groupings of scenes and characters from early modern English dramas, that highlight the most important theatrical conventions – appearance, linguistic

---

[3] See, for example, Eric Lott, *Love and Theft: Blackface Minstrelsy and the American Working Class* (New York: Oxford University Press, 1993); Susan Gubar, *Racechanges: White Skin, Black Face in American Culture* (Oxford and New York: Oxford University Press, 1997); and William J. Mahar, *Behind the Cork Mask: Early Blackface Minstrelsy and Antebellum American Popular Culture* (Urbana: University of Illinois Press, 1999).

[4] David Theo Goldberg, *Racist Culture: Philosophy and the Politics of Meaning* (Oxford: Blackwell, 1993), p. 24.

[5] Quoted from *Titus Andronicus*, ed. Jonathan Bate, Third Arden Series (London: Routledge, 1995), 3.1.206.

[6] Keir Elam, *The Semiotics of Theatre and Drama* (London: Routledge, 1980), p. 10.

tropes, speech patterns, plot situations, the use of asides and soliloquies, and other types of dramatic signification – which shaped the ways black characters were "read" by white audiences.[7] Many of these conventions were repeated from play to play, often with modifications that stretched or inverted audience expectations. Thus blackface – and the theatrical patterns associated with it – accrued a readily recognizable set of meanings that repeated, expanded, and modified over time. While theatrical performance cannot be equated with the everyday performativity that, as Judith Butler argues, helps to construct our conceptions of race and gender, it shares performativity's "repeated stylization of the body, a set of repeated acts within a highly rigid regulatory frame that congeal over time to produce the appearance of substance, of a natural sort of being."[8] The bodies of others, as David Theo Goldberg notes, are "unproblematically observable, confronted and engaged." And the body is "central to ordinary experience and offers a unique paradigm: It is a symbol of a 'bounded system,' a system the boundaries of which are formed by skin at once porous but perceived as inviolable and impenetrable."[9] If Goldberg's analysis is correct, the actor's blackened skin is a particularly powerful signifier of otherness to English audiences, even though its temporary and performative qualities undermine its seeming inviolable nature. Its recurrence on stage was, as

---

[7] Several highly regarded studies have provided ample inventories of the black characters who appeared in dramas from the sixteenth and seventeenth centuries, but their focus is not on performance. Eldred D. Jones's *Othello's Countrymen: The African in English Renaissance Drama* (London: Oxford University Press, 1965) laid the ground-work for studies of the drama's representation of black characters. While anyone working in this area today is deeply indebted to him, his mission, characteristic of the turbulent 1960s, was to prove that there was an awareness of Africa in early modern England, that Africa indeed mattered. Elliot H. Tokson's *The Popular Image of the Black Man in English Drama, 1550–1688* (Boston: G. K. Hall, 1982) cast a wide net over the traditional dramatic canon and showed the negative stereotypes that shaped its impersonations of black characters. But in the process he collapsed chronology, grouping early and late plays together, looking for character types that would recur for centuries. Anthony Gerard Barthelemy's *Black Face, Maligned Race: The Representation of Blacks in English Drama from Shakespeare to Southerne* (Baton Rouge: Louisiana State University Press, 1987) followed five years later, but it, too, flattened the landscape without registering the immense social, economic, and political changes between England's first contacts with Africa (1550s–1580s) and a century later, when many English men owned black slaves and participated in a colonial plantation economy.

[8] In her Preface to the second edition of *Gender Trouble: Feminism and the Subversion of Identity* (New York: Routledge, 1999), Butler warns that race and gender "ought not to be treated as simple analogies" (p. xvi); however, in *Bodies That Matter: On the Discursive Limits of "Sex"* (New York: Routledge, 1993) she shows how heterosexuality and race are mutually constituted, a concept especially relevant to representations of "lascivious Moors" that will be discussed below. Butler's discussion of "performativity" cannot be universally applied to theatrical performance, but her analysis of the ways in which reiteration acts to congeal layers of signification is certainly apropos. Quotation from *Gender Trouble*, pp. 43–44.

[9] Goldberg, *Racist Culture*, p. 54.

Butler contends, "at once a reenactment and a reexperiencing of a set of meanings already socially established."[10]

In the theatre, the repetition of a trope or a gesture or a conventional plot comforts the audience by presenting what is familiar. Moors were expected, for example, to be cruel and lascivious, and in plays of the 1590s new black-faced figures might push those stereotypes a bit further than their homiletic forebears but they might also contradict or complicate audience expectations in new ways. Theatrical performance is by definition a masquerade, which by its very nature negates essentialist notions of reality. The white actor in blackface may speak and act in ways that reinforce stereotypes about black people, but because he is not the thing he pretends to be and the audience knows it, his gestures and attitudes suggest that his identity is adopted, not inherited.[11]

The performer's facial expressions, hand movements, gait, and other forms of body language are particularly expressive. "The moving actor's body," notes Curdella Forbes, can "negotiate relations among multiple levels of consciousness and experience." The actor feeds upon the audience's responses, creating "kinetic energy" in the playing space.[12] Such dynamics are difficult, if not impossible, to recapture for early modern performances for which we have only a script as a record of performance. In the performances under discussion here, however, it is clear that blackface coated the performer's most expressive non-verbal signifier, his face. By reading the scripts that have come down to us with the dynamics of performance in mind, we can tease out some insights as to what the audience might have seen when they looked at a black Moor and how they might have interpreted that experience.

The language of blackness, too, was multivalent. Many blackfaced characters are referred to as "Moors," a slippery term at best.[13] Although in some texts early modern writers distinguished between "tawny" Moors of

---

[10] Butler, *Gender Trouble*, p. 178.

[11] See Butler, *Bodies That Matter*, pp. 187–222. In work that is complementary to mine, Ian Smith discusses the audience's double consciousness that the actor is externally black but internally white in "White Skin, Black Masks: Racial Cross-Dressing on the Early Modern Stage," *Renaissance Drama*, n.s. 32 (2003), 33–67.

[12] Curdella Forbes, "Shakespeare, Other Shakespeares and West Indian Popular Culture: A Reading of the Eroticized Errantry and Rebellion in *Troilus and Cressida*," *Small Axe* 9 (2001), 44–69; quote from 51–52.

[13] See Jack D'Amico, *The Moor in English Renaissance Drama* (Tampa: University of South Florida Press, 1991) for a survey of characters depicted as "Moors" and the use of Moroccan settings in early modern plays. D'Amico's approach is complementary to mine, but he is primarily concerned with the depiction of peoples from northern Africa regardless of pigmentation, whereas I am concerned with European impersonations of blackness.

northern Africa and "blackamoors" from the sub-Saharan region, the two were often conflated in the popular mind. As the *Oxford English Dictionary* notes, well into the seventeenth century, "the Moors were commonly supposed to be mostly black or very swarthy." My focus is the dynamics of performance, and consequently my criterion for discussing characters and plots is not geographical, but rather the cues in the text that indicate that the actor blackened his face in order to perform a particular role.[14] For the most part, the Moors discussed here would have been considered "blackamoors" in the early modern period, as opposed to the tawny Moors of northern Africa. And unlike previous surveys of the black characters in early modern English drama, this book will not discuss *every* blackfaced character. My emphasis is on patterns – character types, plot situations, tropes, and other performative tactics – that are repeated from play to play.[15]

This examination of early blackface performances is intrinsically interesting to theatre historians, but it may also make a contribution to what is now termed "whiteness studies," the examination of the ways in which English men and women in the early modern period came to think of themselves as constituting a "white" norm in opposition to people of darker pigmentation. In *Playing in the Dark*, Toni Morrison asked critics of American literature to reexamine how the black "Africanist" figures in canonical texts such as *Huckleberry Finn* were imagined. "What are the signs, the codes, the literary strategies designed to accommodate this encounter? What does the inclusion of Africans do to and for the work?" Morrison asked us to recognize that "The fabrication of an Africanist persona is reflexive; an extraordinary meditation on the self; a powerful exploration of the fears and desires that reside in the writerly conscious."[16]

The figures discussed in this book are indeed Africanist personae,[17] whose presence shadows and shapes the audience's responses to characters white and black as well as their own sense of identification. When all is said and done, the black characters that populated early modern theatres tell us little about actual black Africans; they are the projections of imaginations that capitalize on the assumptions, fantasies, fears, and anxieties of England's

---

[14] In his study of blackfaced characters, Anthony Gerard Barthelemy maintained a geographical distinction between north African Moors and sub-Saharan Africans by devoting one of his chapters to "white moors." See *Black Face, Maligned Race*, pp. 182–99.

[15] Tokson lists early modern English plays that feature black characters and black characters by name in the Appendices to *The Popular Image*. See pp. 139–41.

[16] Toni Morrison, *Playing in the Dark* (New York: Vintage Books, 1993), pp. 16 and 17.

[17] See also Arthur L. Little Jr., *Shakespeare Jungle Fever: National-Imperial Re-Visions of Race, Rape, and Sacrifice* (Stanford: Stanford University Press, 2000), pp. 99 and 101, for a discussion of how the performance of black personae helps to invent whiteness.

pale-complexioned audiences. An English proverb dating from the early fifteenth century teaches that "Black best sets forth white,"[18] a sentiment reiterated by Edmund Spenser in *The Faerie Queene*:

> But neuer let th'ensample of the bad
> Offend the good: for good by paragone
> Of euill, may more notably be rad,
> As white seemes fayrer, macht with blacke attone.
>
> (III.ix.2)[19]

Blackfaced characters in early modern dramas are often used in just this way, to make whiteness visible so that it can be "read" and in the process to make it seem fairer by contrast.[20]

It is striking how many black characters in these plays call attention to their own complexions, introducing metadramatic elements into their performance. Often they reiterate the proverbial expression that "it is impossible to wash an Ethiop (or blackamoor) white," a saying roughly adopted from Jeremiah 13:23, which in the Geneva Bible reads, "Can the black More change his skin? Or the leopard his spottes?"[21] Geoffrey Whitney's *A Choice of Emblems* depicts two washerwomen scrubbing down a naked black man, accompanied by this motto:

> Leave of with paine, the blackamore to skowre,
> With washinge ofte, and wipinge more then due:
> For thou shalt finde, that Nature is of powre,
> Do what thou canste, to keepe his former hue.[22]

In popular parlance "washing the Ethiop white" could refer to any impossibility or "labor in vain." When stage blackamoors recall this expression, they reference a well-established stereotype about the indelibility of black pigmentation. Ironically, even as they cite the proverb, they undercut it because they are white actors known to the audience. Thus, even though the audience may be caught up in the play's theatrical illusion, the repetition of this proverb creates a fissure in the mimesis. Like Cleopatra's inside joke

---

[18] Morris Palmer Tilley, *A Dictionary of the Proverbs in England in the Sixteenth and Seventeenth Centuries* (Ann Arbor: University of Michigan Press, 1951), B 435, p. 53.

[19] Edmund Spenser, *The Faerie Queene*, ed. A. C. Hamilton (London: Longman, 1977), p. 383.

[20] For a fascinating account of the ways in which the tropes of "fairness" and "darkness" used in early modern love poetry were imbricated with racial resonances, see Kim F. Hall, *Things of Darkness: Economies of Race and Gender in Early Modern England* (Ithaca: Cornell University Press, 1995).

[21] Tilley, *Dictionary*, E 186, p. 190. The Geneva Bible uses the phrase "The blacke Moore" as a page heading above this verse.

[22] Geoffrey Whitney, *A Choice of Emblems* (Leiden, 1586). See also Karen Newman, "'And Wash the Ethiop White': Femininity and the Monstrous in *Othello*," in *Shakespeare Re-Produced: The Text in History and Ideology*, ed. Jean E. Howard and Marion F. O'Connor (New York: Methuen, 1987), pp. 141–62.

LEAVE of with paine, the blackamore to ſkowre,
With waſhinge ofte, and wipinge more then due:
For thou ſhalt finde, that Nature is of powre,
Doe what thou canſte, to keepe his former hue:
Thoughe with a forke, wee Nature thruſte awaie,
Shee turnes againe, if wee withdrawe our hande:
And thoughe, wee ofte to conquer her aſſaie,
Yet all in vaine, ſhee turnes if ſtill wee ſtande:

Eraſmus ex Luciano.
Abluis Æthiopem fru-
ſtrà: quin deſinis arti?
Haud vnquà efficies
nox ſit vt atra, dies.
Horat. 1. Epiſt. 10.
Naturam expellas fur-
ca tamen vſque re-
ſurret.

1 This image from Geoffrey Whitney's *A Choice of Emblems* (Leiden, 1580) illustrates
the proverb, "It is impossible to wash the Aethiop white."

about the actor "boying" her greatness, repeated references to the washing trope constitute a metatheatrical "wink, wink, nudge, nudge" to the
audience.[23]

[23] Andrew Gurr suggests that both playwrights and playgoers were "well aware of their environs" in the
uncomfortable London theatres and, as a result, they seldom forgot that they were watching a play.
Metatheatrical moments were routine. See *Playgoing in Shakespeare's London*, 2nd edn. (Cambridge:
Cambridge University Press, 1996), p. 106.

Another frequently repeated trope resonated with the religious and moral signification of blackness. When black villains boast that they cannot blush, they echo a popular expression describing one who has no shame as "blushing like a black dog."[24] In his response to a Gothic soldier's question, "What, canst thou say all this and never blush?" Aaron explicitly echoes this phrase: "Ay, like a black dog, as the saying is" (5.1.121–22). Another proverb from the period claims, "blushing is virtue's color," a sentiment explained more fully in Thomas Wright's *Passions of the Minde in Generall* (1604):

[T]hose that have committed a fault, & are therein deprehended [sic], or at least imagine they are thought to have committed it; presently if they be . . . that is, of an honest behaviour, and yet not much grounded in vertue, they blush, because nature beeing afrayd, lest in the face the fault should be discovered, sendeth the purest blood, to be a defence and succour, the which effect, commonly, is iudged to proceed from a good and vertuous nature, because no man can but allowe, that it is good to bee ashamed of a fault.[25]

A black, unblushing face indicated, in contrast, that the bearer had no virtue and, hence, no shame. Such sentiments circulated freely and reiterated the medieval correlation between evil and blackness; their repeated utterance on the public stage no doubt contributed over time to their discursive power.[26]

Black pigmentation thus served as a marker in sixteenth- and seventeenth-century English culture that could more easily be signified on stage than other "racial" characteristics.[27] Used prominently in the medieval period as a marker of religious difference, blackened faces became increasingly complicated by inchoate conceptions of race. Fear of the devil overlapped with fear of the black African other; on the stage, the fascinating and sometimes frightening characteristics dark pigmentation came to signify were acted out.[28] Over time, the actor's blackened face hardened into

[24] Tilley, *Dictionary*, D 507, p. 167.
[25] Thomas Wright, *The Passions of the Minde in Generall* (London, 1604), p. 30.
[26] For an insightful discussion of the early modern English conception of "blushing," see Sujata Iyengar, *Shades of Difference: Mythologies of Skin Color in Early Modern England* (Philadelphia: University of Pennsylvania Press, 2004), esp. pp. 103–39.
[27] See, for example, Ania Loomba, "'Delicious Traffick': Racial and Religious Difference on Early Modern Stages," in *Shakespeare and Race*, ed. Catherine M. S. Alexander and Stanley Wells (Cambridge: Cambridge University Press, 2000), pp. 203–24, who argues that the power of blackness as a symbol of alterity should not be underrated, especially as it "articulate[d] itself through other markers of difference such as religion and gender" (p. 204).
[28] Barbara Hodgdon, *The Shakespeare Trade: Performances and Appropriations* (Philadelphia: University of Pennsylvania Press, 1998), discusses how theatrical performance served to contain fears about alterity. See p. 44.

a marker of racial difference;[29] by the Restoration, it denoted slave status, and in the eighteenth century, it could also evoke the audience's pity.

II

The theoretical and practical implications of blackface impersonation depend, of course, upon the material conditions that create it. There is a world of difference, for example, between the exaggerated lips and eyes featured in the make-up used in nineteenth-century minstrel shows and the impersonation of Otello by a world-class opera singer. The performers intend different effects. The former uses grotesque images of black people for comic farce; the latter seeks a convincing representation. Both must use some sort of black make-up, however. Pierre Delacroix's assistant in *Bamboozled* offers the traditional recipe for blackface make-up: "Pour some alcohol on corks and light it, let them burn to a crisp. Make into a powder and then add water. Voila! But please put cocoa butter on your face to protect your skin."

Early modern performers may indeed have used burnt cork, but there were other ways of signifying blackness. In earlier sixteenth-century court performances, vizards, similar to the masks employed in Italy's *commedia dell'arte*, were used. According to Randle Holme's *Academy of Armory* (1688), a compendium of information related to heraldry, the vizard "is made convex to cover the Face in all parts, with an out-let for the nose, and 2 holes for the eyes, with a slit for the mouth to let the air & breath come in and out. It is generally made of Leather, and covered with black Velvet. The Devil was the inventer of it, and about Courts none but Whores and Bauds, and the Devil Imps do use them, because they are shamed to show their Faces." Holme also insists that "this kind of Mask is taken off and put on in a moment of time, being only held in the Teeth by means of

---

[29] See Dympna Callaghan, *Shakespeare Without Women: Representing Gender and Race on the Renaissance Stage* (London: Routledge, 2000), p. 78. My discussion of the racial implications of blackface impersonation has been influenced by David Theo Goldberg's analysis of racism's origins and subsequent incarnations in *Racist Culture*, but I am also indebted to Anthony Appiah's "Race," in *Critical Terms for Literary Study*, ed. Frank Lentricchia and Thomas McLaughlin (Chicago: University of Chicago Press, 1990), pp. 274–87. Also helpful are Margo Hendricks and Patricia Parker's *Women, "Race," and Writing in the Early Modern Period* (London: Routledge, 1994), Ania Loomba's *Shakespeare, Race, and Colonialism* (Oxford: Oxford University Press, 2002), esp. pp. 1–74, and several essays in *Shakespeare Studies* 26 (1998). As should be apparent, I take race to be a socially constructed category with no actual basis in biology. For further discussion of various approaches to the topic of race, see Michael Banton, *Racial Theories*, 2nd edn. (Cambridge: Cambridge University Press, 1998).

a round bead fastned on the in-side over against the mouth."[30] Speaking with a bead between the teeth must have been problematic, though not impossible. Court records show that for some performances vizards were combined with velvet or fine linen covering for the arms. Philip Henslowe listed "The Mores lymes," along with "Hercolles lymes, and Will. Sommers sewtte," in an inventory of 1598. Presumably the "Mores lymes" were a black covering for the actors' arms and legs.[31]

Like the *commedia dell'arte* masks, vizards limited the actor's scope. He had to "work within the limitations of persona and [could not] escape into the complexities of personality." The actor became the "prisoner of the mask" and had to play out his part "in terms of the statement *it* makes, rather than in terms of some complex of emotions that go beyond that statement."[32] Once the actor donned the mask of a black Moor or a black devil, the face's emotional range was static. The actor could adopt a variety of poses in hopes that body language would convey different attitudes, but the scope of emotion was more limited than what could be conveyed through facial expressions. In his survey of the development of the vice figure, L. W. Cushman notes the secundus demon in the Townley cycle did not wear a mask because the text calls for him to make faces: he "gryned and ghast."[33] It seems likely that actors who wished to grimace preferred some other mode of blackening than a heavy leather vizard.

Although vizards probably served well for court masques, in which dance and music were more important than the spoken word, the use of vizards in the public theatre may have been restricted to non-speaking roles, such as the Moors who drew in Bajazeth's chariot in Christopher Marlowe's *Tamburlaine*. The shift from what Dympna Callaghan describes as "exhibition" – the display of black people "as objects, passive and inert before the active scrutiny of the spectator" – to "mimesis" – the simulation of negritude – required a different mode of representation, one which allowed the actor to convey a full range of expressions, not a series of static poses.[34] When actors in the public theatres began to impersonate black characters in speaking roles, the "technology" consequently underwent a profound shift.

[30] Randle Holme, *Academy of Armory* (London, 1688); facs. reprint from Scolar Press (Menston, 1972), V. 64, and III. 87. My thanks to Stephen Orgel for this reference.
[31] Listed in *Documents of the Rose Playhouse*, ed. Carol Chillington Rutter (Manchester: Manchester University Press, 1984), p. 135.
[32] John Rudlin, *Commedia Dell'Arte: An Actor's Handbook* (London: Routledge, 1994), p. 35.
[33] L. W. Cushman, *The Devil and the Vice in the English Dramatic Literature Before Shakespeare* (Halle: Max Niemeyer, 1900), p. 23.
[34] Callaghan, *Shakespeare Without Women*, p. 77.

For over a century, actors in country folk dramas and mystery plays had resorted to coal or some form of charcoal. In the late 1580s when black Moors began to have speaking roles that a vizard would have impeded, actors probably concocted their own make-up materials. A black pigment could be made from a tallow base, suggests Jenny Tiramani of the International Globe Centre.[35] Tallow or a similar grease was probably mixed with some sort of black powder, such as the color bases outlined in Nicholas Hilliard's manuscript, "The Arte of Limning" (ca. 1601). Hilliard describes black pigments made from burnt cherry stones, date stones, peach stones or charcoal, but for velvet black, he recommends a powder manufactured from ivory burnt in a crucible, ground with gum water; "let it settle a whole afternoon, and pour from it the uppermost, which is but the gum and foulness, good to put among ink. The rest let dry, and keep it in a paper or box and use it as aforesaid with soft grinding of it again."[36] How ironic that Hilliard's "best black" originates in white ivory, which suggests that blackness (like the black stage figures this book will describe) is not an originary state but the result of turning white into black.

Or perhaps Delacroix's assistant was right after all. Cork was plentiful in early modern England, and actors may have resorted to what became the staple for black impersonators until the twentieth century. Instructions circulated in actors' handbooks from the late eighteenth well into the nineteenth century, as in this excerpt from Leman Thomas Rede's *The Road to the Stage*:

[T]he performer should cover the face and neck with a thin coat of pomatum, or what is better, though more disagreeable, of lard; then burn a cork to powder, and apply it with a hare's foot, or a cloth, the hands wet with beer which will fix the colouring matter. Wearing black gloves is unnatural for the colour is too intense to represent the skin, and negroes invariably cover themselves with light clothing. Arms of black silk . . . have a very bad effect: armings dyed with a strong infusion of Spanish annatto look much more natural, for a negro's arms it will be observed are generally lighter than his countenance. A strong colouring of carmine should be laid upon the face after the black, as otherwise the expression of countenance and eye will be destroyed.[37]

[35] Private conversation between Jenny Tiramani and the Globe's former Head of Research, Dr. Jacquelyn Bessell.

[36] Nicholas Hilliard, *A Treatise Concerning the Arte of Limning*, ed. R. K. R. Thornton and T. G. S. Cain (Ashington: Mid Northumberland Arts Group, 1981), p. 91. See also Jones, *Othello's Countrymen*, pp. 120–23, for a discussion of costuming practices. Records suggest that Richard Burbage, the actor who first impersonated Othello, also had some experience as a limner; in 1613 he designed an emblem for the Earl of Rutland for which Shakespeare wrote the motto (see E. K. Chambers, *The Elizabethan Stage*, 4 vols. [Oxford: Clarendon Press, 1923], vol. II, pp. 308–09).

[37] Leman Thomas Rede, *The Road to the Stage* (London: J. Onwhyn, 1836), p. 34.

Note the concern that the audience see the actor's expressions. It is not unlikely that a late sixteenth-century actor like Edward Alleyn, who impersonated Muly Mahamet in George Peele's *Battle of Alcazar*, the first speaking black Moor on London's public stage, should have shared that concern. The movement from vizard to black make-up was perhaps inevitable.

Ben Jonson's *Masque of the Gypsies* describes another mixture made from walnuts that was used to fashion gypsies, who were probably not coal black but swarthy:

> To change your Complexion,
> With the noble confection,
> Of Wall-nuts and Hogges-grease:
> Better than Dogs grease.

The grease must have kept the walnut juice from deeply staining the skin, for the Epilogue indicates that this concoction was easily washed off:

> But least it prove like wonder to the sight,
> To see a Gypsie, as an *Aethiope*, white:
> Know, that what dy'd our faces was an oyntment
> Made, and laid on by Mr. *Woolfes* appoyntment;
> The Court *Licanthropos* yet without spells,
> By a meere Barber, and no Magicke ells:
> It was fetcht off with water and a Ball,
> And to our transformation this is all.[38]

Mr. Woolf, apothecary to King James and his court, probably knew a good deal about ointments and other concoctions.

References from the Caroline drama are suggestive, too. The four little boys who "ape" adult black Moors in *Mr. Moore's Revels*, a masque performed at Oxford in 1636, appear on stage, each with "an inkhorne in his hand to blacke themselves To resemble the moores and that they might see to doe it exactly one of them had a lookinglasse."[39] That an inkhorn was used does not necessarily mean that the boys used ink, but presumably it contained some sort of black liquid suitable for face painting. More important, this amateur theatrical demonstrates that, by this period, the impersonation of Moors in theatrical productions had become a cliché,

---

[38] Ben Jonson, *The Gypsies Metamorphosed*, ed. George Watson Cole (New York: Modern Language Association, 1931), pp. 103–04.

[39] From John R. Elliott, Jr.'s transcription. See "*Mr. Moore's Revels*: A 'Lost' Oxford Masque," *Renaissance Quarterly* 37 (1989), 411–20; quote from 417. For a penetrating analysis of the masque's significance, see Kim F. Hall, "'Troubling Doubles': Apes, Africans, and Blackface in *Mr. Moore's Revels*," in *Race, Ethnicity, and Power in the Renaissance*, ed. Joyce Green MacDonald (Madison: Fairleigh Dickinson University Press, 1997), pp. 120–44.

something that could be parodied as the boys "ape" the performance. Similarly, when Quicksilver applies black paint to his wife Millicent's face in Richard Brome's *The English Moor*, he comforts his wife by reminding her that queens (a reference to Queen Anne's *Masque of Blackness*) have worn the same kind of "tincture."

The *Oxford English Dictionary* indicates that "tincture" in this period referred to "A colouring matter, dye, pigment; *spec.* a dye used as a cosmetic" (1), but it could also mean "A physical quality; a taste or flavour, a taint" (5a). The latter definition suggests black make-up's ambiguity; on the one hand it lent exoticism to the character, a "taste" of the forbidden, but because of blackness's traditional association with evil, it also suggested a "taint." As he applies the make-up, Quicksilver tells his wife:

> Take pleasure in the scent first; smell to't fearlesly,
> And taste my care in that, how comfortable
> 'Tis to the nostril, and no foe to feature.[40]

Quicksilver categorizes the black paint he applies as a cosmetic, sweet-smelling and harmless to the wearer. In contrast, Philip Massinger's *Parliament of Love* calls it "varnish,"[41] which as early as the fourteenth century, according to the *Oxford English Dictionary*, denoted as it does today, a "Resinous matter dissolved in some liquid and used for spreading over a surface in order to give this a hard, shining, transparent coat" (1a). In the sixteenth century, "varnish" also meant "A means of embellishment or adornment; a beautifying or improving quality of nature" (3a); at the same time, this covering could figure "a special gloss or outward show; a pretence" (2a). The terms used to speak about blackface suggest its complex, sometimes contradictory, significance, as well as its performative qualities.

Whatever ingredients were used, the application of black pigment must have been messy, and on occasion the paint must have rubbed off from one actor on to another, as in the final scene of Stuart Burge's film of the 1964–65 National Theatre Production of *Othello*, where Maggie Smith's face is visibly smeared with Laurence Olivier's heavy, black make-up. With effort, however, it could be washed off, leaving the actor – unlike the proverbial

---

[40] Richard Brome, *Five New Playes viz The English Moor, or the Mock-Marriage* (London: A. Crook and H. Brome, 1659), p. 38. This passage is omitted in the manuscript version of the play edited by Sara Jayne Steen (Columbia, MO: University of Missouri Press, 1983).

[41] *The Plays and Poems of Philip Massinger*, ed. Philip Edwards and Colin Gibson (Oxford: Clarendon Press, 1976), vol. II, p. 174.

Ethiopian – white.[42] Two texts suggest that this process was comparatively easy. In *The English Moor* the disguised and blackened Phillis is told to leave the stage "and let instant tryall be made / To take the blackness off."[43] She reenters approximately thirty lines later, whitefaced, much to her lover's chagrin. It is conceivable that the stage effect could be achieved through doubling Phillis's role with a second boy actor without blackface, but it seems more likely that the make-up was removed off stage. The second example is Milesia, a white noblewoman in William Berkeley's *The Lost Lady* (1638) who is disguised as a black Moor. After she swoons, the surrounding characters try to revive her by chafing her temples and rubbing water on her face. They are startled to see her black pigmentation rub off: "Oh Heavens! what prodigy / Is here! her blacknesse falls away." "More water, she returns to life, / And all the blacknesse of her face is gone."[44]

Rede's acting handbook describes various techniques for the removal of color. One tragedian "applies pomatum to his countenance, and then drops water upon his forehead." Other actors, "having removed the colour previous to coming on, have played the scene, till the point of discovery, with their backs to the audience." Another tactic is "oiling the inside of your gloves, and burying your face in your hands at the moment of accusation; colour adheres to oil immediately, and, without the appearance of error, the paint will be removed."[45] Such trickery seems by the early nineteenth century to have been standard stage practice.

These quick changes are calculated to amaze the audience. Pleasure emanates from the sudden realization of the actor's legerdemain. Like the spectators' sigh of satisfaction when a talented female impersonator takes off his wig and reveals that he is "really" a male, these theatrical moments please most when the audience is made aware of the difference between the actor and the role he plays. The greater the perceived difference between performer and persona, the more wonder and pleasure we feel. The obese Nutty Professor wouldn't be nearly so comical if we didn't know that the very thin Eddie Murphy was inside his rubber suit.

The moment of revelation when the mask comes off also suggests a fluidity of cultural and perhaps even racial identity, signified by black pigmentation. Such moments remind the spectators that the characters on stage are not really black and that they are watching a performance, a

---

[42] See Barbara Hodgdon's intriguing discussion of this film and other renditions of *Othello* in *The Shakespeare Trade*, pp. 39–73.

[43] Brome, *The English Moor*, p. 81.

[44] William Berkeley, *The Lost Lady: A Tragy Comedy* (London: John Oakes, 1638), p. 43.

[45] Rede, *Road to the Stage*, p. 35.

projection of what the English dramatist (or in the two instances cited above, the European character pretending to be a Moor) thought a black person of African descent should be like. While English racial attitudes were still in the early stages of formation during the early modern period, the blackfaced characters discussed here are often prescient of the dynamic Eric Lott was to find in the black impersonations of the American minstrel shows: "the dialectical flickering of racial insult and racial envy, moments of domination and moments of liberation, counterfeit and currency, a pattern at times amounting to no more than the two faces of racism, at others gesturing toward a specific kind of political or sexual danger."[46] Blackface performances were never static, and as this study will show, their changing nature reflected England's shift from an insignificant European power in the early sixteenth century to a global empire supported by a slave economy in the eighteenth.

III

Chapter two begins with patterns of blackness that circulated in medieval Europe. On the pageant wagons of mystery cycles, a blackened face served as a religious sign, indicating that the bearer was cast out from God's grace. Because saved souls were figured white and damned souls black, the visual code of the cycle plays was a simple binary: salvation versus damnation. In sixteenth-century court pageantry, changes are perceptible. Like *race*, blackface "assumes significance . . . in terms of prevailing social and epistemological conditions at the time, yet simultaneously bearing with it sedimentary traces of past significations."[47] Moorish kings who were figured by a black visor, a leather mask that signified exotic but appealing strangeness, represented plausible human beings from Africa instead of devils. As chapter three demonstrates, when Moorish kings were impersonated in the public theatres during the 1580s and 1590s, their blackened faces took on multiple meanings.[48] The theatre had become secularized and its plots were taken from literary, historical, and contemporary sources rather than the Bible. Audiences looked for stage heroes who seemed humanized rather than completely demonic.[49] While the religious signification of black, as opposed to white, remained deeply entrenched in common proverbs and resonated in stage performances, added to it were geographical, and even racial, modes of identification.

[46] Lott, *Love and Theft*, p. 18.   [47] Goldberg, *Racist Culture*, p. 81.
[48] See Elam, *Semiotics of Drama*, p. 15, for an explanation of code and function switching.
[49] See Gurr, *Playgoing in Shakespeare's London*, pp. 139–41.

Royal court masques also appropriated black royal figures during the Jacobean period, with Ben Jonson's *Masque of Blackness* the best known example. Chapter four examines the ways in which black kings and queens were performed and considers what conventions were borrowed from the popular theatre and what from other types of discourse – mythology, geographical treatises, Ortelius' atlas, for example.

Chapters five and seven analyze particular plot devices in seventeenth-century comedy and tragedy that exploited blackfaced figures for theatrical effect and underlined blackness's erotic implications. Chapter five considers the bedtrick (substituted bedmate), a folkloric device exploited for sexual intrigue, while chapter seven examines the disguised Moor, a European character who covers him- or herself with blackface and assumes the identity of a Moor when the audience knows he/she is "really" white. Most of the plays discussed in these chapters are non-canonical and now are seldom performed or read. In their day, most were performed at the indoor playing houses for elite audiences who apparently relished the sexual intrigues that could be complicated by blackface disguise.

Against the backdrop of recognizable theatrical conventions – metadramatic framing, erotic play, substitution of sexual partners, and emphasis on impersonation – Shakespeare's *Othello*, the subject of chapter six, will appear to us in a different light. Shakespeare wrote the play for his leading actor, Richard Burbage, who from all accounts was very successful in his impersonation, knowing that his audience was accustomed to reading and understanding the visual signifier of blackness in a certain way.[50] How was Othello received by his original audience? Othello is in some respects the "damned soul" of medieval mysteries, but he is also a noble warrior like the Moorish kings who populated court pageants. At the same time, the Moor is *sui generis*, and only when we place him within the theatrical conventions of early modern performance can we realize his uniqueness. Because *Othello* remains such an important yet highly contested text, this chapter will venture outside the book's chronology to highlight the history of blackface performances of Shakespeare's Moor from the Restoration to the

---

[50] A 1618 Elegy on the death of Richard Burbage particularly praises his performance as Othello:

> But let me not forget one chiefest part
> Wherein, beyond the rest, he mov'd the heart,
> The grieved Moor, made jealous by a slave,
> Who sent his wife to fill a timeless grave,
> Then slew himself upon the bloody bed
> All these and many more with him are dead.

See H. H. Furness, ed., *A New Variorium Edition of Othello* (Philadelphia: J. B. Lippincott, 1886), p. 396.

twentieth century, a tradition which culminated in Sir Laurence Olivier's 1964–65 controversial rendition for London's National Theatre.

Theatrical conventions change under the pressure of political and economic events, and thus it is appropriate that blackfaced characters that appear in plays of the Restoration (1660–1700) and exploit newly evolving stage practices should be analyzed apart from their early seventeenth-century predecessors.[51] Chapter eight examines three adaptations of earlier tragedies that were staged during the political unrest leading up to the 1670s Exclusion crisis over the Catholic Duke of York's probable succession to the throne. It shows how changes in characterization, plot, and language reflect a political and social climate that was drastically different, especially with regard to interactions with black Africans. A final chapter considers two of the longest playing and most popular tragedies of the eighteenth century, Thomas Southerne's *Oroonoko* and Edward Young's *The Revenge*. By the middle of the eighteenth century there was a significant population of freed blacks in London, one of whom (Ignatius Sancho) wanted to portray Oroonoko on the public stage. The theatre itself became a vehicle for abolitionist sentiment and the blackfaced actor – whether a villain like Zanga or a tragic hero like Oroonoko – was a sentimentalized site for resistance to the evils of slavery.

The plays discussed here were produced in venues that were to early modern England what television and film are to the twenty-first century; London's theatrical scene circulated a host of complicated, sometimes contradictory, images that shaped public consciousness.[52] *Performing Blackness on English Stages* examines the complex impressions created by the black bodies who walked and talked in early modern England's most popular entertainment medium. It shows the complexity of color consciousness and how white appropriations of "blackness" can be paradoxical combinations of love and theft, or to use Spike Lee's words, of "liking / appreciating a culture and trying to take it over."[53] In the process, it illuminates the drama's crucial role as both a receptor and a creator of racial attitudes in the early modern period.

---

[51] Barthelemy and Tokson tend to conflate Jacobean and Restoration plays, discussing the latter as simply extensions of the former.

[52] Gurr contends that the London theatre was "the only major medium for social intercommunication, the only existing form of journalism and the only occasion that exist for the gathering of large numbers of people other than for sermons and executions." See *Playgoing in Shakespeare's London*, p. 118.

[53] Spike Lee, Director's DVD Commentary, *Bamboozled*, 2001.

CHAPTER 2

Patterns of blackness

When did the custom of blackening actors' faces begin? What were the circumstances in which blackface was used? And when it was used, what did it signify? Historians, anthropologists, and theatre historians have frequently addressed these questions, and, not surprisingly, their answers vary. Through much of the twentieth century, discussions of blackfaced characters on the Elizabethan stage casually attributed their origins to the blackened faces of medieval morris dancers, the appearance of black devils in mystery plays of the late middle ages, and the personation of Moorish characters in Tudor court masques, homogenizing profound differences in traditions that developed in disparate venues and served distinct social purposes. Eldred Jones, and many who followed him, relied on E. K. Chambers's *Medieval Stage* or *The English Folk-Play* for information about folk customs such as morris dancing and St. George pageants.[1] John Forrest's *History of Morris Dancing* cautions that there is little evidence of face blackening in medieval accounts of morris dancing and that the rural practices Chambers observed were customs developed within the specific context of nineteenth-century rural English life,[2] and more likely influenced by grotesque imitation-Negroes in that era's minstrel shows than by early modern cultural practices.[3]

---

[1] See Eldred D. Jones, *Othello's Countrymen: The African in English Renaissance Drama* (London: Oxford University Press, 1965), pp. 27–28, E. K. Chambers, *The Medieval Stage* (Oxford: Clarendon Press, 1903), and E. K. Chambers, *The English Folk-Play* (Oxford: Clarendon Press, 1933).

[2] See John Forrest, *The History of Morris Dancing, 1458–1750* (Toronto: University of Toronto Press, 1999), pp. 1–27, for a thorough discussion of theories of origins.

[3] Chambers's account of Beelzebub from the pageant of King George and the Turkish Knight is a case in point. According to Chambers, Beelzebub enters, saying, "In comes I old Belzebub / And on my back I carries my club / And in my hand the dripping-pan, / I thinks myself a jolly old man. / Round hold, black as coal, / Long tail and little hole." But the "In comes I" construction is more akin to nineteenth-century minstrel shows than medieval English dialects. See Chambers, *The English Folk-Play*, p. 46. For an astute critique of Chambers, see John D. Cox, *The Devil and the Sacred in English Drama, 1350–1642* (Cambridge: Cambridge University Press, 2000). Even so perceptive a critic as Claire Sponsler relies heavily on nineteenth-century sources in her discussion

With this caveat in mind, this chapter will reexamine "face-blackening" in late medieval mystery cycles, court pageantry, urban processions, and the *commedia dell'arte*, looking at each custom within its social and economic context. By the 1580s, when the public theatres' early success sparked a ravenous appetite for new plays on exotic subjects, enterprising playwrights exploited the dramatic conventions that were shaped by these disparate traditions. Although the patterns were sometimes conflated (e.g. the devilish Moorish King in chapter three), their influence on the theatre's representation of black characters was palpable, as was their contribution to the formation of racial attitudes in early modern England.[4]

The blackened figures in mystery cycles and court masques shared one important characteristic: whether the blackness was conveyed through a painted face or a vizard, it disguised the identity of the performer, a quality particularly desirable in carnivalesque pageants in which the performer is playing roles drastically different from his or her everyday identity within the community.[5] This disguising characteristic, as I shall show in chapter three, contributes to the performative qualities we associate with black characters like Muly Mahamet, Aaron, and Eleazar.

I

Religious doctrine, conveyed to the illiterate in countless paintings during the middle ages, was the bedrock of much medieval art. The Bible's great stories from the Creation to the Last Judgment were narrated in statuary, frescoes, and wall paintings throughout Europe.[6] Although depictions of the devil were not common, when he did appear, his status "outside the pale" of Christianity was usually signified by a blackened complexion.

of medieval mumming and morris dancing; see "Outlaw Masculinities: Drag, Blackface, and Late Medieval Laboring-Class Festivities," in *Becoming Male in the Middle Ages*, ed. Jeffrey Jerome Cohen and Bonnie Wheeler (New York: Garland, 2000), pp. 321–47, esp. n. 31.

[4] Robert L. A. Clark and Claire Sponsler argue that blackface was important to "the construction of a fictive cultural coherence" that contributed to an "emerging ideology of race . . . in late medieval Europe." See "Othered Bodies: Racial Cross-Dressing in the *Mistere de la Sainte Hostie* and the Croxton *Play of the Sacrament*," *Journal of Medieval and Early Modern Studies* 29 (1999), 61–87; quote from 81.

[5] Clark and Sponsler show how costumes (which included swarthy skin tones for the impersonation of a Jew) functioned to "facilitate instant recognition." See "Othered Bodies," 71. While the type was recognizable, the identity of the performer was not. Sponsler cites a sixteenth-century act which banned disguises in mummings because they allowed people to hide their identities; see Sponsler, "Outlaw Masculinities," p. 329.

[6] For an overview of the black presence in medieval art see Jean DeVisse and Michel Mollat, *The Image of the Black in Western Art, II: From the Early Christian Era to the "Age of Discovery,"* Part 2: *Africans in the Christian Ordinance of the World (Fourteenth to the Sixteenth Century)* (Cambridge: Harvard University Press, 1979).

This mode of signification extended to medieval saints' legends. Take the story of the Irish saint Modwen (AD 870), for example. Incited by the devil, Bishop Cheuin armed himself to assail the virgin Modwen, "to kill her and to destroy her monasterie." But when Cheuin approached her, she "saw the diuell hanging on his left foote, in forme of a litle blacke boy, also whyspering in his left eare wicked counsell, and inspiring into his hart naughtie desires." Modwen prayed that Cheuin himself would see this figure, and when he did, he repented, gave over his enterprise, and returned to the wilderness "well informed and amended."[7] Like the vice figure of late medieval morality plays, this devil figure shadows the Bishop and whispers in his ear, tempting him away from the path of virtue. When the Bishop sees the blackness of this figure, he recognizes it as a devil, which, in turn, leads to his reformation.

The blackened figure could also signify damnation in medieval cycle plays. Several English cycle plays begin before the creation of Adam and Eve with the story of Lucifer, detailed in Isaiah 14:12–15. Named for the brightest star in heaven, Lucifer, like the classical Icarus, undergoes a dramatic fall. The prophet describes how Lucifer coveted God's place on high: "Yet thou saidest in thine heart, I wil ascend into heauen, and exalt my throne above beside the starres of God," but "thou shalt be broght downe to the graue, to the sides of the pit." After the fall, "How art thou fallen from heauen, o Lucifer, sonne of the morning? & cut downe to the grounde" (Geneva Bible).

The logistics for dramatizing Lucifer's fall are obvious; in the three-tiered space of the medieval pageant, the earth was figured on the central platform, heaven above and hell below. Lucifer should enter on high, sit next to God's throne and try to sit in it; then he is cast down (perhaps pushed), not just to "middle earth" but all the way down, into the pit below. Extant cycles of the fifteenth and sixteenth centuries depict Lucifer's fall from grace in much this way. His transformation is sometimes signified by changes in costume; John D. Cox notes several references to a coat of black feathers, and another to "blak develles cootes," that indicate black as the chromatic signifier for Satan's minions.[8] The most prominent marker of Lucifer's fall, however, is a blackened face. The Chester cycle (early fifteenth century) first presents Lucifer as "wonderous bright," but after the fall, he

---

[7] *The Lives of Women Saints of our Contrie of England*, ed. C. Horstmann (London: Early English Text Society, 1886), pp. 93–95.
[8] Cox, *The Devil and the Sacred*, pp. 5–6.

and his colleague Lightborne are transformed into "2 feendes blacke."[9] In the Wakefield *Creation* (mid-fifteenth century) he announces, "Now ar we waxen blak as any coyll, and vgly taytred as a foyll."[10] The Coventry *Creation* (late fifteenth century) has Lucifer explain that after the fall, "I am a devyl ful derke / that was An Aungell bryht."[11] After his rebellion, observes Glynne Wickham, Lucifer retains "the outline of his former angelic shape, including his wings, but all the details have become grotesque parodies of the original image."[12] His face, which had been white (or sometimes gilded), has now turned black.

Lucifer's blackened complexion indicates his transformation from the moral norm of God's whiteness and his exclusion from the community of believers.[13] It is an easy and convenient signifier for the amateur actor, because he needs only don a vizard or smear some soot on his face. The blackness also disguises his private identity, allowing for doubling (as in the Chester cycle), and making the dramatic illusion more palpable. It also hides any shame the citizen/actor might feel at being, at least for the day, the arch devil and allows him to perform actions that in everyday life would seem transgressive. Carnivalesque disguise, moreover, can be pleasurable. Contemporary American football fans who paint their faces with their team's colors exhibit great glee when the television cameras turn them into public spectacles.

Records of the cycle plays reveal that Lucifer's evil progeny, too, are painted black. Accounts from the Coventry cycle note money "paid for colour and coloryng of Arad [Herod]."[14] Although the coloring may not have been coal black, it was clearly intended to set Herod apart from the other characters. But the most telling evidence for face blackening comes from the Drapers' Company at Coventry, which produced the pageant of Doomsday each year; extant records from 1561 to 1579 (when the cycle was

---

[9] Quoted from *The Chester Plays*, ed. Hermann Deimling (Oxford: Early English Text Society, 1892), pp. 13 and 18.

[10] M. Lyle Spencer, *Corpus Christi Pageants in England* (New York: Baker and Taylor, 1911), p. 229.

[11] *Ludus Coventriae, or The Plaie called Corpus Christi*, ed. K. S. Block (London: Early English Text Society, 1922), p. 19. Although this cycle has traditionally been attributed to Coventry, recent scholarship suggests that it actually came from the East Midlands.

[12] Glynne Wickham, *Early English Stages, 1300–1660*, vol. III (London: Routledge and Kegan Paul, 1981), p. 197.

[13] Sponsler claims that blackface "was associated with inferiority, unruliness, excess, and the grotesque." The transformation in Lucifer's skin color could thus denote a loss of status as well as a proclivity to evil. See Sponsler, "Outlaw Masculinities," p. 334.

[14] Annette Drew-Bear, *Painted Faces on the Renaissance Stage: The Moral Significance of Face-Painting Conventions* (Lewisburg: Bucknell University Press, 1994), p. 33.

discontinued) show that the pageant remained the same over time. The Drapers' representation of the Last Judgment drew upon the homiletic tradition of contemporary morality plays. Perhaps they had Revelations 20:4 in mind when they planned the costumes and make-up:

> I *sawe* the soules of them, that were beheaded for the witnes of
> Iesus, and for the worde of God, & which did not worship the
> Beast, nether his image, nether had taken his marke vpon their forheads, or
>   on their hands.   (Geneva Bible)

Damnation was signified, in other words, by a visual mark, the mark of blackness. The Doomsday pageant represented the drama of salvation by displaying souls who were saved and souls who were damned. The Drapers' account books list money paid every year to hire the "savyd sowles" and the "dampnyd Sowles"; the latter required extra money, however, for the "blacckyng of the Sowles facys."[15] The payments also suggest that the blacking up required some time and effort, not just a quick mark on the cheek. There are no records of payment for whitening the saved souls. Pale skin was the norm in England's isolated market towns where the cycles were performed, and the audience may well have identified with the saved souls and read the blackened skin of the damned souls as the token of God's condemnation.

This chromatic symbolism was carried into the Tudor moral interlude. John Redford's *Wit and Science*, written between 1531 and 1547, uses the device to symbolize Wit's seduction by Idleness; while Wit is sleeping, Idleness announces, "idlenes marke on hym shall I clappe." The text provides no stage directions, but the dialogue implies that Idleness approaches Wit's sleeping figure and applies blotches sufficiently dark and large for the audience to notice. After some wordplay Idleness makes his companion Ignorance take off his cloak and put it on the sleeping Wit; he predicts that when Wit awakes, "he shall soone scantlye knowe hym selfe." Through make-up and costume, Wit is transformed so that even his lover Science cannot recognize him; whereas before he was "fayer plesant & goodlye," now he is "foule dysplesant & vglye." The spots mark him as a "nawghty vycious foole."[16] Later, when Wit examines himself in a mirror,

---

[15] See R. W. Ingram, ed., *Records of Early English Drama, Coventry* (Toronto: University of Toronto Press, 1981), pp. 217, 221, 224, 230, 237, 242, 246, 250, 254, 257, 259, 264, 475–76, 478.

[16] Robert Hornback believes that the black marks on Wit signified his foolishness. The connection between a blackened face and foolishness, he argued, later became conflated with notions of African irrationality, perhaps leading to Shakespeare's creation of a credulous Moor in *Othello*. See "Emblems of Folly in the First *Othello*: Renaissance Blackface, Moor's Coat, and 'Muckender,'" *Comparative Drama* 35 (2001), 69–99.

he finds that either "this glas is shamefuly spotted / or els am I to shamefully blotted." His face, he proclaims, "is abhominable / as black as the devyll."[17]

Similarly, Thomas Lupton's moral interlude *All for Money* (1578) includes the stage direction: "*Iudas commeth in like a damned soule, in blacke.*"[18] The playwright here relies on a recognized symbolic convention; damned souls are coded black. The trope is used metaphorically in John Bale's *King Johan* by the Vice, Sedition, who urges England: "Hold Yowr peace, ye whore, or ellys by masse I trowe / I shall cawse the pope to curse the[e] as blacke as a crowe!"[19]

Transcodification, the transference from a simple sign – here, blackness as a theological sign of condemnation – to other sorts of discourse systems, seems to have been widespread.[20] For example, the political signification of blackface was exploited for political purposes by *An Homilie against disobedience and Willful Rebellion* (1570), which was recited in parish churches throughout England. The *Homilie* proclaimed that the first author of rebellion was "Lucifer, first God's most excellent creature and most bounden subject, who, by rebelling against the majesty of God, of the brightest and most glorious angel is become the blackest and most foulest fiend and devil, and from the height of heaven is fallen into the pit and bottom of hell."[21] Rebellion against the king is equated with rebellion against God.

Lucifer's blackness was also used satirically. Thomas Nashe's description of "Lawrence Lucifer" in *Pierce Penilessse His Supplication to the Divell*, for example, recycles the ancient proverb that it is impossible to "wash an Ethiop white"; Nashe writes, "you went vp and downe London crying then like a lanterne & candle man. I meruaile no Laundresse would give you the washing and starching of your face for your labour, for God knowes it is as black as the blacke Prince."[22] Lucifer's color was a staple of such witcrackers, as in Robert Greene's *Quip for an Upstart Courtier*: "Marry, quot hee, that lookte like Lucifer, though I am blacke I am not the Divell, but indeed a Colier of Croiden." Or, he could be confused with real people

---

[17] John Redford, *Wit and Science*, ed. Arthur Brown (Oxford: Oxford University Press for the Malone Society, 1951; orig. pub. 1908), quotes from pp. 17, 24, 32, and 33.
[18] Thomas Lupton, *A Moral and Pitiefvl Comedie, Intituled, All for Money* (London, 1578), sig. E2r.
[19] John Bale, *King Johan*, ed. Barry B. Adams (San Marino: Huntington Library, 1969), p. 73.
[20] See Keir Elam, *The Semiotics of Theatre and Drama* (London: Routledge, 1980), pp. 84–85.
[21] From Russ McDonald, *The Bedford Companion to Shakespeare*, 2nd edn. (Boston: Bedford Books of St. Martin's Press, 2001), p. 346.
[22] *The Works of Thomas Nashe*, ed. Ronald B. McKerrow, vol. 1 (Oxford: Basil Blackwell, 1958), p. 281.

as Reginald Scot did in his *Discoverie of Witchcraft* when he claimed that
"a damned soule may and dooth take the shape of a blacke Moore."[23]

The association between damnation and blackness became commonplace in Elizabethan discourse. Shakespeare repeated the trope throughout
his career, making black "the badge of hell" (*Love's Labour's Lost* 4.3.250).
Richard III is described as "hell's black intelligencer" (*Richard III*, 4.4.71)
and in *King John*, when the Bastard discovers Arthur's body, he warns
Hubert that if he committed the murder, "Thou'rt damned as black – nay
nothing is so black – / Thou art more deep damned than Prince Lucifer"
(4.3.122–23). Henry VIII claims that Buckingham "is become as black / As
if besmeared in hell" after his treasonous fall (*Henry VIII*, 1.2.124–25), and
on a more comic note, Falstaff is said to have compared a flea on Bardolph's
nose to "a black soul burning in hell" (*Henry V*, 2.3.35). The trope recurs
in the tragedies: Hamlet decides not to kill Claudius while he is praying,
but to wait until "his soul may be as damned and black / As hell whereto
it goes" (*Hamlet*, 3.3.94–95). In the following scene Gertrude exclaims:

> Thou turns't my eyes into my very soul,
> And there I see such black and grained spots
> As will not leave their tinct.   (3.4.79–81)

Macbeth curses the messenger bearing bad news: "The devil damn thee
black, thou cream-faced loon!" (*Macbeth*, 5.3.11). And in sonnet 147 the
speaker compares the dark lady to Lucifer: "For I have sworn thee fair, and
thought thee bright, / Who art as black as hell, as dark as night." Moral
corruption, murder, rebellion and treason, sexual perversion – all manner
of human vices were signified by a blackened complexion.

Thus through repetition and diffusion, the association between black
skin and damnation permeated early modern English culture. References
to blackness were shorthand for the negative associations loosely linked to
Lucifer's original fall from grace. With such ready-made phrases circulating
freely in the culture, it is not surprising that they readily came to the
dramatists' minds when they were fashioning black Moorish characters.

II

Mystery plays were presented in England from the fifteenth well into the sixteenth centuries. The latest record for the Corpus Christi Cycle at Coventry

---

[23] Morris Palmer Tilley, *A Dictionary of the Proverbs in England in the Sixteenth and Seventeenth Centuries*
(Ann Arbor: University of Michigan Press, 1951), D 247; Reginald Scot, *The Discoverie of Witchcraft*
(London, 1585), p. 456.

is in 1579; by the 1580s, such performances were suppressed in a tightening of Protestant authority. While the mystery cycles were thriving in the towns, however, a more elite performative tradition developed in the courts of Henry VII and Henry VIII, which featured black Moors in masques and processions.

The roots of this tradition are difficult to trace, but medieval theologians had included a blackfaced King among the Three Magi beginning in the sixth century to indicate that Christ's birth was a gift to ALL nations. St. Jerome had defined the Magi as representing the three sons of Noah, referring to Psalm LXXII: 8–10's prophecy that

His dominion shalbe also from the sea to sea, and from the Riuer vnto the ends of the land. They that dwell in the wildernes, shal knele before him, and his enemies shall licke the dust. The Kings of Tarshish & of the yles shal bring presentes: The Kings of Sheba and Seba shall bring giftes (Geneva Bible).[24]

The Legend of the Three Kings circulated widely through Europe, and by the early fifteenth century, translations of John of Hildesheim's *Three Kings of Cologne* (written between 1364 and 1375) were readily available to clerics throughout England.[25] Hildesheim, a Carmelite friar, studied at Avignon and was known as a doctor of divinity. In the Lambeth Palace manuscript, Hildesheim describes "Iaspar, kyng of Thars and of the yle of Egrisculle," who brought myrrh to the Christ child as "an Ethiope and blak."[26] The figure of a blackfaced, gift-bearing King, it would seem, came to signify the universality of the Christian faith; as the Psalmist continued, "Yea, all Kings shal worship him: all nations shal serue him" (Geneva Bible, 72: 11).

But the blackened King could also signify alterity. Moors of northern Africa who conquered much of Spain during the early middle ages were often described as black in literature and given black faces in the visual arts. Again, blackness became a sort of shorthand, a way to signify that a character who was Moorish and non-Christian was excluded from the community. The Middle English poem "Rouland and Vernagu," which has come down to us in a fourteenth-century manuscript, describes Vernagu, the sultan of Babylon in this way:

---

[24] Winifred Sturdevant traces the origins of the black Ethiopian King to Sedatus, Bishop of Beziers in 589, who wrote "in eo quod ad Christum primum Aethiopes i.e., gentes ingrediuntur." See *The Misterio De Los Reyes Magos: Its Position in the Development of the Mediaeval Legend of the Three Kings* (Baltimore: The Johns Hopkins Press, 1927), pp. 19–20.

[25] C. Horstmann, who edited this text for the Early English Text Society, notes that the large number of extant manuscripts proves the great popularity of the book. See *The Three Kings of Cologne: An Early English Translation of the Historia Trium Regium*, ed. C. Horstmann (London: Early English Text Society, 1886), p. xi.

[26] *The Three Kings of Cologne*, ed. Frank Schaer (Heidelberg: C. Winter, 2000), p. 69.

> His nose was a fot & more,
> His browe as brestles wore,
>
> . . .
>
> He loked lotheliche [loathly],
> & was swart as piche,
>   Of him men might adrede.[27]

The *Oxford English Dictionary* defines "swart" as generally meaning "Dark in colour; black or blackish," specifically referring to "the skin or complexion," from the time of *Beowulf*. In "Rouland and Vernagu," the poet transmits an identification of Moors as blackened and grotesque that was current in the French *Chanson de Roland*, which described north Africa as "a land accursed," inhabited by a "black race" with "the huge noses, the enormous ears on them." The Saracen Abisme is

> stained with the marks of his crimes and great treasons,
> lacking the faith in God, Saint Mary's son.
> And he is black, as black as melted pitch,
> a man who loves murder and treason more
> than all the Gold of rich Galicia.[28]

When Roland confronts "that unbelieving race, / those hordes and hordes blacker than blackest ink – / no shred of white on them except their teeth – "[29] he knows they are infidels from northern Africa. Their blackness signifies both religious and geographical difference.

The twelfth-century *Chanson de Roland* was inspired by Europe's military confrontations with the Saracens, Muslim peoples of northern Africa. The main focus of the poet's horror of these non-Europeans was, of course, their religion, but attributing black complexions to them was a handy way to underscore visually their devilish nature. In this way, as Anthony Gerard Barthelemy contends, Moorishness and blackness became intertwined in the European mind very early in the middle ages.[30]

Forrest conjectures that morris dancing also has its roots in the twelfth century in the medieval dramatic dance "Moros y Cristianos" which was performed in Spain in 1149 during the celebration of the betrothal of

---

[27] Quoted with slight modification for clarity from *The English Charlemagne Romances, Part VI*, ed. Sidney J. H. Herrtage (London: Early English Text Society, 1882), p. 50. Herrtage translates, "He was a loathsome sight and as black as pitch."

[28] *The Song of Roland*, trans. Frederick Golden (New York: Norton, 1978), pp. 107 and 99.

[29] *Song of Roland*, p. 107. See also Cherrell Guilfoyle, "Othello, Otuel, and the English Charlemagne Romances," *Review of English Studies*, n.s.38 (1987), 50–55.

[30] Anthony Gerard Barthelemy, *Black Face, Maligned Race: The Representation of Blacks in English Drama from Shakespeare to Southerne* (Baton Rouge: Louisiana State University Press, 1987), pp. 11–12.

Petronilla, Queen of Aragon to Ramon of Barcelona. In this dance-narrative, "two armies, one of Moors and one of Christians meet and, having delivered long speeches, attack one another, the Christians ultimately winning the day."[31] This became a custom in many Spanish towns.[32] It may also have been the forerunner of both processional moriscas, which were performed as part of a street pageant, and court moriscas, which narrated a story and were staged in one place. Forrest concludes, "both forms could have arrived in England independently even though both had a common European ancestor."[33]

However he got there, the Moor (and morris dancers)[34] inhabited court revels during the sixteenth century. Records show a disguising of Turks, Russians, Prussians, and Moors during Henry VIII's reign. Like the inclusion of an Ethiopian among the Three Kings, Henry's introduction of foreign figures into his court mummings perhaps underscored his aspirations to transform England from an insular nation absorbed with civil wars to a cosmopolitan European power.

Edward Hall records that "The torchebearers were appareyled in Crymosyn satyne and grene, lyke Moreskoes, their faces blacke: And the kyng brought in a mommerye."[35] On the same occasion, some ladies were disguised: "Their faces, neckes, armes and hands, covered with fyne plesaunce blacke: Some call it Lumberdynes, which is marveilous thinne, so that the same ladies semed to be nigrost or blacke Mores. Of these fforesayd vi ladies, the lady Mary syster unto the kyng was one, the other I name not."[36]

A masque of Moors in 1548 required costumes of "black velett for gloves aboue thelbow for mores," "nether stockes of lether black for mores," "Gootes skynnes" for hose, and caps made with "Course budge"[37] (coarse fur, usually of lambskin), presumably for the Moors' woolly hair. Accounts also call for twelve dozen "belles to hange at the skyrtes of the mores

---

[31] Forrest, *Morris Dancing*, p. 99.
[32] Shakespeareans who gathered in Valencia for the 2001 International Shakespeare Congress could see a procession of Moors and Christians on Shakespeare's birthday, 23 April.
[33] Forrest, *Morris Dancing*, p. 99.
[34] Although we have no record that rural morris dancers painted their faces black, Sponsler is surely right to note the semantic link between "Moor" and "morris" dancing, and it is likely that the morris dancers listed in revels accounts wore some sort of black visor. See Sponsler, "Outlaw Masculinities," p. 333.
[35] Edward Hall, *Henry VIII*, ed. Charles Whibley, 2 vols. (London: T. C. and E. C. Jack, 1904), vol. 1, p. 16.
[36] Hall, *Henry VIII*, vol. 1, p. 17.
[37] Albert Feuillerat, ed. *Documents Relating to the Revels at Court in the Time of King Edward VI and Queen Mary* (Louvain, 1914), pp. 30–31.

garmentes."[38] The bells suggest that the masquers performed the morisco, a wild version of morris dancing. The Christmas revels of 1550–51 include a masque of Irishmen and Moors; the latter wore long black gloves and "small lambe skynnes."[39] King Edward VI joined these masquers as a torch bearer.

Moors also appeared during the festivities celebrating Queen Elizabeth's coronation. Accounts indicate that "the Mask of Moors was apparelled with cloth of gold and blue velvet, with sleeves of silver sarcenet."[40] The Moors also had "corled hed sculles of blacke laune wrethen aboute with redd golde sarsnett and sylver Lawne."[41] Their arms and faces were covered with black velvet. Again, orders for bells indicate that morris dancing was probably incorporated into the masque. The Revels accounts list payments in 1571–72 for "Lambeskins for moores" and in 1576–78 for more "Lambes skynnes" and "ffer Moores Dartes and Irish Dartes."[42]

Forrest suggests that these court entertainments were shaped by their antecedents in stylized medieval tournaments and included mock combats and wooing games that carried on the courtly love conventions of medieval Europe. The King of Moors appeared, as did the Moorish figures in the original "Moros y Cristianos," to "symbolize the remote and exotic worlds at the fringes of Europe."[43] The inclusion of a Moorish king in court festivities was akin in some ways to John of Hildesheim's rendering of a black magi. Just as Christ had come to bring salvation to all peoples, King Henry VIII's court was constructed as a beacon of light to far away nations who needed his civilizing influence. The use of Moors at court seems strangely prescient of what would become England's colonial aspirations in the next century. Moreover, the richness of the costumes suggests that the Moors, like other exotic commodities imported from the east, visually represented the royal court's opulence. The performers, taken from the court's highest echelons and even including Henry VIII, his sister Mary, and later Edward VI, play at wildness in the performance of a morris dance. For these Moors blackening was a carnivalesque sign of a liberation from social norms, a temporary celebration of misrule where the king became equal with his court.[44]

Unlike the blackening paint used in rural mystery cycles, the king's black lawn and velvet could be easily and quickly removed. The use of

---

[38] Feuillerat, *Edward VI*, p. 31. [39] Feuillerat, *Edward VI*, p. 33.

[40] W. R. Streitberger, *Court Revels, 1485–1559* (Toronto: University of Toronto Press, 1994), p. 221.

[41] Albert Feuillerat, *Documents Relating to the Office of the Revels in the Time of Queen Elizabeth* (Louvain, 1908), p. 41.

[42] Feuillerat, *Queen Elizabeth*, pp. 139 and 276. [43] Forrest, *Morris Dancing*, pp. 89–90.

[44] For a fascinating account of the symbolic power of the "Black Lady" in court pageantry, see Louise Olga Fradenburg, *City, Marriage, Tournament: Arts of Rule in Late Medieval Scotland* (Madison: University of Wisconsin Press, 1991), pp. 244–64, esp. p. 248.

velvet coverings for hands and face suggests a disguising quite different from paint, which preserves the performer's individual features. In court masques, the Ethiop could turn white in an instant, for his blackness was a mere cover-up concealing his true nature, which lay intact underneath. Such transformations in court revelry may be akin to medieval conversion narratives, in which an outcast's adoption of Christianity was signified by an instantaneous and seemingly miraculous physical transformation, like the converted Saracen sultan who marries a Christian princess and, after being baptized, turns white.[45] In Henry VIII's Protestant court, however, the miraculous change pointed to his authority as head of the church and state rather than the whitening power of the sacraments.

Moorish figures who appeared in urban processions during the same period connoted misrule. In the first half of the sixteenth century, they occasionally appeared in Midsummer Watch processions, military spectacles that emphasized the "maintenance of social order through the constabulary and the militia,"[46] an important reminder of the need for public control on the longest day of the year when feasting and bonfires could easily lead to social disruptions.

Records from London's trade guilds list their contributions to these pageants, including expenses for costumes, music, dancers, and the construction of sets. The Skinners' Renter Wardens' accounts for 1519, for example, include 20 d. for "10 boys who played the 'morens' at 2 *d.* a piece."[47] The *Oxford English Dictionary* defines "morian," "morien," "morryon," and "moryan" as "A Moor, Blackamoor, Negro," and dates this usage to 1500. The record does not indicate how the boys were dressed, but surely some blackening of the complexion was required. The pageant also called for a "Sowden" (i.e. a Sultan) to play "before the Martyrdom of St. Thomas" and included a Knight and a Jewess, details which recall the clash of Christian and pagan depicted in the Spanish "Moros y Cristianos."

The Drapers' Company accounts for 1521 record payments for a Midsummer pageant that included "a King of Moore & 1 moryans." Money was paid to Godfrey "for the lone of a dymy lawnce that the kyng of the Moore pavillion was born vppon over his hede. & for a long swerd for the said king & a child harnes." Payments for the Moor's costume indicate that he wore a red satin mantle, a special girdle, and a garland made of black satin. His sleeves may have been trimmed with silver paper, and he

---

[45] See Clark and Sponsler, "Othered Bodies," 74.   [46] Forrest, *Morris Dancing*, p. 94.

[47] Cited from *A Calendar of Dramatic Records in the Books of the Livery Companies of London, 1485–1640*, ed. Jean Robertson and D. J. Gordon (Oxford: Oxford University Press for the Malone Society, 1954) under the title, *Collections*, vol. III, p. 4.

appeared with "wyld fyre," probably squibs. In addition, the Drapers paid wages to "lx moryans grete & small . . . & and a woman morian aftir iiijd a pece for bothe nyghte & the woman moryan viijd for both nyghte."[48] The "moryans" apparently carried "dartes" some of which were lost, which suggests that the pageant called for "some kind of martial action."[49] The most interesting item, however, is for "fyre for the moryans aft' they had put of ther clothes & were nakyd."[50] The boys were decribed as being naked by Lodovico Spinelli, secretary to the Venetian ambassador to England, who witnessed the pageant, but Forrest speculates that they actually wore some kind of blackened leather or cloth covering that would represent the Moor's exotic pigmentation.[51] The use of fireworks suggests that the Moors, similar to the wild men who appear in other pageants, were used to gain the crowd's attention and to clear the way for the procession, which included a giant, a castle, children with paper swords, and a morris dance.

The King of Moors who appeared in the Midsummer procession of 1536 was also "well trimmed." The Drapers' Rough Minutes record payment to a painter on the fifteenth of June

for the garnyshyng of the Kyng of Moore well trymmed wt all thynge that shalbelong vnto hym as well his wage as horsse Trapper & leder and also of X moore & trymmyng of them aft' the best ffascyon & the hyer of them & gonstone of pap[er] sufficyent so that ther lack none for defens of the castell & for makyng of v harnes of sylver paper . . . for trymmyng of the Kynge pavylyon of Moore & of the iiij Men that shal bere hym.[52]

The phrase "all thynge that shalbelong vnto hym" indicates that by 1536 the King of Moors had become a conventional figure and that audiences expected him to be brilliantly costumed with recognizable Moorish trappings.

Midsummer Watches disappear from the records by the mid-sixteenth century, their processional and celebratory functions subsumed into lavish Lord Mayors' Shows. The later urban festivals continued many of the conventions that had been established earlier, however, including the use of wild men, morris dancing, and Moors. The Skinners' Court book lists payment for "a 'moryne' and 2 wildmen" for the 1551 pageant, when one of their own, Sir Richard Dobbes, became mayor. As late as 1611, the Goldsmiths' spectacle, *Chrusothriambos*, written by Anthony Munday, featured "two Moores rydeing vppon vnicornes."[53] These Moors have no speaking role in Munday's printed text, probably because they had become disconnected from their military origins in the "Moros y Cristianos" and were by

[48] *Calendar*, pp. 5–10.   [49] Forrest, *Morris Dancing*, p. 101.   [50] *Calendar*, p. 7.
[51] Forrest, *Morris Dancing*, p. 100.   [52] *Calendar*, p. 27.   [53] *Calendar*, p. 81.

this time simply items of display, like the artificial ingots of gold and silver that denoted England's wealth.[54]

III

In addition to pageantry of religious folk drama and court entertainments, early modern English drama may have been influenced during the late sixteenth century by importations from Italy's *commedia dell'arte*. By the middle of the sixteenth century, professional troupes that improvised pre-set plots, or scenari, were performing for court audiences.[55] English travelers to France and Italy reported seeing such entertainments at court, and by 1591 Italian actors were commonly performing in England.[56] While the *commedia dell'arte* arrived on English shores comparatively late, it could have influenced plays from the late sixteenth well into the seventeenth centuries.

These popular Italian entertainments often included the figure of Harlequin or Arlecchino, whose name derives from "Hellecchino" or "Little Devil." His origins have been traced as far back as the Chronicles of Ordericus Vitalis "which recount the experiences of a priest of Saint Aubin de Bonneval who in 1091 claimed to have seen a procession of devils, some armed, some dwarfs, some sooty and scattering fire, conveying the souls of the damned with torture to hell."[57] By the fourteenth century, he appeared in street theatricals as a human being "retaining some devilish and bestial features," who incurred ecclesiastic censure for unlicensed reveling.[58] His origins, in other words, are similar to the blackened devils of England's mystery cycles, and like the comic vice of English morality plays, he makes trouble for the central character.

Harlequin's mask was usually blackened, and at least one master of the *commedia* played him in blackface.[59] K. M. Lea notes that the details of his costume are fairly consistent:

He wears a tight-fitting jacket and trousers, sewn over with odd-shaped patches, laced down the front with a thong and caught by a black belt worn very low on the hips. His shoes are flat and black, his cap small, black, and tufted with a rabbit scut: his mask is black, wrinkled, and hairy, with little eyes and a snub-nose: he carries a pouch and a wooden sword.[60]

---

[54] See Anthony Munday's *Chruso-thriambos: The Triumphs of Gold* (London: Privately Printed, 1962), passim.

[55] See Kenneth Richards and Laura Richards, *The Commedia Dell'Arte: A Documentary History* (Oxford: Basil Blackwell, 1990), pp. 337–40 and K. M. Lea, *Italian Popular Comedy: A Study in the Commedia Dell'Arte, 1560–1620*, 2 vols. (Oxford: Clarendon Press, 1934).

[56] See Lea, *Italian Popular Comedy*, vol. II, pp. 342–69.

[57] Lea, *Italian Popular Comedy*, vol. I, p. 74.   [58] Lea, *Italian Popular Comedy*, vol. I, p. 75.

[59] See John Rudlin, *Commedia dell'Arte: An Actor's Handbook* (London: Routledge, 1994), pp. 76–83.

[60] Lea, *Italian Popular Comedy*, vol. I, p. 86.

Harlequin usually appears as a servant to the old miser, Pantalone. His abject position, plus his black mask with the snub nose, are reminiscent of the black Moorish servant, and it is conceivable that he derived from the African slaves in Roman comedies as well as the black devil of medieval religious drama.[61] A variant of the trusty servant of Plautine comedy, Harlequin is a "shape-shifter" who "frequently adopts disguises and cross-dresses without demur."[62] In his *Apology for Actors*, Thomas Heywood refers to the "Doctors, Zawnyes, Pantaloones, Harlakeenes, in which the French, but especially the Italians have been excellent,"[63] which suggests that by the early part of the seventeenth century, Harlequin was well known to English actors and audiences. While Harlequin's influence on the depiction of black characters was negligible in the sixteenth century, by the Caroline period he may indeed have influenced comedies whose plots are similar to some of the *commedia dell'arte* scenari that feature young men eager to defeat the older generation and attain their sexual desires.[64]

IV

The cultural practices described here arose in different contexts and served different social purposes. The mystery cycles were town affairs, supervised by the local parish and mounted by tradespeople and citizens. They depicted familiar stories from the Bible, entertaining and teaching at the same time. Despite their religious import, cycle plays were performed in an atmosphere of carnival at the celebration of the feast of Corpus Christi. During the longest day of the year everyday routines were broken and members of the community joined together on a "holy day" that was also a "holiday." The devils who appeared in the day's pageants, sometimes with fireworks and other cacophonous effects, were agents of misrule who provided temporary release from the constraints of everyday life, but also threatened the order of the community. However familiar the plots may have been, the plays' dramatic spectacle reenacted a cosmic battle between good and evil. The faces blackened by soot or paint that populated these dramas were dynamic figures who could convey through performance both the attractiveness and the horror of evil. At the cycle's end, they were banished to

---

[61] See Lynne Lawner, *Harlequin on the Moon: Commedia dell'Arte and the Visual Arts* (New York: Harry N. Abrams, 1998), p. 16.

[62] Rudlin, *Commedia dell'Arte*, p. 77.

[63] Thomas Heywood, *An Apology for Actors* (London, 1612), sig. E2v.

[64] See my discussion of John Fletcher's *Monsieur Thomas* and Richard Brome's *The English Moor* in chapter five.

hell, reaffirming the audience's belief that the community of the saved was homogeneous, and that the hard-fought establishment of that harmonious norm was also the story of divine salvation.

Court performances were another story. Nobles and their ladies, kings and queens participated in feasts of misrule, donning leather vizards that could hide their identity and allow liberties beyond the scope of everyday life. The exotic Moorish kings who appeared in such disguising required brightly colored, lavish costumes, often garnished with bells. Urban processions that were enacted on London's streets rather than at court were lavish as well, relying on display rather than dramatic action for effect. The records give no hint as to how these figures were regarded by their respective audiences, but their display alongside giants, wildmen, and other exotica suggests that they were mainly spectacles of strangeness, that the religious meanings that were originally coded into "Moros y Cristianos" had become vestigial rather than visceral. Their significance to the secular arm of authority was more palpable; blackfaced Moors in court pageants and urban processions who could suddenly turn white symbolically enacted the colonizing myth that king and merchants could control and transform the darkened aliens beyond England's shores.

Thus by the 1580s blackened faces on the public stage resonated with traditional rural and urban signifying codes that had developed out of different performance traditions, but which complemented each other in many ways. The black devil and trickster who subverted the Christian community, and the Moorish king who ruled over an exotic realm far from England's shores, were equally enduring symbols of alterity, and, as subsequent chapters will demonstrate, Elizabethan dramatists were not shy about exploiting both.

CHAPTER 3

Talking devils

Even though mystery cycles were banned in the late sixteenth century as England became more militantly Protestant, their association of blackness with the demonic continued to resonate in the plays performed for Londoners in the newly opened public theatres. Moors continued to appear in court pageantry well into Elizabeth's reign, but not as frequently as they had in her father's time. During the 1580s, however, other kinds of coding were superimposed on representations of blackness as geographical awareness of darkly pigmented sub-Saharan Africans became more widespread, fostered especially by the publication of travel narratives.

In the aftermath of John Hawkins's slave-trading expeditions to the coast of Africa in the 1560s, English people could see black slaves in port cities and likely became increasingly aware of the role black Africans played in Iberia's New World empires. Travel narratives compiled in Richard Eden and Richard Willes's *The History of Travayle in the West and East Indies* (1577) and Richard Hakluyt's *Principall Navigations, Voiages, and Discoveries of the English Nation* (1589) circulated images of black Africans that were grotesque and fascinating. English accounts – or translations into English of foreign accounts – repeatedly criticized sub-Saharan Africans for paganism, barbarism, and even sub-human ways of living.[1] Appalled by nakedness that in the authors' culture was equated with lust and lasciviousness, European writers excoriated the Africans for bestial sexual practices and promiscuous lifestyles. Robert Gainsh's report of his 1554 voyage to equatorial Africa claimed, for example, that in Africa "women are common: for they contracte no matrimonie, neyther have respect to chastitie."[2] Hakluyt's *Principall Navigations* included a poem by Robert Baker that describes Africans as "black as coles." He recounts:

---

[1] See Alden T. Vaughan and Virginia Mason Vaughan, "Before Othello: Elizabethan Representations of Sub-Saharan Africans," *William and Mary Quarterly*, 3rd ser., 54 (1987), 19–44, for an analysis of a broad range of texts describing black Africans that circulated from ca. 1560 to 1600.
[2] Richard Eden and Richard Willes, *The History of Travayle in the West and East Indies* (London, 1577), sig. 349r.

> Their Captaine comes to me
>   as naked as my naile,
> Not hauing witte or honestie
>   to couer once his taile.
> By which I doe here gesse
>   and gather by the way,
> That he from man and manlinesse
>   was voide and clean astray.[3]

To at least one fully clothed English observer, nakedness signified not just promiscuity, but bestiality. As English readers learned more about sub-Saharan Africa, blackness took on additional significations, connoting an exotic but forbidden sexuality.

This chapter examines the black characters who were first portrayed on the public stage and considers how these significations worked together to create a new type of villain. In these plays, moreover, blackface's signification was complicated by the actor's new authority as a speaking character, by a shift from display to performance.[4] To be sure, devils sometimes spoke in medieval cycle plays, but their speech acts were limited. Seldom did they participate in the illocutionary acts of self-representation, promising, thanking, greeting, affirming, etc. which automatically add a multitude of possible signifiers to be read as part of the speaker's character. In the 1580s and early 1590s a crucial shift took place from the simple *display* of blackened devils and Moorish kings to the white actor's *impersonation* of black characters who were meant to be imagined as human beings from the exotic and dangerous regions of sub-Saharan Africa.[5]

I

Elizabethan playwrights began by using Moorish kings to teach moral lessons. Royalty was often the issue. The fall of kings, white and black,

---

[3] Robert Baker, "The First Voyage of Robert Baker to Gunie," and "The Second Voyage to Gunie," in Richard Hakluyt, *The Principall Navigations, Voyages, and Discoveries of the English Nation* (London, 1589), pp. 132–42; quote from p. 132.

[4] Keir Elam contends that "Dramatic discourse is a network of complementary and conflicting illocutions and perlocutions; in a word, linguistic *interaction*, not so much descriptive as performative." Characters who talk are consequently far more complex than those who appear on display or in dumb shows. See *The Semiotics of Theatre and Drama* (London: Routledge, 1980), p. 159.

[5] Andrew Gurr describes the London audience's appetite for realism during the 1590s: "It was not simply realism, though that went with it, but something more like an emotional response to staged events which depended for its strength on a conviction that the display was a form of truth." See *Playgoing in Shakespeare's London*, 2nd edn. (Cambridge: Cambridge University Press, 1996), p. 139.

often exemplified the folly of human ambition. In 1566, for example, George Gascoigne's *Iocasta* was presented at Gray's Inn. The opening dumb show included the following tableau: Ambition, figured as Sesostres, king of Egypt, "who beeing in his time and reigne a mightie Conquerour, yet not content to have subdued many princes, and taken from them their kingdomes and dominions, did in like maner cause those Kinges whome he had so ouercome, to draw in his Chariote like Beastes and Oxen, thereby to content his vnbrideled ambitious desire."[6] Sesostres, whose face might have been darkened to suggest his Egyptian origins, was twice drawn around the stage before the play proper began. Twenty years later, Marlowe adapted this stage convention in *Tamburlaine*, with Moors drawing the chariot. Aware that black slaves were commonly employed as beasts of burden in other parts of the world, Marlowe may have added this exotic touch to the humiliation of the Turkish bashaw because horses would not work in the theatre. Stage directions for *Tamburlaine, Part One* read: "[*Enter*] *Tamburlaine, Techelles, Theridamus, Usumcasane, Zenocrate, Anippe, two Moors drawing Bajezeth in his cage.*"[7] Henslowe's accounts for the Rose Theatre list "viij viserdes" along with "Tamberlyne brydell,"[8] which suggests that the actors used masks that could be easily put on for the short time the Moors were on stage and quickly removed when the actors played other roles. The second part of *Tamburlaine*, performed in 1588, has the captured son of Bajezeth promise a reward to his keeper if he will help him escape: "With naked negroes shall thy coach be drawn" (1.3.40).

Other dramatists adapted this convention. Thomas Lodge's *Wounds of Civil War*, also written in the 1580s, calls for the Roman dictator Scilla to enter, "*in his chair triumphant of gold, drawn by four Moors before the chariot.*"[9] George Peele included Moors in *King Edward I* with the stage direction, "*The trumpets sound. Queene Elinor in her litter borne by foure Negro Mores.*"[10] In 1594 King James VI of Scotland imitated this popular theatrical convention at court when a blackamoor was used to draw in a chariot.[11] And Francis Beaumont and John Fletcher's *Four Plays or*

---

[6] *Early English Classical Tragedies*, ed. John W. Cunliffe (Oxford: Clarendon Press, 1912), p. 71.

[7] *The Complete Plays of Christopher Marlowe*, ed. Irving Ribner (New York: Odyssey Press, 1963), 4.2.1sd.

[8] *Documents of the Rose Playhouse*, ed. Carol Chillington Rutter (Manchester: Manchester University Press, 1984), p. 136.

[9] Thomas Lodge, *The Wounds of Civil War*, ed. Joseph W. Houppert (Lincoln: University of Nebraska Press, 1969), p. 43.

[10] George Peele, *King Edward the First*, ed. Horace Hart (Oxford: Oxford University Press for the Malone Society, 1911), sig. E1r.

[11] See the Second Arden Edition of *A Midsummer Night's Dream*, ed. Harold F. Brooks (London: Methuen, 1979), p. xxxiv.

Moral Representations of 1610 introduced "*a Chariot drawn by two Moors.*"[12] Whether Marlowe's use of Moors for the chariot-pulling entrance was influenced by personal acquaintance with black African slaves, one cannot say, but certainly by the late 1580s Londoners might come into contact with black servants in a variety of capacities.[13]

Marlowe's chariot-pullers, the Rose documents suggest, wore black vizards to signify their Moorishness. Black leather masks that covered the entire face were a frequent disguise. The illustrated title page to the 1615 quarto of Thomas Kyd's *Spanish Tragedy* depicts the villain Lorenzo with his face covered by just such a vizard; and the stage directions of the 1592 quarto direct Lorenzo, Balthazar, Cerberin, and Pedringano to enter "disguised,"[14] which suggests that the murderers' use of black vizards was standard practice from the play's initial performances in the late 1580s through its revisions in the Jacobean period. Black vizards did not always signify Moorishness, but *The Spanish Tragedy* suggests that the association between black faces and villainy established in the mystery cycles continued in the early Elizabethan theatre.

Since the Moors prescribed by Marlowe's stage directions had no lines to speak, they appeared simply as the objects of display. Whether they were meant to provide authenticity to exotic locales such as Rome or northern Africa where black slaves were common, or simply serve as a novelty item, their blackness was their most salient feature. And in 1587–88, George Peele decided to exploit that feature in his drama depicting the fate of three kings.

II

Gascoigne had figured ambition in Sesostres, whose chariot was drawn by the kings he had conquered. The fall of kings was a popular literary trope from the *de casibus* tragedies of Chaucer's "Monk's Tale" well into the 1580s, so it is not surprising that the theme should be imposed upon contemporary events, such as the battle fought at Alcazar in northern Africa on 4 August 1578. After a four-hour blood bath, three kings lay dead on the plain: Sebastian, King of Portugal, Mohammed El-Mesloukh, King of Barbary, and Abd-el-Malek, rival claimant to the Berber throne. John Polemon's

[12] Francis Beaumont and John Fletcher, *Four Plays or Moral Representations in One*, in *The Works of Francis Beaumont and John Fletcher*, vol. x, ed. A. R. Waller (Cambridge: Cambridge University Press, 1912), p. 311.
[13] See Peter Fryer, *Staying Power: The History of Black People in Britain* (London: Pluto Press, 1984), chaps. 1 and 2.
[14] Thomas Kyd, *The Spanish Tragedy*, Malone Society Reprint (Oxford: Oxford University Press, 1949), sig. D2v.

The Second Part of the Booke of Battailes was translated into English from Thomas Freigin's Latin narrative *Historia de Bello Africano*, a description of the battle of Alcazar based on Spanish sources. This text served as the source for Peele's *The Battle of Alcazar*, the first English play to represent a black Moor on the public stage as a speaking character. Polemon's translation drives home the moral of this story:

These dead bodies of three kings being brought into one Pauilion, made an horrible spectacle, and wrong teares from the beholders. For what more sorrowfull and horrible a sight could there bee, than to beholde three most mightie kings, that died in one battaile, lying together.[15]

Spectacle is the key word here; the display of the bodies serves as an emblem of the transience of human ambitions.

Like the color-coded opposition of saved and damned souls in medieval pageants, part of this spectacle's message lay in its opposition of white and black, for Mohammed El-Mesloukh (or Muly Mahamet, as both Polemon and Peele term him) was the offspring of a "bondwoman, that was a blacke Negroe"; because he was "of his mothers complection," he "was commonly called the Black King."[16] Polemon describes Muly Mahamet as

of stature meane, of bodie weake, of coulour so blacke, that he was accompted of many for a *Negro* or black *Moore*. He was of a perverse nature, he would neuer speak the trueth, he did all things subtelly and deceitfully. He was not delighted in armes, but as he shewed in all battailes, of nature cowardly, and effeminate.[17]

Muly's opposite, his uncle Abd-el-Malek, is a white Moor. Polemon describes him as

of a meane stature, of a fine proportion of bodie, with brode shoulders, white face, but intermixed with red, which did gallantlie garnish his cheekes, a blacke beard thicke, and curled, great eies and graie. In summe, he was a verie proper man, and verie comelie in all his actions and iestures and verie strong.[18]

The opposition of black and white, evil and good, was thus not Peele's invention, but already coded in his source, a narrative derived from Spanish accounts of the battle. Peele's Muly conforms to Polemon's image of blackness, conveying the deceitful, cowardly Moor through language and action.

The Battle of Alcazar fascinates historically minded critics because it is, as the Presenter proclaims, "contemporary." It dramatizes King Philip II of

---

[15] John Polemon, *The Second Part of the Booke of Battailes, Fought in Our Age* (London, 1587), p. 81v.
[16] Eldred D. Jones, *Othello's Countrymen: The African in English Renaissance Drama* (London: Oxford University Press, 1965), p. 138, n 23.
[17] Polemon, *Second Part*, p. 83r.   [18] Polemon, *Second Part*, p. 82v.

Spain's treachery in promising aid to Sebastian that never materializes; it lauds English heroism in the madcap character of Thomas Stukeley (who abandoned plans to invade Ireland in the Catholic cause to fight alongside Sebastian and then – to Elizabeth's relief – died in the battle); and it presents a positive picture of Ahmed-el-Mansour (Peele's Muly Mahamet Seth) who inherited the Moroccan throne and was to become Elizabeth's ally until they both died in 1603. But for this chapter's purposes, its presentation of the demonized "Negro Moor" in a speaking role (enacted by no less an actor than London's leading tragedian, Edward Alleyn) is its most salient feature.

Peele structured the events of Polemon's narrative into a five-act drama that is part revenge tragedy, part history.[19] Each act begins with a dumb show and Presenter, a "Portingal," who interprets the spectacle and focuses the play's sprawling action. His initial rhetoric is reminiscent of Tamburlaine's; he describes King Sebastian as "An honourable and couragious king," inflamed by honor "that pricks the princely minde, / To followe rule and climbe the stately chaire." Sebastian's ambition is misguided, however, for he aids "the Negro Muly [Ma]Hamet," who is

> Blacke in his looke, and bloudie in his deeds,
> And in his shirt staind with a cloud of gore,
> Presents himselfe with naked sword in hand,
> Accompanied as now you may behold,
> With devils coted in the shapes of men.
>
> (1–20)[20]

The face painted black, the blood-stained shirt, the upheld sword, and the devils are an emblematic display, a tableau taken over from the homiletic tradition of the mystery cycles. Muly expands on the equation between blackness and the demonic through his actions; in the ensuing dumb show Muly and his son smother Muly's brothers as they lie in their beds. Then they strangle Muly's uncle Abdelmunen, rightful heir to the throne of Barbary. The Presenter declares:

> Saie not these things are faind, for true they are,
> And understand how eager to injoy
> His fathers crowne, this unbeleeving Moore
> Murthering his unkle and his brethren,
> Triumphs in his ambitious tyrannie,
> Till Nemesis high mistres of revenge

---

[19] A. R. Braunmuller, *George Peele* (Boston: Twayne, 1983), p. 76.
[20] Quotations from *The Battle of Alcazar* are cited by line number from *The Dramatic Works of George Peele*, vol. II, ed. John Yoklavich (New Haven: Yale University Press, 1961). Yoklavich uses the 1594 quarto for his text, but supplements it with information from the extant theatrical plot used by the Admiral's Men.

> That with her scourge keepes all the world in awe,
> With thundering drums awakes the God of warre,
> . . . to inflict
> Vengeance on this accursed Moore for sinne, . . .
> Sit you and see this true and tragicke warre,
> A modern matter full of bloud and ruth,
> Where three bolde kings confounded in their height,
> Fall to the earth contending for a crowne,
> And call this warre *The battell of Alcazar*.   (30–54)

This opening vignette brings together elements Peele would exploit throughout the play: Marlovian language that evokes faraway, exotic locales and the adventurous deeds of hero-conquerors; the Senecan/Kydian invocation of revenge for bloody wrongs committed by the villain; the fall and death of kings, a *de casibus* reminder of the transitory nature of worldly ambition; the visually terrifying display of devils painted black; and, Peele's most intriguing innovation, the claim that this account is a "true" representation of real people and "modern" events, not a fiction. Muly is a "real" king, not just a painted devil.

After he is presented to the audience much as Lucifer or a devil was introduced in cycle plays, Muly Mahamet makes a dramatic entrance in 1.2. Peele's stage directions read: "*Enter the Moore in his chariot, attended with [a page on each side, Calypolis his wife, Muly Mahamet] his sonne. Pisano his captaine with his gard and treasure*" (190 sd). In fine Tamburlainian iambic pentameters Muly commits himself to a course of action:

> Our enemies keepe upon the mountaine tops,
> And have incampt themselves not farre from Fesse,
> Madame, gold is the glue, sinewes, and strength of war,
> And we must see our treasure may go safe.   (194–97)

Cast in the play's opening dumb show as a one-dimensional devil, Muly switches codes to make his initial appearance here as a Moorish king, complete with family, guard, and treasure; this Moor drives the chariot instead of pulling it. His mastery of the English language is a form of "linguistic insurgency," that demonstrates his control and agency.[21] Muly promises that he will fight his enemies and preserve his treasure.[22] Added to the Prologue's claim that this is "true," that the blackened actor stands

[21] Ian Smith's discussion of Aaron's "linguistic insurgency" seems appropriate to Muly Hamet and to Eleazar in *Lust's Dominion* as well. See "Those 'slippery customers': Rethinking Race in *Titus Andronicus*," *Journal of Theatre and Drama* 3 (1997), 45–58.
[22] In Elam's taxonomy of illocutionary acts, this statement would be categorized as a "commissive." See *Semiotics of Theatre*, pp. 166–67.

in for a human being who actually lived and died in northern Africa, Muly's performative speech incarnates, so to speak, the homiletic marker of blackness in a sixteenth-century person.

After Muly's initial defeat by Abdelmelec and being left to starve in the mountains, Muly brings flesh he has stolen from a lioness to feed his wife Calypolis, a figure reminiscent of Marlowe's Zenocrate. This act further complicates our reading of Muly, for he cannot be a one-dimensional devil or simply a bloodthirsty Moor if he is concerned for his wife's welfare. The play concludes with Muly's unheroic performance on the battlefield, which negates the stereotype of Moors as ferocious fighters; in the heat of battle he cries for a horse "to flie / To swimme the river villaine, and to flie." In his last soliloquy before he exits, Muly curses the black mother who gave him life:

> Thou mother of my life that broughtst me forth,
> Curst maist thou be for such a cursed sonne,
> Curst be thy sonne with everie curse thou hast,
> Ye elements of whome consists this play,
> This masse of flesh, this cursed crazed corpes,
> Destroy, dissolve, disturbe, and dissipate,
> What water, earth, and aire conjeald.   (1279–85)

Blackness, thus, is perceived by Muly as a curse laid on his body from his birth, and it makes him wish the corporeal flesh that bears its mark would dissolve. One wonders whether Peele is here alluding to the "curse of Cham," the theory that sub-Saharan Africans are descended from the reprobate son of Noah. At any rate, it is intriguing that instead of blaming his allies' lack of military prowess or the vagaries of political alliances, Muly locates the source of his troubles in the pigmentation derived from his mother.

The play's final lines report Muly's flight:

> Seeking to save his life by shamefull flight,
> He mounteth on a hot Barbarian horse,
> And so in purpose to have past the streame,
> His headstrong stead throwes him from out his seate,
> Where diving oft for lacke of skill to swim,
> It was my chance alone to see him drowned.
>
> (1430–35)

While the corpse of Sebastian is to be returned to "Christendome," the new King of Barbary decrees that Muly Mahamet will be made into a spectacle to teach the world not to "hall on princes" to injurious war: "His skin we will be parted from his flesh. / And being stifned out and stuft with strawe, / So to deterre and feare the lookers on" (1441–45). Polemon notes that this black-skinned figure was to "bee carried about thorough out all prouinces of his kingdome, for to deterre all other for attempting the like at anie time after."[23]

To be sure, the negative overtones of Muly's blackness are readily apparent in Polemon's narrative which in turn came from Spanish sources, but Peele transformed that blackness into a visual spectacle of strangeness. *The Battle of Alcazar* presents a typology of otherness which moves from England, where "Sacred, imperiall, and holy is her [Elizabeth's] seat / Shining with wisdome, love and mightines" (678–79), to King Sebastian of Portugal who, because he wishes to "plant the Christian fa[i]th in Affrica" (734), initiates a misguided war, to Abdelmelec, a noble barbarian who fights for his rightful throne, to the black "ambitious Negro moor" Muly Mahamet. From the first, Muly is "Blacke in his looke, and bloudie in his deeds." Blackness and villainy are originary conditions, not effect and cause; the opening dumb show acts out what Muly is, not what he becomes. The play's ensuing action complicates that signification, but it does not negate it. The existence of the absolutes of moral corruption (represented in Muly) and English moral perfection (embodied in Sebastian's paeon to Elizabeth) allows a space in between for troubling, slippery categories such as Iberian Catholicism and the heathenism of the Moorish king el-Mansour, whom England courts as a trade partner.

Muly Mahamet has roughly 210 lines to speak for himself, not a terribly large part for the Admiral's Company's leading actor. True, he has a wonderfully Marlovian soliloquy:

> Now have I set these Portugals aworke,
> To hew a waie for me unto the crowne,
> Or with your weapons here to dig your graves,
> You bastards of the night and Erybus,
> Fiends, Fairies, hags that fight in beds of steele,
> Range through this armie with your yron whips,
> Drive forward to this deed this christian crew,
> And let me triumph in the tragedie,
> Though it be seald and honourd with my bloud.
>
> (1133–41)

---

[23] Polemon, *Second Part*, p. 82r. Muly makes a brief appearance in the anonymous play, *The Famous Historye of the Life and Death of Captaine Thomas Stukeley* (London, 1605), which was probably patched together in the 1590s and printed in 1605. Muly first appears with Calipolis "drawne in their chariot"; Stukeley notes that 'He speaks all Mars," but as in *The Battle of Alcazar*, he runs away from the battle. At the play's finale, the victor commands Muly's skin to be flayed "from of the flesh: from foote vnto the head, / and stuft within: and so be borne about, / through all the partes of our Dominions, / to terefie the like that shal pursue / to lift their swords against their souerayn" (sig. L3v).

Despite many such lines of glorious rant, Muly must compete for the audience's attention with the Christian martyrs Thomas Stukeley and King Sebastian. Even so, the blackfaced and flamboyant Muly was probably an automatic guarantee that, from the spectacular chariot-driving entrance to his final lines, the audience's gaze would focus on Edward Alleyn.

III

Peele's Muly Mahamet is deceitful and cruel, but, in contrast to his successors on the Elizabethan stage, he is not sexually corrupt. We see him in a monogamous marriage to Calypolis, and in 2.3 he is solicitous towards her. Muly's color, a biological curse laid upon him by his mother, is never associated with the bestial, merely the cruel and demonic. The theatrical representation of blackness becomes vastly more complex when we turn to Shakespeare's *Titus Andronicus*, however, where Aaron the black Moor is a self-pronounced villain and adulterer.[24] Aaron's sexual relationship with a white woman suggests Shakespeare's fascination with what Eric Lott describes as the myth of "black male sexual potency."[25] Spurred, perhaps, by travelers' accounts of Africans' promiscuity, the dramatist may have shared a widely circulated notion that black African males were lascivious, even bestial, in their desires. Whatever the reasons, Aaron is the first in a long line of black male heroes (crafted by white authors) who flaunt their sexuality as a quality inherent in their blackness.

Shakespeare's audience may well have assumed that a character called Aaron would be gifted with unusual oratorical abilities. His name originates in the book of Exodus, where he appears as Moses's brother; noted for his eloquence, Aaron is appointed by God to be the spokesperson before Pharaoh and to demand the release of the children of Israel from bondage. Shakespeare's Aaron is also notable for his eloquence. His role is the second lengthiest in the play; after a long silence in the opening act, his words and actions direct much of the plot. From his devilish antecedents on the medieval stage, he inherits a special relationship with the audience in soliloquies and asides that express delight in his ability to deceive and manipulate. Many of these speeches are commissives that promise a particular course

---

[24] Mary Floyd-Wilson argues in her study of early modern geohumoral and climatic theories that Aaron is not presented as lascivious because he denies interest in venereal desires in 2.2.30–37 when he meets Tamora in the woods outside Rome. But Floyd-Wilson takes this speech as an expression of his general character and neglects the specific context – he is busy planning a rape and a murder. Elsewhere in the play he is quite pleased that he has "done" Tamora (4.2.78). See *English Ethnicity and Race in Early Modern Drama* (Cambridge: Cambridge University Press, 2003), pp. 43–44.

[25] Eric Lott, *Love and Theft: Blackface Minstrelsy and the American Working Class* (New York: Oxford University Press, 1993), p. 57.

of action and highlight his evil plans. This special relationship to the audience explains much of his appeal, for Aaron's obvious zest for violence and mayhem makes him the wittiest and most energetic character in the play. In this, as many commentators have noted, he is also strongly reminiscent of Marlowe's Barabas, the Machiavellian villain/hero of *The Jew of Malta*. According to Jonathan Bate, Aaron's catalogue of misdeeds (5.1.124–44) is modelled on the exchange between Barabas and Ithamore (a son of Aaron in the Old Testament) in which "they outdo each other on outrageous ill-doing."[26]

The most important source for Aaron is the seventeenth story from the second part of Matteo Bandello's *Novelle* (1554), translated into French by François de Belleforest in his *Histoires Tragiques* (1570). Bandello tells the story of a Moorish slave in Majorca who takes revenge on his master by abducting his wife and three sons and sequestering them in a nearby tower; after raising the drawbridge so that no one could gain access, he rapes his master's wife. When the husband hears her screams and those of the children, he curses the Moor, who replies by tossing the eldest son out of the tower to his death. The Moor promises the husband he will restore his wife and remaining sons if the husband will cut off his nose. The husband does so, but the Moor laughingly reneges on the bargain, dashes the other two boys against the wall and throws them to the ground. Still laughing, the cruel Moor slits the lady's throat and lets her fall from the top of the tower. Then in a gesture of defiance, claiming his thirst for vengeance is at last satisfied, the Moor throws himself headlong from the tower onto the rocks below. The moral is that "men should not make use of slaves of this sort, for that they are seldom found faithful and are mostly full of all manner of filth and uncleanness and stink at all seasons like buck-goats."[27] Bandello thus incorporates the travel narratives' derogatory tone into his story, suggesting the danger to white women of bringing a black male slave into the household.

This story provides the basis for Aaron's gleeful deception of Titus in act 3, but it does not account for the Moor's paternity in act 4, scene 2, a scene which Francesca T. Royster has recently argued "complicates whiteness" and reflects the play's "preoccupation with miscegenation and mixed-race children."[28] An illegitimate mixed-race baby does appear in

---

[26] William Shakespeare, *Titus Andronicus*, ed. Jonathan Bate, Third Arden Series (London: Routledge, 1995). See Bate's introduction, p. 84. Quotations from *Titus Andronicus* are taken from this edition.

[27] *The Novels of Matteo Bandello Bishop of Agen Now First Done into English Prose and Verse*, 6 vols. (London: Villon Society, 1890), vol. v, p. 278.

[28] Francesca T. Royster, "White-limed Walls: Whiteness and Gothic Extremism in Shakespeare's *Titus Andronicus*," *Shakespeare Quarterly* 51 (2000), 432–55; quotes from 447 and 449.

The History of Titus Andronicus, an eighteenth-century chapbook, which some scholars believe is the printed version of an earlier manuscript. The chapbook describes how the Empress "grew pregnant, and brought forth a Blackmoor Child: this grived the Emperor extreamly, but she allayed his Anger, by telling him it was conceived by the Force of Imagination, and brought many suborned Women and Physicians to testify the like had often happened. This made the Emperor send the Moor into Banishment."[29] If we accept the chapbook as Shakespeare's source, it is clear that Shakespeare transformed the episode of the black baby from a mere aside into a crucial building block of Aaron's character.

To early twentieth-century editors, such as John Dover Wilson, the black baby seemed "an excrescence on the plot,"[30] but as the biological product of a sexual union between a white woman and a black man, he is crucial to any discussion of race in Shakespeare's earliest tragedy. The baby also sets up an intertextual relationship between Shakespeare and George Best, whose *True Discourse of the Late Voyages of Discoverie* was first printed in 1578 and later included in the second edition of Richard Hakluyt's compendium of travel narratives, *The Principal Navigations* (1600).[31]

Best begins with a description of "the people of Africa, especially the Ethiopians" who are "so cole blacke, and their haire like wooll curled short";[32] even so, Aaron describes his "fleece of woolly hair that now uncurls" in act 2 (2.34), and in act 3, Titus refers to him as "a coal-black Moor" (3.2.79). But the bulk of Best's analysis is a rejection of the climatological explanation for the Ethiop's black skin. He argues that "I my selfe have seene an Ethiopian as blacke as a cole brought into England, who taking a faire English woman to wife, begat a sonne in all respects as blacke

[29] Geoffrey Bullough, *Narrative and Dramatic Sources of Shakespeare Plays*, vol. VI (London: Routledge and Kegan Paul, 1966), p. 39. Bullough and Oxford editor Eugene Waith believe the chapbook represents a legitimate source, whereas Bate believes it was compiled after Shakespeare's play. See Bate's introduction to *Titus Andronicus*, pp. 83–90.

[30] William Shakespeare, *Titus Andronicus*, ed. John Dover Wilson (Cambridge: Cambridge University Press, 1948), p. xi.

[31] Quotations from Best are taken from *The Principal Navigations Voyages Traffiques and Discoveries of the English Nation* by Richard Hakluyt, vol. VII (Glasgow: James MacLehose and Sons, 1904). In "'And wash the Ethiop white': Femininity and the Monstrous in *Othello*," in *Shakespeare Re-produced: The Text in History and Ideology*, ed. Jean E. Howard and Marion F. O'Connor (New York: Methuen, 1987), pp. 141–62, Karen Newman demonstrates how Best served as an "enabling discourse" for the association between blackness and monstrosity that circulated in England during the 1580s (p. 148), but she does not specifically relate his analysis to *Titus Andronicus*. Joyce Green MacDonald links the two in her essay, "'The Force of Imagination': The Subject of Blackness in Shakespeare, Jonson and Ravenscroft," in *Renaissance Papers 1991*, ed. George Walton Williams and Barbara J. Baines (Durham, NC: Southeastern Renaissance Conference, 1992), pp. 53–74.

[32] Best, *True Discourse*, p. 261.

as the father was, although England were his [the child's] native countrey, and an English woman his mother: whereby it seemeth this blacknes proceedeth rather of some natural infection of that man, which was so strong, that neither the nature of the Clime, neither the good complexion of the mother concurring, coulde any thing alter."[33]

Shakespeare dramatizes just such a scene in 4.2. The Nurse presents Aaron with his son:

> A joyless, dismal, black and sorrowful issue.
> Here is the babe, as loathsome as a toad
> Amongst the fair-faced breeders of our clime.
> The empress sends it thee, thy stamp, thy seal,
> And bids thee christen it with thy dagger's point.
>
> (4.2.68–72)

Demetrius rushes to kill the baby, the accursed "offspring of so foul a fiend" (81), but Aaron quickly seizes the child and declares:

> What, what, ye sanguine, shallow-hearted boys,
> Ye white-limed walls, ye alehouse painted signs!
> Coal-black is better than another hue
> In that it scorns to bear another hue;
> For all the water in the ocean
> Can never turn the swan's black legs to white,
> Although she lave them hourly in the flood.
>
> (4.2.99–105)

Aaron cleverly exploits the proverb that it is impossible to wash the Ethiop white, turning the tables on Chiron and Demetrius by accusing *them* of being "painted." Moreover, when Chiron confesses to blushing, Aaron decries the blush as a sign of weakness that will betray "The close enacts and counsels of thy heart" (120). "Black, says Aaron, is better than white because white is characteristically subject to black inscription: it can be defaced," observes Dympna Callaghan. "Black, in contrast, can neither be written on, nor can it be returned to white."[34] Although Tamora is a "fair-faced breeder" of a northern clime, Aaron's blackness predominates over her whiteness, marking his paternity on the child's skin. Shakespeare thus racializes both Aaron and Tamora as the binary opposites of black and white, put in contestatory relation to each other.[35]

[33] Best, *True Discourse*, p. 262.
[34] Dympna Callaghan, "'Othello Was a White Man,'" in *Shakespeare Without Women: Representing Gender and Race on the Renaissance Stage* (London: Routledge, 2000), p. 80.
[35] See Royster, "'White-limed Walls,'" 442–3 for a perceptive discussion of Gothic "whiteness" as opposed to Aaron's "blackness."

Aaron admits another possibility when he describes the child of his countryman Muly, a baby born to a white wife: "His child is like to her, fair as you [Demetrius] are" (4.2.156). Assuming we accept Steevens's textual emendation from Q's "Muliteus" to "Muly lives," the name suggests Peele's Muly Mahamet, and this echo of *The Battle of Alcazar* (which presented Moorish brothers, one white and one "Negro") repeats the common Elizabethan confusion concerning pigmentation and genetics. The black pigmentation that indelibly marks his baby as his own flesh and blood is strangely lacking in the offspring of his countryman, who can "pass" for Saturninus' child.

George Best concludes that "this blacknesse proceedeth of some naturall infection of the first inhabitants of that Countrey, and so all the whole progenie of them descended, are still polluted with the same blot of infection."[36] Like a congenital disease, blackness carries with it a curse from generation to generation. Best locates this curse in the biblical story of Noah. One of Noah's sons, Cham, disobeyed his father and "used company" with his wife in the ark in hopes that "the first child borne after the flood (by right and Lawe of nature) should inherite and possesse all the dominions of the earth." Instead, God ensured that "a sonne should bee borne whose name was Chus, who not onely it selfe, but all his posteritie after him should bee so blacke and lothsome, that it might remaine a spectacle of disobedience to all the worlde."[37] Blackness reiterates its meaning generation after generation.

As Kim F. Hall persuasively argues, essential to Best's *True Discourse* is the opposition between Ethiopian blackness and English whiteness. The offspring of a black father could not be white because "[t]o include him in the nation would be to break the desired homology between land, skin, and group identity, thereby overturning the associations of England with whiteness and fairness."[38] To Best, blackness is also performative; like the fall of Lucifer from heaven, Cham's disobedience is a "spectacle," a display of the indelible mark that sets him off as abnormal and "other," making whiteness the norm of the saved as opposed to the blackness of the damned. But unlike Lucifer's proud defiance, this disobedience is sexual, and thus the legend of Cham begets the indelible link between blackness and ungoverned sexuality.

Whether *Titus Andronicus* was influenced by George Best or not, Aaron's characterization seems to cross the line from color-coding into the murky

---

[36] Best, *True Discourse*, pp. 262–63.   [37] Best, *True Discourse*, p. 264.
[38] Kim F. Hall, *Things of Darkness: Economies of Race and Gender in Early Modern England* (Ithaca: Cornell University Press, 1995), p. 12.

2 The Peacham drawing of a conflated scene from Shakespeare's *Titus Andronicus*.

territory that George Fredrickson terms "proto-racism".[39] In Aaron, Elizabethan audiences saw blackness as a causative factor. Aaron was not black because he was evil, but evil because he was black; as he himself proclaims, "Let fools do good and fair men call for grace, / Aaron will have his soul black like his face" (3.1.204–05). Unlike Lucifer who is blackened as a consequence of his fall, the Moor implies that his dark pigmentation predisposes him to evil.

We have a unique opportunity to imagine how Aaron may have looked on stage in 1594.[40] Henry Peacham's drawing of a reconstructed scene from *Titus Andronicus* in the Longleat manuscript provides the only contemporary costume sketch we have for a Shakespearean play. As many commentators have noted, the drawing is not a replica of any specific performance moment, but a reading of a scene drawn from the artist's memory. The drawing features opposed groups of characters: three helpless Goths kneeling on the right and three powerful Romans on the left. On the side, as Richard Levin astutely observes, "the artist has designed his treatment of the figure of Aaron so that it will stand out as a startling violation of

[39] George M. Fredrickson, *The Black Image in the White Mind* (Middletown, CT: Wesleyan University Press, 1987).

[40] For a discussion of the date on the manuscript, see Herbert Berry, "The Date on the 'Peacham' Manuscript," *Shakespeare Bulletin* 17 (Spring 1999), 5–6.

this symmetrical design." Moreover, Aaron "is distinguished from both the Goths and the Romans by his color and nationality."[41]

The drawing also suggests how the actor performing Aaron would have been costumed and what his characteristic posture might have been. His face, hands, and legs are black. Presumably, the actor's face and neck were painted, while black gloves and leggings could have been used for his appendages. Something like a bandana encircles his head under his short black hair (presumably a wig of "coarse budge"). His costume is a long-sleeved tunic, which reaches only to the top of his thighs. He also wears boots that come up to the mid-calf. His right arm is raised aloft, with a finger pointing out, as if he were demanding something. In his left hand he brandishes a sword. As Levin argues, this posture indicates that he represents a threat to the Andronici.[42] This Aaron is a menacing figure who stands out from the other characters by his color, his placement, his posture, and his upraised sword.

The language of other characters also calls attention to Aaron's outsider status and notes his physical characteristics. In addition to the play's many references to his coal-black skin, Lucius describes him as a "wall-eyed slave" with a "fiendlike face" (5.1.44–45). The *Oxford English Dictionary* cites these lines as an early usage of the term "wall-eyed": "having one or both eyes of an excessively light colour, so that the iris is hardly distinguishable from the white . . . Also, having a divergent squint, which exposes an excessive portion of the white of the eye." Perhaps the black make-up used by the actor who played Aaron emphasized the whiteness of his eyes in an effect similar to the exaggerated white eyes that were characteristic of nineteenth-century American minstrel shows. Lucius' reference to his "fiendlike face" suggests that this effect may have also been true of the devil figures in earlier plays. At any rate, this utterance, coming late in the play, reiterates that Aaron's blackness is a conventionally recognized marker of his damned condition.

But Aaron is more than a character on display. After his appearance in the first scene, he assumes agency and uses language effectively. Despite his evil deeds, his fierce determination to protect his child humanizes him, complicating and thickening blackness's signification. As Joyce Green MacDonald

[41] Richard Levin, "The Longleat Manuscript and *Titus Andronicus*," *Shakespeare Quarterly* 53 (2002), 323–40; quote from 334. Levin also persuasively rebuts June Schlueter's widely discussed contention that the Peacham drawing is based on another play, *A Very Lamentable Tragedy*, which survives in a German version. See Schlueter, "Rereading the Peacham Drawing," *Shakespeare Quarterly* 50 (1999), 171–84.

[42] See Levin, "The Longleat Manuscript," 333, for a discussion of the significance of Aaron's appearance.

contends, Aaron demonstrates a "dangerous implacability" and "scorn of the standards of a white society" that is indifferent to the value of human life.[43] By the play's finale, when he is sentenced to be buried waist-deep in the earth, he loses the power to act and becomes the demonized scapegoat – like the black-skinned and stuffed figure of Muly Mahamet – who allows Roman and Goth to unite, opposing their civic values to his "barbarism." Despite Roman attempts to "enforce a silence on the alien," in his last defiant words Aaron once again uses the power of speech to resist.[44]

Aaron's role as a scapegoat was reinforced by the compositor who set the closing lines for the second quarto. Anxious to fill out a page, he modified Q1's last line and added four more:

> And being so, shall haue like want of pitty.
> See iustice done on *Aron* that damn'd Moore,
> By whom our heauie haps had their beginning:
> Than afterwards to order well the state,
> That like euents may nere it ruinate.[45]

The compositor seems to have forgotten the deaths of Alarbus and Mutius, which started the play's bloody chain of events. To him Aaron is the author and engine of the tragedy's violent plot.

As I have argued elsewhere, Shakespeare's *Titus Andronicus*, composed during England's first attempts at building New World colonies, reflects English cultural anxieties about what was barbaric and what was civilized.[46] Shakespeare's manipulation of Gothic and Roman behavior throughout the play undercuts the easy assumption that civilized Rome cannot be barbaric, but the play's closure seeks to erase such ambiguities by naming Aaron and Tamora, the demonized black and the sexualized woman, as the loci of evil. Miscegenation thus became a marker for a variety of social problems, and *Titus Andronicus* established a pattern that would be repeated in English and American literature and culture for centuries.

IV

Lust's Dominion, or The Lascivious Queen, conventionally identified with *The Spanish Moor's Tragedy* by Dekker, Haughton and Day and dated in 1599/1600 even though the text was not printed until 1657, reiterates

---

[43] MacDonald, "Force of Imagination," p. 65.   [44] Smith, "Those 'slippery customers,'" 54.

[45] See Eugene Waith, ed., *Titus Andronicus* (Oxford: Oxford University Press, 1984), p. 194.

[46] See Virginia Mason Vaughan, "The Construction of Barbarism in *Titus Andronicus*," in *Race, Ethnicity, and Power in the Renaissance*, ed. Joyce Green MacDonald (Madison: Fairleigh Dickinson University Press, 1997), pp. 165–80, esp. pp. 175–76.

the sexual motif of *Titus Andronicus*. Cyrus Hoy describes the text that
has come down to us as "a fascinating compendium of Elizabethan and
Jacobean tragic themes . . . To the subjects of ambition and revenge as
treated in the Marlovian and Kydian tragedy of the late 1580s and early
1590s, *Lust's Dominion* adds a third tragic subject, lust."[47] The dedicatory
poem to Mr. F. K. (Francis Kirkman, the publisher) summarizes the play's
action:

> A Queen is Pictur'd here, whose lustful Flame
> Was so Insatiate, that it wants a Name
> To Speak it forth, Seeking to Bastardize
> Her Royal Issue that a MOOR might rise.
> He flatter'd Her, on purpose to Obtain
> His Ends to sit on th' Royal Throne of Spain.
> Black as his Face his Deeds appear'd at last,
> And What he Climb'd by, Did his Ruine hast.[48]

Whoever prepared this dedicatory poem in the 1650s equated the hero's
blackness with villainy, reiterating once again the centuries-old link between
a blackened face and damnation.

Eleazar appears in the Old Testament as the son of Aaron. In Numbers
22:25–26, Moses is commanded to take Aaron and "Eleazar his sonne,
& bring them vp into the mount of Hor. And cause Aaron to put of
his garments and put them vpon Eleazar his sonne; for Aaron shal be
gathered *to his fathers*, and shall dye there" (Geneva Bible). Whether or
not the author(s) of *Lust's Dominion* intended the audience to recognize an
intertextual relationship to *Titus Andronicus*, Eleazar's descent from Aaron
seems clear. Like Aaron, Eleazar is a black Moor who obtains power through
a sexual relationship with a royal white woman. Like Aaron, he is power-
hungry, ambitious, and vengeful. Like Aaron, Eleazar uses asides to establish
a special intimacy with the audience, who are likely to find the other
characters insipid by comparison. But unlike Aaron, Eleazar comes from a
noble lineage and has plausible political and psychological motives for his
villainy.

In the opening scene, the Moor reveals that his father (later identified as
King Abdala of Fesse) was killed in battle by King Philip, "a Spanish tyrant"
who took Eleazar captive (1.1.159). He claims that in his veins "Runs blood
as red, and royal as the best / And proud'st in *Spain*" (1.1.155–56). In the

[47] Cyrus Hoy, Introductions, Notes, and Commentaries to texts in *The Dramatic Works of Thomas
Dekker*, 4 vols. (Cambridge: Cambridge University Press, 1980), vol. IV, p. 67.
[48] *Lust's Dominion* in *The Dramatic Works of Thomas Dekker*, ed. Fredson Bowers, vol. IV (Cambridge:
Cambridge University Press, 1961), p. 130. Quotations from the text will be cited by act, scene, and
line numbers.

3 The figure of a "well-to-do" Moor from Cesare Vecellio's *Degli habiti* (Venice, 1590).

following act, the dying King Philip attests to Eleazar's "wise and war-like" behavior; because of his noble blood and the valor he showed in "victories / Achieved against the Turkish Ottoman" (2.2.120), Eleazar has risen to the heights of Spanish nobility and married Maria, the daughter of a grandee. More than that, he is the beloved of Spain's queen, who uses her wiles and her power on his behalf through most of the play.

Although Eleazar is like Aaron a Marlovian overreacher, a Barabas figure who uses stratagems and brute force to attain his vengeful purposes, the text does not allow us to forget his roots in the homiletic tradition. The King's son Philip charges: "Thou true stamp'd son of hell, / Thy pedigree is written in thy face" (4.1.40–41). Eleazar is a man who "hath damnation dy'd upon his flesh" (5.2.20). Cardinal Mendoza describes him as "that feind; / That damned *Moor*, that Devil, that Lucifer" (2.1.50–51). To the King of Portugal, he is

> a Devill, never did horrid feind
> Compel'd by som Magicians mighty charm,
> Break through the prisons of the solid earth,
> With more strange horror, then this Prince of hell,
> This damned Negro Lyon-like doth rush.
>
> (4.2.29–33)

Eleazar, however, relishes his blackness:

> Ha, ha, I thank thee provident creation,
> That seeing in moulding me thou didst intend,
> I should prove villain, thanks to thee and nature
> That skilful workman; thanks for my face,
> Thanks that I have not wit to blush.
>
> (2.2.66–70)

Eleazar's repetition of the trope that Moors cannot blush and thus have no shame suggests that he is playing a role that had become conventional. Later he counsels his Moorish followers, "Your cheeks are black, let not your souls look white" (2.2.81), and before he kills Fernando, he threatens: "Now by the proud complexion of my cheeks, / Tane from the kisses of the amorous sun . . . Thus shou'd my hand . . . Requite mine own dishonour" (3.2.164–68). Blackness is the mark of his villainy, but it is also connected to agency – almost as if Eleazar could, like the white actor who performs his role, choose to be black.

Blackness also marks, as Kim F. Hall observes, sensuality;[49] in this play lasciviousness spreads from Eleazar to permeate the court of Spain (in the

---

[49] Hall, *Things of Darkness*, p. 97.

person of the Queen Mother and her son Fernando) as well as the Church (in the Cardinal, who lusts after the Queen). Eleazar's warning to Isabella, the princess he seeks to seduce, suggests that his lust, like the black paint that covers the actor's hands, leaves a mark: "I'le touch you, yes, I'le taint you, see you this, / I'll bring you to this lure" (5.1.281–2). The paint, described by Prince Philip and Cardinal Mendoza (as they don Moorish habits) as the "oil of hell" (5.2.171), is difficult to remove from oneself, yet how easily it can spread to others!

Painting references are also metadramatic, reminding the audience that Eleazar's blackness/evil is a disguise worn for performance. In fact, much of Eleazar's power comes from his ability to play a part, whether the role of the aggrieved lover, the proud warrior, the devilish revenger, the trickster, or the seducer. The drama moves through a plot too convoluted to summarize here, but its culmination – similar in many respects to Marlowe's spectacular closure of *The Jew of Malta* – underlines Eleazar's actorly qualities. *Lust's Dominion* here draws upon two senses of the verb "to act"; the performer "acts" when he is playing a role, but in the process he is also taking action and assuming agency.

Eleazar does not know that his enemies Prince Philip and Hortenzo have killed his Moorish servants Zarack and Balthazar and donned the servants' clothes and painted their own faces black when he shows them his chamber of tortures. Then the Moor asks them to act out the parts of Philip and Hortenzo. Thus in a multi-layered impersonation, actors in the roles of Philip and Hortenzo, impersonating Zarack and Balthazar, pretend to be Philip and Hortenzo. Eleazar shows them where to stand and describes the tortures he has in mind; then he joins the performance himself, trying on the engine he has prepared for his enemy Cardinal Mendoza:

> This Iron engine on his head I'le clap,
> Like a Popes Miter, or a Cardinalls Cap.
> Then Manacle his hands as thou dost mine:
> So, so, I pray thee *Zarack*, set him [Balthazar] free
> That both of you may stand and laugh at mee.
>   (5.3.97–101)

Eleazar is hoisted with his own petard. As he sits imprisoned in an engine of his own devising, his enemies gather around him and taunt him as the "Devill of hell" (5.3.113). Philip stabs "the *Moor*, the actor of these evills" and thrusts "him down to act amongst the devills" (5.3.146–47), a role that Eleazar defiantly adopts in his final words:

Devills com claim your right, and when I am
Confin'd within your kingdom then shall I
Out-act you all in perfect villany.

(5.3.164–66)

Pinioned in the engine, the Moor has lost the power to take action, but he can still perform with brio. Despite his noble birth and his prowess on the battlefields of Spain, in death as in life, Eleazar's chosen role is that of the black devil. His entrapped body, like those of Muly Mahamet and Aaron, is a spectacle, a visual signifier of white Europe's power to contain the blackened and alien "other."

Lust's Dominion's final scene attempts to exorcize anxieties about miscegenation, the monstrous mating of black and white that would bastardize and pollute all of Spain. Eleazar, the visible locus of blackness, and his confederates are dead. The Queen Mother enters, repentant for her misdeeds, and proclaims her son Philip to be the legitimate heir to the Spanish throne – in contrast to announcements she had made earlier in the play. But this is still not enough. In the play's concluding couplet Philip seeks further containment by announcing: "And for this Barbarous *Moor*, and all his black train, / Let all the Moors be banished from *Spain*" (5.3.182–83). Pinioning is not sufficient; the spectacle of blackness must be removed from sight and from the realm. Only this drastic move can insure that the oil of blackness will no longer "taint" Spanish purity.

Lust's Dominion is generally dated ca. 1600, though many suspect that it is based on an earlier play in a Marlovian vein. From the mid-1580s into James's reign, England was at war with Spain; the play's depiction of a Spanish court torn apart by lust, deception, and political intrigue no doubt fed English prejudices. But as Jean Howard has shown in her discussion of *The Fair Maid of the West, Part I*, "While the Spanish are obviously intended to be seen as the antithesis of the English in matters of religion and moral decency, they are, however, also constructed *in relation* to the English in a way that suggests a subterranean fraternal bond between the two nations, a bond defined precisely by rivalrous antipathy."[50] No Englishmen appear in *Lust's Dominion*, but at the play's closure, its white audience might well have suppressed hatred of Spain and displaced its antagonism, as Howard suggests audiences of *Fair Maid* did, onto the blackened skin of an African Moor.

[50] Jean E. Howard, "An English Lass Amid the Moors: Gender, Race, Sexuality, and National Identity in Heywood's *The Fair Maid of the West*," in *Women, "Race," and Writing in the Early Modern Period*, ed. Margo Hendricks and Patricia Parker (London: Routledge, 1994), pp. 101–17; quote from p. 111.

It is easy to see how the eyes of white English spectators would have been drawn to the black bodies displayed at the conclusions of *The Battle of Alcazar*, *Titus Andronicus*, and *Lust's Dominion*. Like the medieval portrayal of black devils, their evil is coded by a blackened complexion, but, particularly in *Alcazar* and *Lust's Dominion*, the black Moors are constructed as being "true" – not fictional at all, but representative of real people in real places of northern Africa and Spain. During the course of the plays, these characters are given scope to act out their villainy, and in the process they are transformed from passive objects of display into impersonators who speak and take action. Then the plays conclude with spectacles – or at least the description of offstage spectacles – that fetishize and immobilize the villain's black body. Muly's black skin is to be stuffed and paraded through northern Africa as an object lesson, Aaron's body is to be pinioned waist-deep in the earth for all to see, and Eleazar is trapped in the engine he had devised, his body front and center. In the plays' final moments, the black body, the object of the fascinated white gaze, is at least theatrically and physically contained, robbed of agency and transformed from impersonation into silent – and safe – display. Like their devilish forebears on medieval pageant wagons, these blackened figures can then serve as a one-dimensional symbol against which white society can coalesce. The semantic complications that flourished during the plays' actions are, for the moment, forgotten. They would, however, reappear in later plays that distance the blackfaced character even further from his medieval origins.

CHAPTER 4

Kings and queens

In the decade after *The Battle of Alcazar*'s first performance, English people increasingly encountered actual people from Africa; impressions from real life now mixed with the earlier, quasi-fictional travelers' tales. The Barbary Company, founded in 1585, sought commercial ventures between Morocco and England; merchants in the sugar trade traveled between the two countries. Soon after the defeat of the Spanish Armada, a Moroccan emissary arrived in England. The best-known evidence of such contacts can be seen in the haunting portrait of Abd el-Ouahed ben Messaoud ben Mohammed Anoun, ambassador to Elizabeth from Muly Hamet (the only claimant to the throne of Morocco to survive the real battle of Alcazar), which now hangs in the Shakespeare Institute at Stratford-upon-Avon. El-Ouahed, who spent six months in London during 1600, was sent to Elizabeth's court to negotiate an alliance against Spain. Muly Hamet wanted an English fleet to help him invade Spain, a design too quixotic for Elizabeth's pragmatic diplomacy; his ambassador had to be content with trade agreements instead.

El-Ouahed's fascinating portrait features a distinguished but severe-looking man dressed in white. He wears a white turban and white flowing robes, covered by a black cloak. Hung from his side is an ornately carved sword and scabbard. The portrait states that his age is forty-two. His complexion is that of a Caucasian; English observers probably described him as a "tawny Moor," the usual term for Moroccans. Bernard Harris, who first brought the portrait to the attention of Shakespearean scholars, summarized contemporary accounts of the Moroccan entourage's visit: "To Elizabethan Londoners the appearance and conduct of the Moors was a spectacle and an outrage, emphasizing the nature of the deep difference between themselves and their visitors."[1] English merchants who came into contact with the Moroccan ambassador and his cohort frequently noted

[1] Bernard Harris, "A Portrait of a Moor," *Shakespeare Survey* 11 (1958), 89–97, quote from 97.

4 Portrait of Abd el-Ouahed ben Messaoud ben Mohammed Anoun, ambassador to Elizabeth I from Muly Hamet, King of Morocco (1600).

differences in dietary laws, religious practices, living arrangements, dress, and language and often described their visitors as "barbarians." Still, El-Ouahed was ambassador from a king to the Queen, a man of high status who was treated with the tact and respect reserved for visiting dignitaries.

The image of El-Ouahed has sparked speculations, in particular, from editors of Shakespeare's *Othello*, who see in this noble figure a possible model for Shakespeare's Moor.[2] More important to my purposes, his visit and the other Moroccan embassies and mercantile contacts that preceded him provide an important backdrop for the representations of Moorish kings on public stages. The drama of the 1590s and early 1600s boasts many such figures, and more often than not they are juxtaposed with English or European women who are textually inscribed as "fair." In this sense, the stage figure of the Moroccan king, whether his face was darkened by brownish (tawny) face paint or perhaps a darker shade, contributed to the construction of a normative English female "fairness" that dominates so much of the period's poetic discourse.

The Merchant of Venice illustrates this dynamic. Shakespeare's comedy was entered in the Stationer's Register in 1598, shortly after Essex's raid on Cadiz, and the opening line's reference to a "wealthy Andrew" among Antonio's ships alludes to the English capture of the Spanish galleon, the *San Andres*. As Joan Pong Linton contends, the capture of the *San Andres*, well known to Shakespeare's audience, recalled "the European scramble for gold in America, to which Portia's marriage lottery is thematically linked."[3] Set in Venice, the crossroads of Mediterranean traffic and trade, Shakespeare's *Merchant* brings to Belmont embassies from Morocco and Spain. The Folio stage directions describe the former's entrance: "*Enter Morochus a tawnie Moore all in white, and three or foure followers accordingly, with Portia, Nerissa, and their traine. Flo. Cornets.*" The "three or foure" is considerable, given the size of the Lord Chamberlain's Company, and all were to be dressed and made-up "accordingly," that is, to appear in guises similar to Morocco's. It was a royal entourage, much like the train that accompanied El-Ouahed to London.

"Tawny" is usually glossed as "light-skinned," but the color was light only insofar as it was not coal black. While the actor who impersonated the Prince of Morocco would not have worn full blackface, his complexion was nevertheless darkened. His opening words draw attention to his skin color:

---

[2] For the most recent, see E. A. J. Honigmann's introduction to the Third Arden Series edition (London: Arden Shakespeare, 1997), pp. 2–4 and 14–15.

[3] Joan Pong Linton, *The Romance of the New World* (Cambridge: Cambridge University Press, 1998), p. 30.

"Mislike me not for my complexion, / The shadowed livery of the burnished sun" (2.1.1–2). "Complexion" would have been pronounced as four syllables to make up the iambic pentameter line, perhaps a deliberate attempt on Shakespeare's part to emphasize Morocco's affected (or non-native) speech patterns. In any event, the unusual pronunciation emphasizes Morocco's most salient feature, his darker-than-English pigmentation.

The actor is also directed to appear in white robes. Editor M. M. Mahood notes that "Shakespeare, who may have known that white was a ceremonial colour in Islam, visualises a theatrically effective contrast between the strangers and the rich colours worn by Portia's 'train.'"[4] The white also contrasts with Morocco's darkened complexion, a "hue" that the Prince boasts is attractive to the "best-regarded virgins" of his country. Using the climatological explanation for the darkened skin of Africans, Morocco contrasts sunburned skin with the fairness of creatures born in northern climes, where "Phoebus's fire scarce thaws the icicles." He boasts that this "aspect" of his darkened complexion "Hath feared [terrified] the valiant." Yet under the skin his blood runs as red as any creature from the north. "Complexion," "aspect," "hue," – Morocco's words insist on his skin color as a determinant in his appearance. Even though Portia graciously trumps Morocco's wordplay by claiming that Morocco stands "as fair / As any comer I have looked on yet / For my affection" (2.1.20–22), his language marks himself as dark, Portia – the object of desire – as fair.

Like Aaron before him, Morocco carries a scimitar, a short, curved sword associated with Turks and Persians, and here (as in *Titus Andronicus*) with Moors. The scimitar is the physical signifier of Morocco's prowess in battle. He claims his weapon slew the Sophy (Shah of Persia); Mahood wryly notes that "No Shah was slain in battle in the sixteenth century, so either Shakespeare has got his facts wrong or he is making Morocco a boastful liar."[5] Morocco's account of his prowess is remarkably reminiscent of the "Negro Moor," Muly Mahamet from *The Battle of Alcazar*; he describes plucking sucking cubs from their mother and mocking the lion "when a roars for prey" (2.1.28–29), a line that recalls the scene in which Muly stole food from a lioness to feed Calipolis. He also compares himself to Hercules, the great Alcides caught in a rage. The overall portrait of Morocco, in sum, consorts with a stage tradition that was already well

---

[4] William Shakespeare, *The Merchant of Venice*, ed. M. M. Mahood (Cambridge: Cambridge University Press, 1987), p. 79.

[5] Shakespeare, *Merchant*, ed. Mahood, p. 80.

established: he is a prince with a substantial retinue, his dark complexion is "burnished by the sun," and his rhetoric strikes fear (he hopes) in the hearts of his auditors. His white robes associate him with Islam; his scimitar, as the *Oxford English Dictionary* notes, is common to Turks and Persians.

Morocco makes his choice in act 2, scene 7. Although his lengthy monologue is sometimes played for laughs, it can be taken seriously. As he ponders the meaning of the caskets' inscriptions, he immediately rejects lead, because he wonders, who would hazard all he hath for base metal. Silver is a possibility, for it promises as much as he deserves, and in his mind he deserves Portia – in birth, fortunes, graces, and in qualities of breeding (2.7.32–33). Morocco finally settles on gold because the inscription promises "what many men desire." He thus makes a commercial argument. Portia is the object of a global economy: "From the four corners of the earth they come" in search of her. "The Hyrcanian deserts and the vast wilds / Of wide Arabia are as throughfares now / For princes to come view fair Portia" (2.7.39–43). She is like an "angel," the golden coin that men seek throughout the world to satisfy their desires for wealth and power. As Bassanio's quest for the "Golden Fleece" demonstrates, Morocco's assessment is more accurate than frivolous.

Belmont is framed, however, as an ideal space in opposition to the mercantile economies of Venice. Morocco learns that in Portia's world, "All that glisters is not gold." Dismissed to a barren life, a life without marriage, he speedily takes his leave. And Portia, despite her earlier protestations to his face, closes the scene with the wish, "Let all of his complexion choose me so" (2.7.79). The lady rejects the Moroccan lover, not because of his merits, but because of his complexion. Color coding is crucial in the construction of his and her worth.

I

Other plays from this period reiterate the visual and verbal codes established in plays of the late 1580s and developed so clearly in Shakespeare's *Merchant*. George Chapman's *The Blind Beggar of Alexandria* (1598) presents an interesting twist on the four kings motif of 1580s plays; the kings who lose battles are not humiliated by drawing the victor's chariot. Rather, they marry the hero's cast-off mistresses. Porus the King of Ethiopia is described as black, and presumably his fellow kings of Phasiaca, Bebritia, and Arabia wore lighter make-up by contrast. Porus fits what had by then become a stock figure, the martial Moor. Before the battle, he threatens:

> If *Porus* liue to weild his martiall sworde,
> His [Cleanthes'] Citty walles shall not preserue him safe,
> But he shall dye by *Porus* and his freindes.   (E3r)[6]

The sword, presumably a scimitar, accompanied by his vain boast, conveys the impression of a braggart soldier. When the four kings lose the battle, Porus is the first to yield:

> First by thy valoure and the strength of armes,
> *Porus* the welthie *Aethiopian* king,
> Doth yeeld his crowne and homage vnto thee,
> Swearing by all my Gods whom I adore,
> To honor Duke *Cleanthes* whilst he liue,
> And in his ayde with twentie thousand men,
> Will always march gaynst whom thou meanst to fyght.
>   (F1v)

Cleanthes' conquest of the Ethiopian king thus dramatically increases his military capabilities and his status as a European power. It also illustrates how the medieval symbol of the black magi – who represents Christ's mission to *all* people – can be appropriated to signify the power of an earthly king to conquer the world.

Porus' color marks his exotic, foreign nature as much as his military status. While his complexion is repellent to some, to Elimene, presented as the widow to Count Hermes (Cleanthes in disguise), it arouses desire. She chooses him to be her new husband:

> In my eye now the blackest is the fayrest,
> For euery woman chooseth white and red,
> Come martiall *Porus* thou shalt haue my love.

When King Bebritius responds "Out on thee foolish woman thou hast chose a deuill," Porus quips, "Not yet sir til he haue hornes" (F3v). In this bawdy interchange, George Chapman exploits two longstanding theatrical conventions: the exotic king, an African warrior whose blackened skin suggests strangeness and geographical alterity, and the black devil associated with lust and cuckoldry. The casualness of this jest suggests that these character traits had become by the turn of the century something of a cliché, losing Muly's and Eleazar's spectacular power.

But even as a cliché, the figure of the black king served, as Jean Howard has shown, as a building block in the discourse of national identity that was

---

[6] Citations from *The Blind Beggar of Alexandria* are taken from the Malone Society reprint, ed. W. W. Greg (Oxford: Oxford University Press, 1928).

emerging in England at the end of Elizabeth's reign. Howard's perceptive analysis of Thomas Heywood's *The Fair Maid of the West, Part I* shows how "skin color functions in this play as a defining mark of difference and one basis for establishing relations of dominance and subordination between the English and Mullisheg and his court."[7] Heywood's drama presents Mullisheg as a black man in clear opposition to Bess Bridges, the "fair maid" who signifies the twin English bourgeois values of female chastity and mercantilism. Mullisheg is the desiring "other" who threatens English chastity. When told of Bess's arrival in a ship called "the Negro," Mullisheg almost salivates: "she in a *Negro* / Hath sail'd thus far to bosom with a Moor" (5.1.9–10).[8] Bess is unveiled to him (in a comic inversion of the practice of displaying foreign curiosities in Europe), and he is so impressed with her fair beauty that he exclaims she is "some bright angel that is dropp'd from heaven" (5.1.35), suggesting once again the angelic qualities of whiteness in opposition to his own blackness. The comic conclusion is assured by Bess's chaste constancy; Mullisheg decides that "Lust shall not conquer virtue" (5.2.119) and relinquishes his suit so that she can marry Spencer, her long lost love. Even so, Clem the Clown responds to Mullisheg and Bess's conciliatory kiss with disgust: "Must your blackface be smooching my mistress's white lips / With a Morian? I would you had kissed her a – " (5.2.80–81). Clem's humorous hijinks minimize any distrust of Bess's virtue and underscore the English norm of "fairness."

One of Mullisheg's bashaws is named Alcade, the Spanish word for "sheriff" or "magistrate" – a name recycled a year later when Alcade, King of Africa, appeared in the anonymous romance, *The Thracian Wonder, A Comicall History* (ca. 1599). We do not see Alcade until act 3, scene 3, when he promises to assist Sophos, the Thracian king's brother, with an invasion:

> Our sable ensigns, never yet before
> Displayed beyond the Mediterranean Sea,
> Shall now be seen to fly. Men have livers there
> Pale as their faces, and, when we appear,
> Will frighted run from such a golden soil.
> (3.3.148–51)[9]

---

[7] Jean E. Howard, "An English Lass Amid the Moors: Gender, Race, Sexuality, and National Identity in Heywood's *Fair Maid of the West*," in *Women, 'Race,' and Writing in the Early Modern Period*, ed. Margo Hendricks and Patricia Parker (London: Routledge, 1994), pp. 101–17; quotation from p. 113.

[8] Citations from *The Fair Maid of the West, Parts I and II* are from the Regents Renaissance Drama edition, ed. Robert K. Turner, Jr. (Lincoln: University of Nebraska Press, 1967).

[9] Cited from *The Thracian Wonder, a Comical History*, ed. Michael Nolan (Salzburg: Institut für Anglistik und Amerikanistik, 1997) by act, scene, and line numbers.

This passage suggests that Alcade is black (sable) in opposition to Europe's whiteness (paleness), yet the King's daughter, Lillia Guida, is a white Moor, and he orders that she be guarded by "demi-negroes" (5.1.133–35), presumably mulattos. At the play's conclusion, Lillia marries the Thracian king's grandson, Eusanius, but because she is white (despite her father's blackness), the union is not deemed transgressive.[10] Alcade's virtues as a just king suggest that in this case the child inherited what an English audience would perceive as the color of the king's character, not the color of his skin.

But moral assessments could go the other way as the figure of the Moorish king became a multivalent signifier. William Rowley's *All's Lost by Lust* (ca. 1619) recycles the devilish Moor of the 1590s in the character of Mulymumen, a King of the Moors. Based on the story of Roderick, the ruler who lost Spain to the Moors in the eighth century, this tragedy sets sexual intrigue within the larger backdrop of war between Christian Spain and Islamic Africa, a conflict that centers on the struggle to possess, once again, the body of a white woman. King Roderick's lust for Jacinta, the daughter of his military commander Julianus, leads him to attack the Moors so that he can bed the daughter while her father is away. After a successful campaign, Julianus takes Mulymumen prisoner. Then, when his daughter (who has been raped by Roderick in the meantime) appears before him, he swears vengeance, frees his Moorish prisoners, and asks them to join him in league against the Spanish king. When the Moorish king offers to take the "damaged goods" off Julianus' hands and to marry Jacinta, she exclaims that the Moor is even worse than the ravisher. Mulymumen swears to avenge her resistance, to which Jacinta cries:

> Tis naturall to thee, base African;
> Thine inside's blacker then thy sooty skin.[11]

Here Rowley reverts to blackened skin as a signifier of African bestiality, and the Moor lives up to the "cruel" stereotype by having Julianus' eyes gouged out and arranging for him to stab his own daughter. Before he dies, Jacinta's father agrees with his daughter's assessment by proclaiming that even though Roderick was a tyrant, the Moor is worse, and that it is always wrong to raise your hand against an anointed king.

As these plays indicate, by the early decades of the seventeenth century, the figure of a black African (Moorish) king had become familiar to

---

[10] Joyce Green MacDonald discusses the significance of the "whitening" of exotic heroines and the "removal of dark-skinned women from representation" in *Women and Race in Early Modern Texts* (Cambridge: Cambridge University Press, 2002), p. 17 and passim.

[11] William Rowley, *A Tragedy Called All's Lost by Lust* (London, 1633), sig. H4v.

London's theatre audiences. His color could signify a range of meanings, from deviltry to primitive nobility. Frequently his blackened complexion was contrasted to the "fairness" of a European woman in ways that coded her as an object of desire; often he engaged in military or diplomatic competition with a white man to win her favor. The fair English woman, in turn, was imbricated in mercantile ventures, standing as a sort of synecdoche for Londoners' growing participation in worldwide trade. Her ability to subdue the Moorish king thus bespoke English aspirations as a nascent colonial power.

II

Moorish royalty was not limited to public performances before middle-class audiences. During the reign of James I, they frequently appeared in court masques where they helped to establish an ideal of English "fairness." Four naked "Negroes" danced in the snow to entertain Queen Anne on her marriage to James in 1589, and the following year, when she arrived in Scotland, she was greeted with townsmen dressed like Moors. In both cases, the black-faced Moors served to highlight her "'fair' white beauty."[12] Her most famous courtly appropriation of blackness is, of course, Ben Jonson and Inigo Jones's 1605 *Masque of Blackness*. Jonson reports in his account of the masque that Queen Anne had requested him to write a court masque in which she and her ladies could pretend to be black Moors. This was not wholly unprecedented, because as indicated earlier, Moors had appeared in court masques during the reigns of Henry VIII, Edward VI, and Elizabeth. But those figures wore coverings of lawn and velvet on their arms and hands and black vizards on their faces. What is radical in Queen Anne's request is *her* desire to use black pigment. Why, one wonders, would a Queen of England, six months pregnant, wish to appear in public, her face and arms coated with black grease? The answer may lie in the song that opens the *Masque of Blackness*, which was performed in the Banqueting House at Whitehall on 6 January 1605. Two "Sea-Maids" welcome Niger, who appears "in forme and colour of an *Aethiope*; his haire, and rare beard curled, shaddowed with a blue, and bright mantle: his front, neck, and wrists adorned with pearle, and crowned, with an artificiall wreathe of cane, and paper-rush":

---

[12] Bernadette Andrea, "Black Skin, the Queen's Masques: African Ambivalence and Feminine Author(ity) in the Masques of *Blackness* and *Beauty*," *English Literary Renaissance* 29 (1999), 246–81, quotation from 261.

Now honord, thus,
With all his beautious race:
Who, though but blacke in face,
Yet, are they bright,
And full of life, and light.
To Proue that beauty best,
Which not the colour, but the feature
Assures vnto the creature.[13]

A vizard would have concealed the Queen's features and those of the eleven ladies who joined her as Niger's beautiful daughters; perhaps the request for black paint was motivated instead by the desire to be recognized through the extravagant disguise. Anne may have used black make-up to experience her own "to-be-looked-at-ness." As her biographer Leeds Barroll notes, using black make-up, Anne and her ladies "devised a structure in which she and her court became a spectacular presence in a glittering and politically symbolic social season."[14]

The use of black paint, however inspired, was particularly transgressive. As Bernadette Andrea notes, "patriarchal spectators at the Jacobean court did not accept, and perhaps could not comprehend, the Queen's assertion of herself as a black(ened) feminine author(ity)."[15] In the most frequently quoted gloss on this performance, Dudley Carleton's letter to Sir Ralph Winwood, the courtier noted:

Their Apparell was rich, but too light and Curtizan-like for such great ones. Instead of Vizzards, their Faces, and Arms up to the Elbows, were painted black, which was Disguise sufficient, for they were hard to be known; *but it became them nothing so well as their red and white, and you cannot imagine a more ugly Sight, then a Troop of lean-cheek'd Moors.*[16]

Although according to Carleton, the courtiers struggled to discover who the ladies were under the blackface, with some effort they were knowable as "aristocratic ladies who are part of the 'golden world' of the court."[17] As Richmond Barbour argues, "the novel means of representation exacerbates racial and sexual anxiety: what troubles Carleton is that, in effect, the masquers' skin is indelibly black. Vizards would signal a safer distance

---

[13] *The Works of Ben Jonson* (London, 1616), pp. 894–95.
[14] Leeds Barroll, *Anna of Denmark, Queen of England* (Ithaca: Cornell University Press, 2001), p. 103.
[15] Andrea, "Black Skin," 273.
[16] *The Complete Works of Ben Jonson*, ed. C. H. Herford and Percy Simpson, 11 vols. (Oxford: Clarendon Press, 1925–52), vol. x, p. 448.
[17] Kim F. Hall, *Things of Darkness: Economies of Race and Gender in Early Modern England* (Ithaca: Cornell University Press, 1995), p. 141.

between the women and their roles."[18] Nor would vizards contaminate the rest of the court. Carleton wryly noted that the Spanish Ambassador took the Queen out to dance "and forgot not to kiss her Hand, though there was Danger it would have left a Mark on his Lips."[19] In another letter he wrote that "Theyr black faces, and hands wch were painted and bare vp to the elbowes, was a very lothsome sight, and I am sory that strangers should see owr court so strangely disguised."[20] The Queen had turned the court into a "spectacle of strangeness."

Wearing blackface was, as commentators have often noted, a subversive act, an assertion of Anne's identity as opposed to that of her husband James and of her authority as opposed to that of the poet, Ben Jonson;[21] in the words of Hardin Aasand, "Flirting with the grotesque parodies of carnival, the masquers are their own anti-masquers, replete in a blackness that vitiates traditional emblems of royalty and challenges the court's dominance as a center of social regulation."[22] At first the women's transgression seems contained in Jonson's design for the masque. The purpose of their pilgrimage from Africa to Britannia is, after all, to be "beautified" through the transforming power of a "Svnne" (James), "Whose beames shine day, and night, and are of force / to blanch an AETHIOPE, and reuiue a *Cor's*."[23] In what was to become the conventional ending for a Jacobean court masque, *The Masque of Blackness* concludes with extravagant praise for James and his plan for a peaceful, united Britain. If we accept the text at its word, "*The Masque of Blackness* presents an idealized world in which normally intransigent blackness is subdued by a European order predicated on white, male privilege and power."[24]

But in other ways the text is equivocal. The masque's hyperbole aside, evidence of James's beautifying power is sadly lacking. Because they used paint, the ladies cannot be transformed instantaneously, and their transformation back to their natural hues had to be delayed until the black grease was washed off. Jonson accounts for this in his conclusion. Aethiopia promises the ladies' return in a year; in the meantime, they are to steep their "bodies in that purer brine, / And wholsome dew, call'd *Ros-marine*."[25] Sea-dew from

---

[18] Richmond Barbour, "Britain and the Great Beyond: *The Masque of Blackness* at Whitehall," in *Playing the Globe: Genre and Geography in English Renaissance Drama*, ed. John Gillies and Virginia Mason Vaughan (Madison, NJ: Fairleigh Dickinson University Press, 1998), pp. 129–53; quotation from p. 141.

[19] Jonson, *Complete Works*, vol. x, p. 448.

[20] Jonson, *Complete Works*, vol. x, p. 449.   [21] Andrea, "Black Skin," 270.

[22] Hardin Aasand, "'To Blanch an Ethiop, and Revive a Corse.' Queen Anne and *The Masque of Blackness*," *Studies in English Literature* 32 (1992), 271–85, quotation from 281.

[23] Jonson, *Works*, p. 898.   [24] Hall, *Things of Darkness*, p. 137.   [25] Jonson, *Works*, p. 900.

Venus, Beauty's Queen, perhaps with suggestions of the intervention of the Virgin Mary (rosemary), will wash them clean. The ladies' transformation is consequently a feminine enterprise.

Although Queen Anne and her ladies put their blackened bodies on display in *The Masque of Blackness*, they had no speaking roles. The delivery of Jonson's lines was left to professional male actors, and in Niger we see some continuities with the "African King" typology of the public theatres. Like Aaron, Niger inverts the commonplaces that Ethiops cannot be washed white and have no shame to blush into praise of blackness's immutability. He claims that in his daughters,

> the perfectst beauty growes;
> Since the fix't colour of their curled haire,
> (Which is the highest grace of dames most faire)
> No cares, no age can change; or there display
> The fearefull tincture of abhorred *Gray*;
> Since *Death* her selfe (her selfe being pale and blue)
> Can neuer alter their most faithfull hiew;
> All which are arguments, to prove, how far
> Their beauties conquer, in great beauties warre;
> And more, how neere *Diuinitie* they be,
> That stand from passion, or decay so free.[26]

For Niger, the ladies' black hue signifies constancy – even immortality – not the "curtizan-like" behavior suggested by Carleton's response. According to Mary Floyd-Wilson, "Even as Jonson equates physical blackness with a lack of beauty, his imagery acknowledges the associations between 'blackness' and wisdom, constancy, antiquity, and piety."[27]

The Masque of Blackness, similar to *The Fair Maid of the West, Part I*, constructs white Englishness in opposition to African blackness, making room for a chromatic scale between. Moving from "Black *Mauretania*" northwards, Niger and his daughters move through "Swarth *Lusitania*," and "Rich *Aquitania*." Spain's swarthiness suggests its propinquity to Africa, while "rich" Aquitania (France) is closer to England.[28] Britannia's snowy cliffs are the ultima thule, "*A world, diuided from the world.*"[29] Jonson thus appropriates Niger's African blackness to differentiate England from the rest of the world, and once again the construction of "Africanism" becomes an instrument of nation formation.

---

[26] Jonson, *Works*, p. 896.
[27] Mary Floyd-Wilson, "Temperature, Temperance, and Racial Difference in Ben Jonson's *The Masque of Blackness*," *English Literary Renaissance* 28 (1998), 183–209, quote from 206.
[28] Floyd-Wilson, "Temperature, Temperance, and Racial Difference," 187, n. 13.
[29] Jonson, *Works*, p. 898.

Recent interest in *The Masque of Blackness* has focused on the text's embedded significations, but we should not underestimate the sheer beauty of this spectacle. The orient pearl used to deck the masquers' arms and necks provided a stunning visual contrast between textures of black and white. The costumes, of azure and silver, however curtizan-like they seemed to Carleton, must have contrasted nicely with Oceanus' robe of sea-green.[30] Some spectators, contra Carleton, found the experience enjoyable. Nicolo Molin, the Venetian Ambassador, wrote home to the Doge and the Senate that the performance "was very beautiful and sumptuous,"[31] and the only political aspect of it he mentioned was the dispute among foreign ambassadors over precedence and seating arrangements. To many of the courtiers assembled at James's court on 5 January 1605, the spectacle of the black-faced Queen and her ladies was a source of visual pleasure, with blackness the exotic focal point for the white, English "gaze."

Queen Anne's blackness was perhaps imitated in Thomas Campion's *The Discription of a Maske in Honour of the Lord Hayes* (1607) in the figure of Night, who appears "in a close robe of blacke silke & gold, a blacke mantle embroidered with starres, a crowne of starres on her head, her hair blacke and spangled with gold, her face blacke, her buskins blacke, and painted with starres, in her hand shee bore a blacke wand, wreathed with gold."[32] Night is an agent of transformation in this mask, with the power to change trees into nine knights of Apollo and, at the play's conclusion, to provide respite for the royal onlookers and consummation for the bride and groom.

It is not surprising that Night should be figured black in an allegorical pageant, but the association between blackness, night, darkness, and ignorance is more palpable in Thomas Middleton's 1613 Lord Mayor's pageant, *The Triumph of Truth*, written in honor of Sir Thomas Middleton (no relation to the poet) who became Lord Mayor on 29 October 1613. Mayor Middleton, a member of the Grocers' Company, had traveled in foreign countries during his youth, and the *Dictionary of National Biography* reports that he was an adventurer in the East India voyage of 1599 and a charter member of the East India Company; he was also an adventurer in 1623 in the Virginia Company and wrote "A Discourse of Trade from England

---

[30] Barbour notes that the costumes described for *The Masque of Beauty* three years later are far skimpier, including at least one masquer who appeared "naked-breasted," but there were no complaints about curtizan-like attire; he posits that the equation between blackness and unbridled sexuality sparked Carleton's critique. See "Britain and the Great Beyond," p. 140.

[31] *Calendar of State Papers Venetian*, vol. x, ed. Horatio F. Brown (London, 1900), p. 213.

[32] Thomas Campion, *The Discription of a Maske in Honour of the Lord Hayes* (London, 1607), sig. B1v.

unto the West Indies" – biographical facts that indicate Mayor Middleton's interest and investment in England's burgeoning overseas enterprises.

Middleton's plan for the public celebration of Sir Thomas's installation includes a meeting with a "King of the Moors" partway through the procession. This King, accompanied by his Queen and "two Attendants of their owne colour," approaches the procession from a "strange Ship" on the Thames; like Niger and his daughters in *The Masque of Blackness*, he seeks transformation, only this time the quest is for "true religion" rather than beauty. As Queen Anne had earlier, the King recognizes that the black color of his skin will draw the audience's gaze. He addresses the crowd:

> *I see amazement set upon the faces*
> *Of these white people, wondrings, and strange gazes,*
> *Is it at mee? Do's my Complexion draw*
> *So many Christian Eyes, that neuer saw*
> *A King so blacke before? No, now I see*
> *Their entire obiect, the're all meant to thee*
> *(Graue Citty Gouernour) my Queene and I*
> *Well honor'd with the Glances that by,*
> *I must confesse many wilde thoughts may rise.*
> *Opinions, Common murmurs, and fixt Eyes*
> *At my so strange arriuall, in a Land,*
> *Where true Religion and her Temple stand.*[33]

The Moor assures the crowd that although his face is dark, there is truth in his soul:

> *And though in daies of Error I did runne*
> *To giue all Adoration to the Sunne,*
> *The Moone & Stars; nay Creatures base and poore,*
> *Now onely their Creator I adore.*

The Moor and his people have been converted to the true Christian faith through "*Religious Conuersation / Of English Merchants, Factors, Trauailers, / Whose* Truth *did with our Spirits hold Commerse.*"[34] This message, presumably spoken by a white actor in black make-up, articulates the spread of the Christian religion as the major rationale for England's colonial enterprises, with the profit from trade as a by-product. At the end of this speech, "All in the shippe and those in the Castle" bow "their bodies to the Temple of Saint *Paul.*"[35] After the English Church is signified as the agent of transformation and subjugation, Error, dismayed that "deuout humility" should

---

[33] Thomas Middleton, *The Triumph of Truth* (London, 1613), sigs. B4v–C1r.
[34] Middleton, *Triumph*, sig. C1r.   [35] Middleton, *Triumph*, sig. C1v.

take hold of that complexion, cries: "*What, haue my Sweete-fac'st Deuils forsooke me too, / Nay, then my charmes will haue enough to doo?*"[36] Time saves the day, however, leading the procession onward to Cheapside where Truth will outspeak Error.

Middleton's pageant demonstrates how the "black-faced devils" of the homiletic tradition had become amalgamated with the figure of the black Moor of Africa in a conventional symbol of the qualities – barbarism, ignorance, impudence, and falsehood – in opposition to white Englishness and true religion. The battle between the forces of good and evil no longer figured in the next world, but in the here and now of exploration and trade.

By 1613, Africa's subjugation had been figured visually in multiple editions of Abraham Ortelius' *Theatrum Orbis Terrarum*. The frontispiece to the 1606 English translation shows Africa as a nearly naked black-skinned female who stands beneath the fully clad figure of Europe, who is seated on a throne and holding a scepter. Thomas Campion exploited this convention in his 1614 *Maske Presented in the Banqueting Room at Whitehall . . . at the Marriage of the right Honourable the Earle of Somerset and the right noble the lady* Frances *Howard*. As part of an antimasque, the four "parts of the earth" dance in a confused measure. Europe is "in the habit of an Empresse, with an Emperiall Crowne on her head"; Asia appears in "a Persian Ladies habit with a Crowne on her head"; America is in a "skin coate of the colour of the iuyce of Mulberies, on her head large round brims of many coloured feathers, and in the midst of it a small Crowne"; while Africa is simply "like a Queene of the Moores, with a crown." Black skin tone is all she needs to indicate who she is.[37]

The confusion of the antimasque disappears in Campion's masque through a scene change to London, where "*Bel-Anna*" stops the hubbub and brings union (in a reference to James's plans for the union of England and Scotland):

> All that was euer ask't, by vow of *Ioue* [Jove].
> To blesse a state with, Plentie, Honor Loue,
> Power, Triumph, priuate pleasure, publique peace,
> Sweet springs, and *Autumn's* filld with due increase,
> All these; and what good els, thought can supplie.
> Euer attend your Triple Maiestie.[38]

---

[36] Middleton, *Triumph*, sig. C1v.
[37] Thomas Campion, *Maske Presented in the Banqueting Room at Whitehall* (London, 1614).
[38] Campion, *Maske*, sig. B4r.

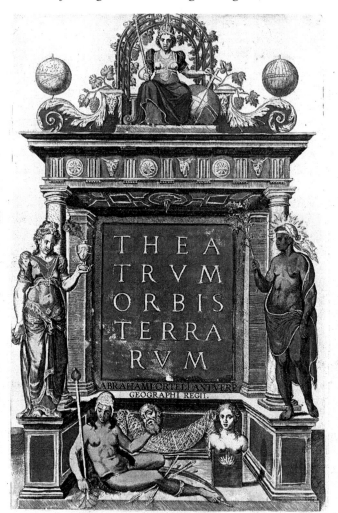

5 The frontispiece to Abraham Ortelius' *Theatrum Orbis Terrarum* (London, 1606) figures Africa as a scantily clad black woman.

Similar to Middleton's *Triumph of Truth*, this court masque constructs "London" by setting it in opposition to the other places of the earth, most profoundly to black Africa. By the middle of James's reign, the widely recognized figure of the black African King or Queen was a major contributor to the English conviction that their country was, indeed, "a world divided from the world."

CHAPTER 5

Bedtricksters

"The devil, devil, devil! O the devil!" shrieks young Thomas when he discovers a blackfaced servant in bed instead of his white love Mary. John Fletcher here capitalizes on a theatrical convention borrowed from mythology and folklore known as the bedtrick. Simply stated, a man or woman unknowingly has sexual relations (or comes close to it) with someone other than the person he or she had intended to bed. The device requires a trickster who sets up the assignation and a victimized dupe. Although such mix-ups may seem implausible in real life, as Wendy Doniger contends, the bedtrick raises a host of questions about sexuality and identity even as it reifies the common feeling after sexual experience that one's partner is not the same – psychologically if not physically – as one thought. Bedtrick stories, she argues, "represent the tension between the urge to diverge and the urge to merge, between the desire to masquerade, to assume the identity of another in addition to one's own, and the desire to lose one's own identity through intimate union with the other."[1] More important to this study, in early modern English drama, the blackfaced figure of a Moor frequently appears in such plot devices, sometimes as the trickster, but more often as the substitute bedmate.

More than thirty years ago William P. Bowden wondered whether a psychologist "might be curious as to why a surprisingly large number of bedtricks involve Moors, real or pretended."[2] The use of Moors in bedtricks is surely a theatrically significant and socially revealing Renaissance phenomenon. Its most common pattern – substituting a black servant in the

---

[1] See the Preface to Wendy Doniger's *The Bedtrick: Tales of Sex and Masquerade* (Chicago: University of Chicago Press, 2000); quotation from p. 7.

[2] William P. Bowden, "The Bed Trick, 1603–1642: Its Mechanics, Ethics, and Effects," *Shakespeare Studies* 5 (1969), 112–23, quotation from 122. Although Marliss C. Densens mentions race as a factor in John Fletcher's *Monsieur Thomas* and Richard Brome's *The Novella*, she never directly addresses the issue of race in her analysis of the bedtrick in English Renaissance drama. See *The Bed-Trick in English Renaissance Drama: Explorations in Gender, Sexuality, and Power* (Newark: University of Delaware Press, 1994), esp. pp. 99–100.

bed for a chaste white mistress – connects issues of gender and sexuality with clearly defined racial constructions and class consciousness. As Arthur L. Little Jr. has recently shown, the "presence of the black body" in or around the bed "becomes a way of visualizing, of fantasizing the pornographic narrative across the border of racial difference."[3] Like the rape narratives Little discusses, the bedtrick fashions visual images of white female chastity as the object of desire. When the bedtrick ends happily, as it does in many comedies where it traps a philandering male into having sex with his own wife, its temporary flirtation with miscegenation creates an erotic fantasy of sex with a black person, usually a female, who serves as the forbidden double of the chaste female heroine.

Marliss C. Desens attributes the popularity of the bedtrick after 1598 to a *fin de siècle* shift from romantic comedy (where a bedtrick would darken the tone) to satire, tragedy, and tragicomedy – genres which highlight lust rather than love.[4] Lust is a crucial element in plays featuring the bedtrick, and when the substituted bedmate is discovered to be black, the dupe's horror is magnified by the grotesque image of intercourse with the devil. The blackness = devil sign system of the homiletic tradition remains, as I will demonstrate, close to the surface in the resulting dialogue. The plays I will discuss here, which were written and performed in the early seventeenth century, also demonstrate that at a time when mercantile efforts in the New World and the Mediterranean were bringing English men and women into frequent contact with people of color, fears and fantasies of sexual pollution were often acted out and dissipated on stage through the folkloric device of the bedtrick

Most often the substituted bedmate is a blackfaced Moorish servant. In this way the public theatre reflected changing social realities, especially the increasing number of black servants in London from the late 1590s onward and emergent resentment toward them among some segments of English society. In 1596, the Privy Council had ordered Casper van Senden to gather "blackamoores here in this realme and to transport them into Spaine and Portugall"; it claimed that "those kinde of people" could be "well spared in this realme, being so populous," whereas "numbers of hable persons[,] the subjectes of the land and Christian people . . . perishe for want of service, wherby through their labor they might be mayntained."[5]

---

[3] Arthur S. Little, Jr., *Shakespeare Jungle Fever: National-Imperial Re-Visions of Race, Rape, and Sacrifice* (Stanford: Stanford University Press, 2000), p. 60.

[4] Desens, *The Bed-Trick in English Renaissance Drama*, pp. 34–35.

[5] *Acts of the Privy Council of England*, n.s., vol. xxvi, ed. John Roche Dasent (London: Mackie and Co., 1902), pp. 20–21.

Later, in her oft-quoted proclamation of January 1601, Elizabeth expressed concern about the welfare of her subjects who were "greatly distressed in these hard times of dearth" by competition from "the great number of Negroes and blackamoors which . . . are carried into this realm since the troubles between her highness and the King of Spain," and ordered "such Negroes and blackamoors to be transported."[6] The effort to rid the realm of "blackamoors" in "these hard times of dearth" suggests that black slaves and servants were perceived to have taken food, not to mention employment, from England's white citizens, and that there was, by the Privy Council at least, a desire to ease the problem by deporting them.

While Elizabeth and her Council expressed concern about the numbers of black servants in England, dramatists began to represent them on stage. The best-known instance from the mid-1590s occurs in *The Merchant of Venice* when Lorenzo tries to ease Jessica's real or pretended anxieties about converting from a "Jew's daughter" to a good Christian by charging Lancelot with "getting up of the Negro's belly." Lancelot playfully replies that "It is much that the Moor" – this nameless serving woman – "should be more than reason, but if she be less than an honest woman, she is indeed more than I took her for" (3.5.32–36). The black servant epitomizes English concerns about amalgamation and opens a space for Jessica, the Jew's daughter, to slip inside the Christian polity. As Peter Erickson astutely observes, "The point here is the contrast: Jessica's new identity has been absolved of any taint of darkness." In Renaissance visual and verbal images, "black and white are relational."[7] Because she is white, Jessica can pass from her Jewish heritage into Christian culture; the nameless Negro, in contrast, is ineluctably black, and however briefly she is mentioned, her shadow highlights, as it were, Jessica's lighter complexion and ability to "pass."

The Merchant of Venice is set in the Mediterranean city best known for multi-cultural contacts and trading relations during the early modern period. By the early sixteenth century, the presence of black servants in Venice would have been commonplace, and as art historian Peter Mark notes, by the later part of the century, the visual arts "reflect the servile status to which most blacks were . . . relegated."[8] The slave trade began

---

[6] Quoted from *Tudor Royal Proclamations*, ed. Paul L. Hughes and James F. Larkin, vol. III (New Haven and London: Yale University Press, 1969), pp. 221–2.

[7] Peter Erickson, "Representations of Blacks and Blackness in the Renaissance," *Criticism* 35 (1993), 499–527; quotations from 521 and 505.

[8] Peter Mark, *Africans in European Eyes: The Portrayal of Black Africans in Fourteenth and Fifteenth Century Europe* (Syracuse: Maxwell School of Citizenship and Public Affairs, 1974), p. 95.

a century later in England than on the Iberian peninsula, but as early as the 1570s black Africans were in England, working as household servants, prostitutes, and court entertainers. And by the time Shakespeare wrote *Merchant*, notes historian Peter Fryer, "it was beginning to be the smart thing for titled and propertied families in England to have a black slave or two among the household servants."[9] Not surprisingly, Jacobean dramas often mirrored this trend in their depiction of aristocratic households. Like the servants in Sir Walter Ralegh's and the Earl of Dorset's households, the stage Moor added a touch of exotic "color" to a nobleman's retinue and reflected the power and prestige of the master.

Critics have long noted how such servants, the Moorish waiting woman in particular, are sexualized. Elliot Tokson observes that "black women on the stage were ... often portrayed as bawds, serving the lusts of white men by acting as procurors of white women,"[10] and Anthony Barthelemy suggests that the black Moorish woman "stands as a symbol of everything evil and low. Legitimately, she functions in the community solely as a waiting-woman, illegitimately as a bawd and whore."[11] But the black servants were more than simple signifiers of debased sexuality. Plays that combine the black servant with a bedtrick show black and white women in a relationship similar to the image in Titian's painting of *Diana and Actaeon*, where Diana's naked body is framed by the image of her black female servant while the male figure of Actaeon accosts her. According to Peter Erickson, the black and white women's bodies are together at a moment "of male intrusion into the field of female sexuality."[12] In the bedtricks described below, the black servant, usually but not always female – like the shadowy figure in Titian's painting – diffuses male lust away from the white female onto her own black body, which is read as a site of forbidden erotic pleasure. Substituted for her white mistress in the bed, she serves as an iconic double, a negative version of the white positive that embodies hidden desires and fantasies.

Lynda E. Boose contends that black women presented a particular challenge to patriarchy in this period because their pigmentation – not the white fathers' – was replicated in their offspring; they were "unrepresentable" because they did not fit patriarchal conceptions of biology

---

[9] Peter Fryer, *Staying Power: The History of Black People in Britain* (London: Pluto Press, 1984), p. 9.

[10] Elliot H. Tokson, *The Popular Image of the Black Man in English Drama, 1550–1688* (Boston: G. K. Hall, 1982), p. 84.

[11] Anthony Gerard Barthelemy, *Black Face, Maligned Race: The Representation of Blacks in English Drama from Shakespeare to Southerne* (Baton Rouge: Louisiana State University Press, 1987), p. 123.

[12] Erickson, "Representations," 510.

6 Titian's painting of *Diana and Actaeon* uses the figure of a black serving woman to highlight Diana's whiteness.

and heredity.[13] But in several plays of the period, black waiting women are indeed represented, both in their own right and as key players in sexual negotiations between their white mistresses and the men who seek to possess those women. In the process, "blackamoor" servants are framed – to use Kim Hall's term as – "the site for crucial negotiations of sexual politics and cultural and racial difference."[14] The bedtrick's traffic in women – black and white – is thus not simply an engaging plot device, but an indicator of England's emerging anxiety about contamination with alien others.

[13] Lynda E. Boose, "'The Getting of a Lawful Race': Racial Discourse in Early Modern England and the Unrepresentable Black Woman," in *Women, "Race," and Writing in the Early Modern Period*, ed. Margo Hendricks and Patricia Parker (London: Routledge, 1994), pp. 35–54.
[14] Kim F. Hall, *Things of Darkness: Economies of Race and Gender in Early Modern England* (Ithaca: Cornell University Press, 1995), p. 116.

I

"The Tale of the Blacke Moore" from the popular *Pasquil's Jests*, first published in 1604, typifies the dramatic pattern of the bedtrick. *Pasquil's* compendium of jokes and anecdotes published material that had probably
circulated orally for some time. This tale describes a foolish young fellow,
"hauing more money in his purse then he knew well how to use," who
is gulled by a "crafty companion." Noticing that the young fool likes the
ladies, the companion offers to help him find a wife and promises that "she
should be fayre, and wealthy, and wise." The companion arranges a time
and place for the fool to meet the lady, but – and here the tale bears quoting
at length –

while the goose was gaping, for one bayt, he was catcht with another. For the
cunning rascall, intending to make himselfe merry with his [the fool's] money,
told him he must be finely apparrelled, and bestow a supper or two . . . The
foole . . . made himself new apparel according to the fashion, gaue money to
bestow upon a supper or two, where met him a fine boy, drest woman-like, to
whom he made such loue that a Dog would not abide to beare it. The counterfeit
young mistris with kind words and knauish wiles, finding the length of his foot,
gate [got] many tokens of his loue, as Gloues, Skarfes, and such like, besides a
Ring or two, and a bracelet; all which he did bestow so louingly, that he must
needes be used like himselfe, and so he was; for nothing was refused that came so
gently to passe. But after many kind meetings, in the end it was agreed betwixt
them that, in a friends house of his, the matter should be made up; which, being
little better then a bawdy house, it serued the turn as well as could be. There they
met, and being both agreed, upon assurance of e[a]che others loue, to bed they
should go that night, and be maried shortly after. Wel, that night there lacked no
good cheere, nor wine to make the heart merry; which, being taken in full cups,
wrought the matter as they would haue it; for after they had well supped and sate
awhile by a good fire, the good Asse fell asleepe; in which, being layd in his bed,
instead of the fayre boy, they had layd a blacke Moore wench by him, with whom
I know not how he handled the matter; but in the morning, seeing what a sweet
bed-fellow he had gotten, suddenly starting out of the bed, [he] ran to his clothes,
and taking them in his hand, ran out into another chamber, crying that he was
undone, for he had lien with the ugliest thing that euer was, and he feared it was
the deuill. In which feare, [he] blessing himself as from sprites, running out of the
house, with the expence of his money, almost losse of wits, and laught at of all that
knew him, like a good Woodcocke, fled away so farre, that I neuer heard more
what became of him.[15]

---

[15] *Pasquil's Jests, Mixed with Mother Bunches Merriments*, ed. W. Carew Hazlitt (London, 1866), pp. 31–
34. I am grateful to Barbara Hodgdon for drawing my attention to this anecdote.

This anecdote lays out several crucial dynamics of the bedtrick. It begins with competition between two males, one of whom seeks to dominate the other both psychologically and financially. The crafty companion not only fleeces the fool but humiliates him sexually. First he substitutes a boy for the "fayre" woman, raising through transvestism the specter of homosexuality and monstrousness, which the fool is too stupid to recognize, but which is readily apparent to the reader (or auditor). Then he replaces one "monster" with another by placing a black woman in the fool's bed; her sex removes the taint of homosexuality from the consummation but substitutes the grosser fear of copulation with the devil.

"The Tale of the Blacke Moore" is akin to the charivari, described by Michael D. Bristol as the practice of "noisy festive abuse in which a community enacted its specific objection to inappropriate marriages and more generally exercised a widespread surveillance of sexuality." The fool's desire for a woman is punished by a parody of the wedding ceremony that is "organized by a carnivalesque wardrobe corresponding to a triad of dramatic agents – the clown (who represents the bridegroom), the transvestite (who represents the bride), and the 'scourge of marriage,' often assigned a suit of black (who represents the community of unattached males or 'young men')."[16] *Pasquil's Jests* approximates this tripartite pattern with a mock marriage in which the foolish bridegroom takes a transvestite for his bride, and later awakes to a different scourge of marriage – the sight of a female Moor in his bed. Like the object of a charivari, the fool is punished for his violation of the community's norms through a theatrical spectacle that includes a blackened figure.

Many of *Pasquil's Jests* are based in popular folklore, and the story of the black Moor is no exception. Just as a fairy tale enables children to experience and then exorcise their worst fears, this anecdote displaces fears of sexual (and financial) inadequacy onto the foolish yokel, while the "bogeyman" black Moor strikes him with terror.

II

This pattern recurs in John Fletcher's *Monsieur Thomas*, written between 1614 and 1617, only here the homoerotic element is suggested in the seducer-victim's decision to disguise himself as a woman. The cast list includes Kate,

---

[16] Michael D. Bristol, "Charivari and the Comedy of Abjection in *Othello*," *Renaissance Drama* 21 (1990), 3–21; quotations from 3 and 6.

"*a blackamoor maid to MARY*,"[17] who appears only once, in act 5, scene 2, but her brief minutes on stage encapsulate much of the plot that rages around her. Set in Jacobean London, the play begins with the homecoming of two "travellers," Valentine and Thomas, who have been seeking their fortunes at sea. The main plot's hero, Valentine, has lost his wife and son in a seafight off Genoa. The subplot is an inversion of the prodigal son motif in that Thomas needs to win his father's admiration not by being virtuous but by being a rapscallion in the family tradition.[18] Most of the comedy centers on marriage negotiations complicated by issues of patriarchal inheritance, and both plots show males in sexual competition. The play's complex interpersonal relationships reflect contemporary England's conflict between two models of upward mobility – one through an arranged marriage approved by the father, the other based on competition in a market economy.

Thomas is trapped by his desire for Mary. While his father wishes him to be a madcap, Mary wants an upright, serious husband. The comedy lies in Thomas's inept attempts to please them both. His initial efforts climax in act 3, scene 3, when he sings country wooing songs outside Mary's window. Madge, one of Mary's maids, appears to him, and "*with a devil's vizard, roaring, offers to kiss* [*him*] *and he falls down.*" This is a shorthand bedtrick, a prolepsis of what happens later. Next Thomas, disguised in his twin sister's clothing, crawls into Mary's bed in hopes of dalliance with the woman he desires. Mary, knowing of the disguise, has her black serving woman, Kate, lie there instead. The stage direction reads: "*A bed discovered with a Blackamoor in it*" (5.2.2). Thomas whispers to the supposed Mary of the "sweet, sweet joy" of kisses (5.2.12), but after he discovers he has kissed a black woman, he cries out:

> Holy saints defend me!
> The devil, devil, devil! O the devil! . . .
> I am abused most damnedly, most beastly;
> Yet if it be a she-devil –   (5.2.30–35)

These lines are ambivalent. At first, Thomas is horrified and reads Kate as the blackfaced devil of the homiletic tradition. His fourth line, "Yet . . .," suggests that after the initial shock dissipates, Thomas has second thoughts; perhaps if the devil is female, she is beddable after all. But then he beats Kate, crying, "Plague o' your Spanish-leather hide!" (5.2.39) and runs away.

---

[17] Quotations from *Monsieur Thomas* are from *A Critical Edition of John Fletcher's Comedy Monsieur Thomas or Father's Own Son*, ed. Nanette Cleri Clinch (New York: Garland, 1987), and will be cited by act, scene, and line number.

[18] Andrew Gurr notes the popularity of "prodigal plays" in this period. See *Playgoing in Shakespeare's London*, 2nd edn. (Cambridge: Cambridge University Press, 1996), pp. 103–04.

After some painful exclamations, Kate tells her mistress, "Pray lie here yourself next, mistress, /And entertain your sweetheart" (5.2.44–45); Kate is, in effect, Mary's black doppelgänger. Mary promises her a new petticoat as compensation for the beating. That is the last we see of Kate.

Because Kate is loyal to her mistress, she is sometimes cited as a rare representation of a "good" black woman, in contrast to treacherous characters in other plays.[19] But Kate is more complex. When Thomas describes her as a devil, he reiterates the folkloric fear of copulation with the supernatural. Kate's most important function in the plot is to enable Mary to keep her virtue. As a double, she can also be read as an unconscious projection of Mary's own transgressive desires.[20] In other words, Kate allows Mary, trapped in a patriarchal marriage economy, to determine her sexual and marital destiny. Desens observes: "Fletcher demonstrates that the women have a thorough understanding of the male fantasies that lie behind Thomas's attempted rape, but he also shows them presenting an alternative fantasy as their defense rather than challenging those fantasies directly."[21] This is a fantasy for the audience too; and although Desens does not pursue this point, it seems clear that the "alternative fantasy" involves illicit sex with a black woman. The "alternative fantasy" that the women dramatize for Thomas was to become a reality in Britain's overseas colonies, where countless slave women became substitute bedmates, so to speak, for their white mistresses.

As a substitute bedmate, Kate becomes the object of illicit male desire, competition, and intrigue, leaving Mary untainted and free to pursue her own marriage choice. And marriage in this play is a venture, which, like the sea voyages that form the play's backdrop, can lead to rags or to riches, misery or happiness, depending upon how the game is played. Because Fletcher's drama is a comedy, the audience expects the hero and heroine to succeed in their marriage ventures, and however attracted Thomas might be to Kate, he is to "come home" to Mary at last.

Richard Brome's *The Novella*, acted at the Blackfriars by the King's Company in 1632, replicates this bedtrick, but with an even stronger sense of gender ambiguity. The heroine, Victoria, comes to Venice disguised as "the novella," a courtesan, and offers her virginity for 2,000 ducats. She arranges a tryst with one of her suitors, the aged Pantaloni, and then substitutes her Moorish servant, Jacconetta, in the bed. Pantaloni's servant Nicolo reports what happened:

[19] See Barthelemy, *Black Face*, p. 134 and Tokson, *The Popular Image*, p. 59.
[20] See Doniger, *The Bedtrick*, p. 71.
[21] Desens, *The Bed-Trick in English Renaissance Drama*, p. 99.

> He bargain'd with her; and for some large price
> Shee yeilded to be his. But in the night
> In the condition'd bed was laid a *Moore*;
> A hideous and detested *Blackamore*,
> Which he (demanding light to please his eye,
> As old men use all motives)
> Discovered and inrag'd forsook the house;
> Affrighted and asham'd to aske his coyne againe.[22]

At the play's conclusion, when the masks are taken off, the audience learns that Jaconnetta is really Jacomo, "a eunuch Moore," the servant of Victoria's lover and Pantaloni's son Fabritio and that the sexual danger suggested in this scene was a phantom all along. Desens contends that "Brome not only makes the substituted bedmate male, but then feels compelled to render him sexless. He wishes to make it absolutely clear to his audience that no sexual activity, either heterosexual or homosexual, could have occurred."[23] The worst can be imagined – homosexual intercourse with a black devil – but in this play it never happens. The nightmare is used, instead, to punish the old pantaloon.

Such theatrical trickery is intended to titillate the audience, but it also embodies sexual and financial competition between men, this time a father and his son, in which the younger man humiliates the senex who blocks his sexual desires. The monstrousness of the threatened union of black and white, male and male, epitomizes the monstrousness of Pantaloni's lust, and public humiliation is his proper punishment.

Brome repeats the plot device of the substituted bedmate in *The English Moor* (1637)[24] to humiliate the predatory male, Nathaniel Baneless, who has deflowered and abandoned a gentlewoman, Phillis. Brome's bedtrick is an example of what Doniger describes as a "double back"; the wronged woman tricks her philandering partner "in such a way that he ends up in bed not merely with someone other than the intended erotic object but with the very person he was trying *not* to sleep with, usually his wife."[25] Pregnant and penniless, Phillis chooses service rather than prostitution. Her mistress, Millicent, is married to an old miser who has disguised her as a black Moor so that she will seem unattractive to would-be cuckolders. Yet

---

[22] Cited from Richard Brome, *Five New Playes* (London, 1653), sig. I6r.
[23] Desens, *The Bed-Trick in English Renaissance Drama*, p. 101. Desens does not consider the possibility of anal penetration, a possibility that might have occurred to some members of the audience.
[24] Richard Brome, *The English Moore; or The Mock-Marriage*, printed in *Five New Playes* (London, 1659). See also Sara Jayne Steen's edition of a manuscript version (Columbia, MO: University of Missouri Press, 1983).
[25] Doniger, *The Bedtrick*, p. 13.

when Nathaniel encounters Millicent, blackface and all, he associates her pigmentation with sexual pleasure and tries to seduce her. To trick Nathaniel into marriage, Phillis dons black make-up, dresses in her mistress's finery, and yields to his sexual advances.

Brome assumes that his audience will accept the theatrical convention that characters in disguise are never recognized, even by those who know them best. He thereby underscores a basic characteristic of racist and sexist behavior; the blackened female is rendered invisible, beyond recognition. They all, in a sense, look alike.[26] When the young wastrel later agrees to marry the Moor he has seduced, he is surprised to find that his cast-off mistress was the woman in blackface. Brome provides a new twist for the old adage that "All women are alike in the dark" by providing darkness in the form of a blackened face.

Like *The Novella* and *The English Moor*, Philip Massinger's comedy, *The Parliament of Love*, uses a similar ploy (the double back) to publicly humiliate a sexual predator. The play survives in a badly deteriorated manuscript; it was licensed in 1624, but there is no evidence it was ever performed. Still, it reveals Massinger's intent to use the bedtrick as a plot device. Because the first part of the manuscript is missing, we cannot be sure exactly how Beaupre's disguise is arranged, but we learn from the list of characters that she is to appear as "Calista, A Moor." In the first surviving scene, the nobleman Chamont presents her as a servant to the noblewoman Bellisant, who describes Calista as "the hansomest / I ere saw of her cuntry; shee hath neither / Thick lips nor rough curld haire." Chamont replies that her manners are even better than her shape; moreover

> Shee speakes our language to[o], for being surprisd
> In *Barbarie*, shee was bestowd vppon
> A pirat of *Marselles*, with whose wife
> Shee liu'd five yeares and learnt it; there I bought her
> As pittyinge her hard vsage; yf you please
> To make her yours, you maie.[27]

Thus Beaupre disguises herself as an attractive and accomplished black slave who serves as the substitute bedmate in the play's bedtrick.

Bellisant refuses all of her importunate suitors. Challenged by such resistance, Clarindor wagers his friends 3,000 crowns that he will bed her within the month. One of his tactics is to court the black servant Calista (Beaupre)

---

[26] See Doniger, *The Bedtrick*, p. 303.
[27] Cited from *The Plays and Poems of Philip Massinger*, ed. Philip Edwards and Colin Gibson, vol. II (Oxford: Clarendon Press, 1976), p. 112. Quotations will be cited by page numbers within the text.

as a way to get to her mistress, but the Moor exclaims, "Like mee sir? / One of my dark complexion?" Clarindor anticipates the bedtrick with his response:

> I am serious;
> The curtains drawne and envious light putt out,
> The soft tuch hightens appetite, and takes more
> Then culler, *Venus* dressinge in the daie tyme,
> But neuer thought on in her midnight revells.
> Come, I must haue thee myne.   (124)

The emphasis here, as in the other bedtricks, is on what is seen and what is not seen. The victims of the bedtrick in *Monsieur Thomas* and *The Novella* draw back in horror when there is enough light to reveal their partner's dark skin. Clarindor states openly what is implicit in the device itself, that as long as the man does not see the woman he is copulating with, her color does not matter.

In a later scene, we see Clarindor after he has slept with Bellisant (or so he supposes), and it's not a pretty picture. Like a proud rooster, he boasts of his conquest and rushes off to tell his friends, violating the oath of secrecy he had made to Bellisant. In the play's conclusion before King Charles, this crime is judged even worse than the conquest itself. Charles denounces Clarindor for it: "In this / Thou dost degrade thie self of all the honors / Thie ancestors left thee, and in thie base natu[re] / Tis to[o] apparent that thou art a peasan[t]" (173). By breaking his word to a lady, Clarindor has been untrue to the aristocratic code of honor. When the King lets Bellisant select the rogue's punishment, she commands him to marry the Moor, and his reaction is characteristic: "A divell, hange me rather!" (174). Only then does he reveal that he has a wife, the good Beaupre whom he had abandoned. Calista is transformed into the good wife Beaupre when "this varnish from her face" (174) is washed off. Her desires are lawful because they were directed toward her husband; the only crime Clarindor committed was to sleep with his own wife. Even so, Beaupre has been transformed, if only temporarily, by imagining herself to be someone else, a sexually active black serving maid.

Of the four comedies that substitute a black female servant for her chaste mistress, sexual consummation actually takes place only in the double back plots of *The Parliament of Love* and *The English Moor*. In both cases, the Moor is not really black, but a white woman in blackface; the sexual act fulfills the fantasy of cross-racial coupling without the reality. Moreover, the female's transgressive sexual initiative is condoned because of her need, and society's need, to police the wandering appetites of her lover or husband through public humiliation. Potential virgin-violators would not escape so easily in early seventeenth-century tragedies.

III

While the bedtrick is a useful comic device in comedies like *Monsieur Thomas, The Novella, The English Moor,* and *The Parliament of Love,* in John Marston's *The Wonder of Women: or, The Tragedy of Sophonisba* (1606) it prevents the chaste heroine from being brutally raped. Set in the context of Rome's war with Carthage, the tragedy depicts the beautiful Sophonisba as the focus of competition between two north African kings, one the virtuous Massinissa who marries her, and the other Syphax, the villain who wants her body. Syphax arranges with the Romans that Massinissa will be called to war before his marriage to Sophonisba can be consummated.

Contrasts of black and white frame *Sophonisba,* and the plot summary that follows will highlight just how the specter of miscegenation haunts the text. The opening scene depicts Syphax confessing his desire for Sophonisba to Vangue, the servant he addresses as "Dear Ethiopian Negro" (1.1.60).[28] Vangue's black body suggests the exoticism of northern Africa. His female counterpart, Zanthia, Sophonisba's serving woman, attends her through the first half of the play.[29]

In the drama's second scene, Sophonisba prepares for her marriage bed in staging reminiscent of Titian's rendition of *Diana and Actaeon;* displayed before us is the white female body readied for sexual consummation, shadowed by a black figure. When Sophonisba asks Zanthia to help "undo" her, Zanthia replies with a bawdy jest: "You had been undone if you had not been undone" (1.2.4). Sophonisba seems eager for the consummation. She rues the ceremonies of the marriage bed that force the bride to hide her anticipation, but Zanthia reflects that women are "imperfect creatures" who without such ceremonies would "fall to all contempt. O women, how much, / How much are you beholding to ceremony!" (see lines 17–28).

---

[28] Quotations from *Sophonisba* are taken from *The Selected Plays of John Marston,* ed. Macdonald P. Jackson and Michael Neill (Cambridge: Cambridge University Press, 1986) and are cited by act, scene, and line number.

[29] Critics of the play have generally agreed that although Zanthia is never referred to as being "black," as a Moorish waiting woman she would have been represented in black make-up. See Eldred D. Jones, *Othello's Countrymen: The African in English Renaissance Drama* (London: Oxford University Press, 1965), p. 76; Tokson, *The Popular Image,* pp. 84–86; and Barthelemy, *Black Face,* p. 126. Joyce Green MacDonald discusses the reasons why the dramatist figures Sophonisba, a north African, as white; see *Women and Race in Early Modern Texts* (Cambridge: Cambridge University Press, 2002), pp. 76–86.

Zanthia's frank sexuality is crucial in the construction of Sophonisba as the chaste heroine because the Moor deflects anxieties about female desire onto herself, accentuating her mistress's white virtue. The scene, which ends without the anticipated consummation because Massinissa is called to war, affirms Massinissa's view of Sophonisba:

> Nature made all the rest of thy fair sex
> As weak essays, to make thee a pattern
> Of what can be in woman!
>
> (1.2.228–30)

The interrupted consummation recurs in mid-play when Syphax tries to rape Sophonisba. The initial stage direction for act 3, scene 1, reads: "SYPHAX, *his dagger twon* [twined] *about her hair, drags in* SOPHON-ISBA *in her nightgown petticoat; and* ZANTHIA *and* VANGUE *following*." Syphax threatens that if Sophonisba does not yield,

> Look, I'll tack thy head
> To the low earth, whilst strength of two black knaves
> Thy limbs all wide shall strain.   (3.1.9–11)

The visual image is clear: the white body of Sophonisba will be held open by two black servants (presumably Zanthia and Vangue) for Syphax to penetrate. Though the black figures will only assist in the rape, they nevertheless serve "to mark rape with racial pollution without insisting on a literalization of this contamination."[30]

But Sophonisba is too smart for Syphax. She puts him off for an hour by promising that she will yield once she has made a special sacrifice. Syphax leaves after bribing Zanthia to spy for him and ordering Vangue to remain. While he is gone, Sophonisba gives Vangue a sleeping potion, places his black body in her bed, and departs through a secret exit. The next stage directions reads, "*Enter* SYPHAX *ready for bed*"; and after several lines of sweet talk (which Zanthia tries to interrupt but to no avail), "*Offering to leap into bed, he discovers* VANGUE." His response, like those of Thomas and Nathanial, equates the black body with the devil: "Ha! Can any woman turn to such a devil?" (3.1.183). Because the object of illicit desire turns out to be both male and black, and a servant to boot, Syphax kills him: "Sleep there thy lasting sleep, / Improvident, base, o'er-thirsty slave. / Die pleased, a king's couch is thy too-proud grave" (193–95). Syphax is incensed at the prospect of a homosexual assignation, but, more importantly, he reacts violently to Vangue's servant class and his blackness, which mark the

---

[30] Little, *Shakespeare Jungle Fever*, p. 60.

intended assignation as socially and racially – not just sexually – monstrous.[31]

Syphax discovers the bed trick in this scene before the consummation can take place. He is not so lucky in act 4, however, when he copulates with the witch Erictho, supposing her body to be that of Sophonisba. The stage directions for act 5, scene 1 show the aftermath: "SYPHAX *draws the curtains and discovers* ERICTHO *lying with him.*" He cries: "Thou rotten scum of hell – / O my abhorred heat! O loathed delusion!" (5.1.2–3), but when he offers to strike the witch with his sword, she slips "*into the ground*" (presumably through the trap door). Although Erictho's cheeks are pale (4.1.103), her rites and her tongue (4.2.112 and 120) are figured black, and the actor who impersonated Vangue could easily have doubled her role. In him/her the figurative black devil is reified.

Marston's tragedy concludes with Rome's triumph over Carthage. But even on this broader political plane, Sophonisba's body is the object of male competition and negotiation. The Roman commander Scipio offers Massinissa peaceable terms and the kingship of Carthage, but only if he will turn over Sophonisba, whom he deems a traitor. Just as husband and wife are reunited, the promised consummation is thwarted once again. To save her country and her husband's honor, Sophonisba takes poison, fulfilling the sacrificial role of the virgin martyr and becoming the "wonder of women" promised in the play's title.

William Rowley's *All's Lost by Lust* (written ca. 1619) also features a bedtrick in the tragedy's subplot, which centers on masculine sexual competition and traffic in women. Lovesick with desire, which he cloaks in romantic protestations of undying love, Antonio marries Margaretta, a poor woman of lower rank. Later he meets Dionysia, a woman of greater rank and means, and repents to his friend Lazarello his earlier choice, voicing the common belief that Islamic cultures were sexually permissive:

> Perswade me to turne Turk, or Moore, Mahometan,
> For by the lustfull lawes of *Mahomet*
> I may have three wives more.[32]

Lazarello's solution is to impersonate Antonio and sleep with his wife, so that his friend can denounce Margaretta's unfaithfulness and marry again. But Margaretta has become so jealous of her husband that she conspires with her Moorish waiting woman, Fidella, to strangle him when he comes

---

[31] Desens notes Syphax's sexual insecurity and fear of homosexuality but ignores the impact of Vangue's class and blackness on his would be seducer. See *The Bed-Trick in English Renaissance Drama*, p. 96.

[32] William Rowley, *A Tragedy Called All's Lost by Lust* (London, 1633), sig. D3v.

to her bed. When the lusty Lazarello pretends to be Antonio and is slain by mistake, Margaretta rewards Fidella with gold for her service and sends her away. Here one of the substitute bedmates is a male, and instead of losing his maidenhead, he loses his life. The black Moorish maid remains true to her name in that she is "faithful" to her mistress. In addition, Fidella's complicity in this sexual intrigue serves as a mode of upward mobility. The sexual subplot reinforces the idea that marriage, like exploits against the Moors of northern Africa, is a venture, a way to better one's economic and social condition, and that like foreign adventures, it carries a host of risks.

The most violent bedtrick (and the most grotesque) from this period comes from an academic play by Samuel Harding while he was in residence at Exeter College, Oxford. Harding took the BA in 1638, and the text of *Sicily and Naples* was printed in 1640 by William Turner of Oxford. The volume includes several commendatory verses from fellows of Exeter College who praise Harding's play and regret that it was never performed. "PP"'s address to the readers notes that the drama was published against the author's will. Added together, the circumstances suggest that *Sicily and Naples* was Harding's exuberant attempt to write the kind of sensational revenge tragedy perfected by John Ford and Cyril Tourneur, but like many youthful imitators, he went too far; the Oxford authorities refused to let the play be performed at the College.

Among Harding's lengthy cast of characters is Zisco, a Moor. He appears in the play's third scene kicking Fungoso, a lackey to Ursini, favorite of the King of Sicily. Fungoso responds with the conventional equation of blackness with the demonic: "A Moore! a divell! A meere divell! his very lookes spake him so, but for his club-foote, his damnable club-foote, (Asse that I was not to see it, I'me sure I feel it now,) 'tis an infallible sign" (8).[33] Ursini describes Zisco as "one that's fit to kill a King, / A thing, whose soule is nothing but a spot / Transmitted from foule parricides, whose thoughts / Weare a more deepe and horrid blacke, than that / Which spreads upon his body –" (11).

Harding's plot uses three bedtricks, piling complication upon complication; at the risk of tediousness, here is an overview of the play's major action. Ursini and Zisco conspire to bring the Moor into King Ferrando's service by fabricating a history (perhaps in an intertextual reference to Shakespeare's *Othello*) of "stout service done against the Turkes / In the Lepanto battle" where he turned Christian and was baptized (11).

---

[33] Quotations from *Sicily and Naples, or the Fatall Vnion. A Tragoedy* (Oxford, 1640) are cited by page number within the text.

But this Moor is a fake. Ursini realizes that Zisco is really Frederico, son of the slain Alberto, and that the young man now seeks revenge against King Ferrando for seducing and abandoning his sister Felicia. Ursini also tells the audience that he does not really want to kill the King, that he is playing along with Zisco, and that Felicia did not lose her virginity to King Ferrando as she thought, but to himself, disguised as the King. This is the play's first bedtrick.

Meanwhile, King Ferrando is in love with Calantha, the Princess of Sicily. Disguised as a page, Sylvio, the lovesick and pregnant Felicia visits Calantha and tells her that Ferrando is married to her and that she carries his child. She proposes to take Calantha's place on the wedding night, hoping that this arrangement will enable her to reform Ferrando and win him back. Calantha agrees to this plot and hopes to use it to her advantage so that she can escape the court. This "double back" is the second bedtrick.

The third bedtrick is less benign. Zisco anticipates it: "The night comes on apace, streight every thing / Will be as blacke as I, and alike terrible, / Nay, out-doe mee too" (63–64). He plans to keep Ferrando's assignation with Calantha and – in revenge against the King – to rape and kill her. Thus when Ferrando goes to what he thinks will be his marriage bed, he finds, according to Harding's stage directions: "*Curteine drawne, Felicia discovered lying upon a bed. Zisco as hauing ravish't, and then slain her*" (90). Zisco kills Ferrando and "*puls off his disguise*" (91).[34] This stage direction suggests that Harding conceived Zisco as wearing a visor that could be immediately removed on stage rather than the blackface make-up of the professional actor. Ursini is stunned when he recognizes Frederico underneath the Moor's disguise. Later in the scene, when Frederico/Zisco discovers that he has raped and killed his own sister, he stabs himself. The play concludes with all the villains satisfactorily and sensationally dead.

Harding's grotesque play deconstructs, as Doniger observes, "first marriage, then adultery, and then the pretense of adultery. The bedtricks whirl around and around into a *mise en abime*, a sexual vortex in which no one ever knows who is tricked and who is tricking."[35] Harding's plot also reifies fantasies of miscegenation and incest. The sudden removal of Zisco's black disguise mitigates the fear of miscegenation but it confirms the commission of incest. In Harding's Naples, as Arthur Little noted of Shakespeare's

---

[34] This intriguing stage direction may suggest Harding's ignorance of staging practices in this period. By the 1630s black make-up was used on the professional stage for Moorish characters (cf. Richard Brome's *The English Moor* [1637]), but the disguise that is pulled off in Harding's imagined scene need not be a mask and could be Moorish garments or even a turban.
[35] Doniger, *The Bedtrick*, p. 48.

Rome, "incest is better than miscegenation,"[36] for miscegenation is the worst thing that could be imagined. No doubt Harding intended to shock his audience by stocking his play with every conceivable horror, which probably explains Oxford's censorship (if that is, indeed, what happened).

IV

Four of the seven dramatic bedtricks described here are abortive. The lover calls for light, discovers the black body in the bed, and rushes from the room in horror, shouting, "a devil!" This spontaneous exclamation reiterates the centuries-old association of Satan and his minions with a blackened complexion and reveals the tenacious hold of the "black devil" trope in early modern England. The reiterated equation of blackness with the demonic has by the early seventeenth century hardened into a cliché that marks English contempt for people of black pigmentation. Copulation with the devil was the ultimate taboo. While it is unfashionable in much recent criticism to label such associations "racist," surely they illustrate early modern England's readiness to generalize freely about the demonic origins of blackness and its connection to forbidden erotic experiences.

Only three plays depict a completed sexual act: *The English Moor*, *The Parliament of Love*, and *Sicily and Naples*. In all three the audience would have been aware that the Moorish figure having sex with a white person is not really a black Moor, but a European in disguise.[37] Thus while the specter of miscegenation is raised, it is never literalized on stage. In the comedies, the hero's erotic fantasy of copulation with a Moor marks his philandering nature. His female partner's willingness to submit to the blackface disguise is a sign of her resourcefulness. The lying of the trickster is thus mitigated by the lying fantasies of the one who is tricked.[38]

As should be clear by now, the bedtrick depends upon the substitutability of bodies as objects of desire. The unsuspecting lover is never completely confident of what he is going to find when the anticipated moment of consummation finally arrives. Substitutability in sexual intrigue works, I believe, in the same way that the light–dark oppositions animate Elizabethan sonnet sequences, where, as Kim Hall contends, lightening "signals

---

[36] Little, *Shakespeare Jungle Fever*, p. 57.

[37] The exposition of *The Parliament of Love* has been lost, but it seems highly likely that Beaupre's disguise as Calista would have been revealed to the audience in an early scene before Chamont presents her to Bellisant. See Edwards and Gibson's introduction to *The Plays and Poems of Philip Massinger*, p. 98.

[38] Doniger, *The Bedtrick*, p. 8.

a wish for an ordered, stable language rather than the dark, unconquered territory of slippery linguistic 'alienness.'"[39] The lover approaching the bed anticipates the fulfillment of conquering and possessing, of taking a woman's virginity; instead he finds "alienness," something unanticipated, foreign, and unconquerable, lying in wait. When the presumed object of desire turns out to be black, its alterity is emphatically represented on stage.

The bedtrick can also be seen as symptomatic of the cultural anxieties that ebb and flow through these plays. Not always, but often, the bedtrick is the site of masculine competition, not just over the body of a woman, but also the wealth and power that could be attained through marriage to an aristocratic female. The aborted bedtrick depicts the frustration of that drive; one man loses possession even as another wins. Often the loser is publicly humiliated, mainly through the revelation that he has been polluted through sexual contact with a black woman.

In the bedtricks described here, the black body, however marginalized, functions as a crucial building block in the construction of a white norm for early modern England.[40] Consistently excoriated by other characters as the devil incarnate, the black figure between the sheets suggests that Stuart audiences – and perhaps the culture at large – assumed that black pigmentation inevitably embodied an ineluctable difference that was both racially and sexually charged. The black Moor's imbrication in this recurring plot device of the substituted bedmate shows that dramatists increasingly exploited cross-racial sexuality as an exotic element that was simultaneously attractive and forbidden. The bedtricks described here graphically demonstrate how early modern English attitudes toward female sexuality were entwined with emerging notions of racial difference.[41]

---

[39] Hall, *Things of Darkness*, p. 72.

[40] Other examples of "whiteness studies" that trace the development of race consciousness in early modern England are Hall, Erickson, and Little, as well as Dympna Callaghan's "'Othello Was a White Man'" in *Shakespeare Without Women: Representing Gender and Race on the Renaissance Stage* (London: Routledge, 2000), pp. 75–96.

[41] See Ania Loomba, *Shakespeare, Race, and Colonialism* (Oxford: Oxford University Press, 2002), pp. 59–63.

CHAPTER 6

Shakespeare's Moor of Venice

Othello is undoubtedly the most famous role that required an actor to perform in blackface. Unlike any of the other plays discussed in this book, *Othello* has held the boards for four centuries, been translated into nearly every language on earth, and is frequently adapted for film and television.[1] However much attention – including my own – has already been devoted to Shakespeare's tragedy, this book would not be complete without some discussion of that most canonical play. My *Othello: A Contextual History* provides historical contexts for the tragedy's inception and the history of its performance. Here my focus is on the dynamics of blackface impersonation.

It was politically correct in the nineteenth and early twentieth centuries to lighten Othello's skin tone and make him a "tawny Moor," but however light the make-up may have been, Othello was always darker than the play's other characters.[2] The dark–light contrast is highlighted in the text's language – Desdemona is the pearl, the chrysolite, the monumental alabaster, whereas Othello is "black". Throughout its acting history, performances of *Othello* have reified the verbal imagery in visual contrasts of light and dark, and there is no reason to doubt that Richard Burbage wore blackface for the role. He was a painter as well as an actor, and as Julie Hankey points out, he was sensitive to visual effects. Standing before the Globe's magnificent

---

[1] Tim Blake Nelson's 2001 film *O*, for example, moves the plot into a southern preparatory school, with the Othello figure named Odin as the star of the basketball team; Geoffrey Sax's *Othello*, made for British and American television, moves the action to London's Metropolitan Police Force, where the newly appointed John Othello is betrayed by his friend Ben Jago. George Cukor's 1948 *A Double Life* has the actor playing Othello (Ronald Colman) become so obsessed with the role that he kills a woman while imagining her to be Desdemona.

[2] In addition to my *Othello: A Contextual History* (Cambridge: Cambridge University Press, 1994), see Carol Jones Carlisle, *Shakespeare from the Greenroom: Actors' Criticism of Four Major Tragedies* (Chapel Hill: University of North Carolina Press, 1969), pp. 172–263, Marvin Rosenberg, *The Masks of Othello* (Berkeley: University of California Press, 1971), Gino J. Matteo, *Shakespeare's "Othello": The Study and the Stage, 1604–1904* (Salzburg: Institut für Sprache und Literatur, 1974), and Lois Potter, *Othello*, Shakespeare in Performance Series (Manchester: Manchester University Press, 2002).

façade, and "no doubt gorgeously costumed . . . Othello would have stood out in bold contrast."[3]

Several lines in the play attest to the Moor's blackness. Iago describes him as an "old black ram" underneath Brabantio's window, and Brabantio angrily refers to Othello's "sooty bosom," which makes him a "thing" to be feared, not for delight (1.2. 70–71).[4] To Brabantio, Othello's black countenance is so monstrous that Desdemona should fear "to look on" it (1.3.98). In addition to a black color, "sooty" suggests contamination; according to the *Oxford English Dictionary*, a sooty object or person is "foul or dirty with soot; covered or smeared with soot." As a coating, soot makes the wearer black in appearance but not essentially black, and thus Brabantio's image is ambiguous. Edward Pechter perceptively analyzes the effects of Brabantio's and Iago's charges: "The indiscriminate mixing of black and Moorish impressions serves to endow Othello with an unstable quality that adds to and may indeed be at the heart of his terrifying strangeness."[5]

During the temptation scene, Othello ponders, "Haply for I am black" (3.3.266), and once he is convinced of Desdemona's perfidy, he insists that "Her name, that was as fresh / As Dian's visage, is now begrimed and black / As mine own face" (3.3.389–91). Like "sooty," "begrimed" suggests a dirty, unattractive coating. "Grime" echoes in Othello's "I here look grim as hell," the Quarto and Folio reading for act 4, scene 2, line 65.[6] After the murder (5.2), Emilia claims Othello is "the blacker devil," a "filthy bargain," and as "ignorant as dirt." "Soot," "grime," and "dirt" denote a black coating that can be rubbed on and off, and perhaps serve as subliminal references to the black make-up that Richard Burbage wore. The words' connotations – filth and uncleanness – make blackness seem repulsive.

"Soot," "grime," and "dirt," as John R. Ford astutely observes, also evoke "an actor's dressing table." They create "metatheatrical moments, intended or not, that simultaneously create a character and deconstruct an actor's craft."[7] Desdemona's deathbed fear when Othello's "eyes roll so" suggests that the black paint highlighted the whites of Burbage's eyes, akin to Aaron's "wall-eyed" look. While I would not go so far as Sheila Rose Bland and

[3] Julie Hankey, ed., *Othello: Plays in Performance* (Bristol: Bristol Classical Press, 1987), p. 17.

[4] Quotations from *Othello* are taken from the Third Arden Series, ed. E. A. J. Honigmann (London: Arden Shakespeare, 1997) and are cited by act, scene, and line number.

[5] Edward Pechter, *Othello and Interpretive Traditions* (Iowa City: University of Iowa Press, 1999), p. 35.

[6] Editors modernize "I" to "Aye" but the original spelling is nevertheless suggestive. See Pechter, *Othello and Interpretive Traditions*, p. 89.

[7] John R. Ford, "'Words and Performances': Roderigo and the Mixed Dramaturgy of Race and Gender in *Othello*," in *Othello: New Critical Essays*, ed. Philip C. Kolin (New York and London: Routledge, 2002), pp. 147–67; quotation from p. 163.

describe Shakespeare's original *Othello* as a "minstrel show" with Iago in the role of Mr. Interlocutor,[8] cues in the text do call attention to the Moor as an impersonation, sporadically reminding the audience that the actor's blackness is a façade.

The text also ascribes an exotic geographical otherness to the Moor. His descriptions of "antres vast" and "anthropophagi" in the Senate scene set him apart from the "wealthy curled darlings" of Venetian society. His references to the handkerchief given to his mother by an Egyptian charmer recall the mysterious realms of northern Africa. And Othello's final speech echoes these suggestions of alterity. If one accepts the Quarto's "Indian," the Moor's line that he "threw a pearl away / Richer than all his tribe" (5.2.345–46) suggests cultural difference in a comparison to East or West Indians who were ignorant of proper values. If one accepts the Folio's "Iudean," the speech resonates with religious overtones, with the suggestion of Judas, the Judean who betrayed Christ. Thus blackness is not the only signifier in the play of Othello's alienation from the white Venetian majority; he is marked throughout, as Brabantio claims, as an "extravagant and wheeling stranger."

Most pertinent to this study are the ways in which Othello fits with the other theatrical conventions I have examined. The most obvious change, one that has been noted by myriads of critics, is that the black character in Shakespeare's *Othello* is not the talking devil with a special relationship to the audience he was in the plays of the 1580s and 1590s. Iago, the white Venetian who feels betrayed by his general's promotion of Cassio, takes this role. Until the final scene, Iago shares his diabolic plans with the audience in soliloquies that only dimly suggest any plausible motivation except sheer enjoyment. In crafting Iago, Shakespeare takes the convention of the stage Moor/devil that he had exploited so successfully in *Titus Andronicus* and turns it upside down. This surprising tactic, which provides the actor performing Iago with the longest role in the play, may have been calculated to shock an audience that by 1604 was quite used to blackfaced devils.

Robert Hornback notes another type of inversion in Shakespeare's creation of Othello. He argues that the Moor's first appearance with a blackened face, in a Moor's coat, and with the handkerchief (which Hornback identifies with the "muckender," a piece of cloth hanging from the fool's waist), would have reminded the audience of the "natural fool" of medieval folk plays. The audience's initial response, posits Hornback, would have

[8] Sheila Rose Bland, "How I Would Direct *Othello*," in *Othello: New Essays by Black Writers*, ed. Mythili Kaul (Washington DC: Howard University Press, 1997), pp. 29–41, esp. p. 31.

made them complicit in Iago's jeers. Although this impression is turned topsy-turvy in the Senate scene, it recurs in the play's final moments with Emilia's charge that Othello is a "gull," as "ignorant as dirt."[9]

Othello resonates with previous stage Moors in other ways, even though he is not a Moorish King. He relates that he had once been sold into slavery, and while he is a respected military officer, he remains a "servant" to the Venetian state, not a Machiavel trying to take it over. At the same time, Othello's position remains liminal throughout the play – he is inside Venetian culture but also very much outside of it. In the play's final scene, Emilia charges him with being a "devil" and a "cruel Moor" (5.2.142 and 247), terms reminiscent of the talking devils, Muly Hamet, Aaron, and Eleazar. Othello is, in other words, a hybrid who finds he cannot assimilate without killing "the turbaned Turk" within.

There is no bedtrick in *Othello*. The convention, however, is suggested in the characters' suspicions of each other. Roderigo wishes to be in bed with Desdemona in place of her husband Othello. Iago suspects that Othello and Cassio have both bedded his wife. Othello is brought to believe that Cassio hath the act "a thousand times committed" with Desdemona. While Cassio seems attracted by Desdemona's grace and beauty, he substitutes a Cypriot whore, Bianca, in his bed. For all the talk of sexual consummation and bedding, the only male and female we ever actually see in bed together are Desdemona and Othello, coupled in death. Even that consummation is compromised by the presence of Emilia, the serving woman who wishes to be laid on the bed next to her mistress.[10] So while the plot device of the bedtrick is omitted, its complicated sexual intrigue, not to mention the attraction and revulsion that it inspires, resonate throughout the play.

Sir Laurence Olivier once described the role of Othello as "a terrible study and a monstrous, monstrous burden for the actor." He went on to speculate that "Shakespeare and actor Richard Burbage got drunk together one night and Burbage said, 'I can play anything you write, anything at all.' And Shakespeare said, 'Right, I'll fix you, boy!' And then he wrote *Othello*."[11] The challenge was the role's intense theatricality. Shakespeare introduced "too many climaxes – 'all beckoning you to scream to the utmost.'"[12] As Elise Marks persuasively argues, the role's histrionic quality – the way "Othello's

---

[9] Robert Hornback, "Emblems of Folly in the First *Othello*: Renaissance Blackface, Moor's Coat, and 'Muckender,'" *Comparative Drama* 35 (2001), 66–99.

[10] James R. Siemon's analysis of the performance history of *Othello*'s final scene indicates that Emilia's request has usually been ignored in the theatre. See "'Nay, That's Not Next': *Othello*, V.ii in Performance, 1760–1900," *Shakespeare Quarterly* 37 (1986), 38–51.

[11] Quoted from John Cottrell, *Laurence Olivier* (Englewood Cliffs, NJ: Prentice Hall, 1975), p. 337.

[12] Cottrell, *Laurence Olivier*, p. 342.

tremendous passion overtakes and even overwhelms the actor who plays him, and 'swells' or 'surges' out into the bodies of those who watch him perform" – is simultaneously "unnerving and deeply pleasurable." The audience identifies profoundly with Othello's emotional experiences even as it notices the signs of his alterity.[13]

We can never recapture what the original performances of *Othello* were like, but we do know that however he was conceived, the Moor was one of Burbage's outstanding roles. An epitaph that circulated after his death describes "the greued Moore"[14] as among his best impersonations, and *Othello* seems to have been a popular play, judging by the number of recorded performances before the closing of the theatres in 1642. Olivier's joke highlights *Othello*'s great appeal; both the protagonist's and the antagonist's roles make horrific demands on the performers' actorly resources, and audiences enjoy seeing their technique at work.

I

We have very few clues as to how Richard Burbage performed his Othello, so it may be helpful to venture beyond this book's chronology to examine the history of *Othello* in performance. The bits and pieces of business revealed in memoirs, anecdotes, and reviews suggest that a major ingredient in the audience's fascination with the Moor is the pleasure of seeing the white actor personate a black man and knowing that this is what he or she is seeing.[15] Colley Cibber's description of Thomas Betterton, the Restoration's great Othello, claims that "*in spite of his Complexion*, Othello has more natural Beauties than the best Actor can find in all the Magazine of Poetry, to animate his Power, and delight his Judgment with."[16] Reporting on Spranger Barry, the eighteenth century's premier Moor, John Bernard wrote that the speech, "I'll tear her all to pieces" was particularly effective because "You could observe the muscles stiffening, the veins distending, and the red blood boiling through his dark skin – a mighty flood of passion accumulating for several minutes – and at length bearing down its barriers, and sweeping onward in thunder, love, reason, mercy, all before

---

[13] Elise Marks, "'Othello/Me': Racial Drag and the Pleasures of Boundary-Crossing with Othello," *Comparative Drama* 35 (2001), 101–24; quote from 101.

[14] See E. K. Chambers, *The Elizabethan Stage*, 4 vols. (Oxford: Clarendon Press, 1923), vol. II, p. 309.

[15] For detailed overviews of *Othello* in performance, see Carlisle, *Shakespeare from the Green Room*; Rosenberg, *The Masks of Othello*; Matteo, *Shakespeare's "Othello"*; Potter, *Othello*; and Hankey, *Othello*. See also my *Othello: A Contextual History*, and Pechter, *Othello and Interpretive Traditions*.

[16] Colley Cibber, *The History of the Stage* (London: J. Miller, 1742), p. 20; italics mine.

it."[17] Samuel Foote noted the same phenomenon in the murder scene: "We see Mr. Barry redden through the very black of his face; his whole visage becomes inflamed, his eyes sparkle with successful vengeance, and he seems to raise himself above the ground."[18] Barry's rendition was so effective that, according to the *Biographical Dictionary*, "when he played Othello he looked so like the Moor it was no easy matter for the audience to remember he was not a real Negro; the story was told of a simple country girl in the gallery who cried out, 'Lord, Lord! where did they hire that Neeger [sic] to act for 'm!'"[19] Even as this anecdote highlights the realism of Barry's performance, it suggests that in contrast to the ignorant country lass who confused the actor with his role, sophisticated urbanites in the audience were always aware of the difference. These nuggets of theatrical history emphasize the same phenomenon, a sort of double consciousness on the audience's part, a recognition that the actor underneath the blackened skin is actually white.

Bits of theatrical business also emphasized this dual awareness. James Quin, who played a ponderous Othello in the first half of the eighteenth century, was noted for slowly taking off his white glove at his first appearance to display the black hand underneath.[20] The audience clearly expected to see the actor's white hand and was pleased at Quin's willingness to blacken hands as well as face in order to create the illusion of verisimilitude. Gloves created a different kind of recognition for Lena Ashwell, who "recalled an Othello that she saw as a child: 'His face was very black – he wore black gloves and appeared to be black all over until he waved his arms about, and then where the gloves ended, he was very white, and that was exciting to watch.'"[21] What made it so exciting was that it was a stunning performance, and the white skin of the actor's hand reminded Ashwell that what she was watching was great acting, not reality.

The actor's body could also be used to emphasize the Moor's blackness. In the early nineteenth century, William Hazlitt praised Kean's display of hands and head in the middle of the temptation scene: "One of his finest instantaneous actions was clutching his black hand slowly round his head

---

[17] John Bernard, *Retrospections of the Stage*, 2 vols. (London: Henry Colburn and Richard Bentley, 1830), vol. i, p. 28.
[18] Cited in Pechter, *Othello and Interpretive Traditions*, p. 142.
[19] *Biographical Dictionary of Actors, Actresses, Musicians, Dancers, Managers and Other Stage Personnel in London: 1660–1800*, ed. Philip Highfill et al., 16 vols. (Carbondale: Southern Illinois University Press, 1973–1993), vol. i, p. 338.
[20] Francis Gentleman, *The Dramatic Censor, or Critical Companion*, 2 vols. (London: J. Bell, 1770), vol. i, pp. 151–52.
[21] Quoted from Potter, *Othello*, p. 30.

as though his brains were turning, and then writhing round and standing in dull agony with his back to the audience."[22] The Victorian actor William Charles Macready embellished the murder scene; he thrust out "his dark despairing face through the curtains," forming in its contrast with the drapery a marvellous piece of color.[23] Clara Morris responded to the color contrast between the Othello of Tommaso Salvini (who spoke in Italian) and his white Desdemona: "Passion choked, his gloating eyes burned with the mere lust of the 'sooty Moor' for that white creature of Venice. It was revolting, and with a shiver I exclaimed aloud, 'Ugh, you splendid brute!'"[24]

When color is not mentioned in the accounts of critics and audience members, the thrill of watching a brilliant impersonation still comes through. Take for example this description of Edwin Forrest in the collaring scene:

Suddenly, with one electrifying bound, he leaped the whole gamut from mortal exhaustion to gigantic rage, his eyeballs rolling and flashing and his muscles strung, seized the cowering Iago by the throat, and, with a startling transition of voice from mellow and mournfully lingering notes to crackling thunderbolts . . . shrieked, –

> 'If thou dost slander her and torture me,
> Never pray more; abandon all remorse.'[25]

Forrest's muscular Moor epitomizes a characteristic of successful Othellos through the eighteenth and nineteenth centuries: physicality. David Garrick failed not only because his short stature made him look like the negro servant Pompey with a tea kettle, as Quin is said to have quipped, but because his physical mannerisms did not allow such display. Henry Irving's Othello also annoyed reviewers with his nervous ticks and movements. Tall handsome actors such as Spranger Barry, in contrast, appealed to audiences because the *display* of the body is integral to the role.

II

For most of its acting history, blackface has been essential to that focus on the body. Mr. Crummles, the itinerant actor of Charles Dickens's *Nicholas Nickleby*, reminisces about a colleague: "We had a first-tragedy man in our

[22] Cited in Rosenberg, *Masks of Othello*, p. 63.
[23] Arthur Colby Sprague, *Shakespeare and the Actors: The Stage Business in His Plays (1660–1905)* (Cambridge: Harvard University Press, 1944), p. 216.
[24] Clara Morris, *Confidences: Talks about Players and Play Acting* (London, 1902); cited in Hankey, *Othello*, p. 88.
[25] Quoted in Rosenberg, *Masks of Othello*, p. 97.

company once, who, when he played Othello, used to black himself all over. But that's feeling a part and going into it as if you meant it; it isn't usual; more's the pity."[26] This fictional actor wanted to make the role "real," so he blacked himself, not just on the hands and face as was customary, but all over. Crummles admires this man for his willingness to subsume himself in the role of a black man, a sign of his dedication to the art of impersonation. Again, it is the actorly quality that appealed.

Crummles's colleague seems strangely prescient of the most notable blackface performance of Othello in the twentieth century, Sir Laurence Olivier in the National Theatre's 1964–65 production directed by John Dexter. In a publicity puff for *Life* magazine, Olivier wryly noted: "It's terribly hard to say what they were like, those boys from Morocco. The whole thing will be in the lips and the color. I've been looking at Negroes' lips every time I see them on a train or anywhere, and actually, their lips seem black or blueberry-colored, really, rather than red. . . . I'll use just a little tiny touch of lake and a lot more brown and a little mauve."[27] In addition to creating the illusion of "thick lips," Olivier blackened his entire body for the role. Biographer Anthony Holden describes the process Olivier used to make himself into Othello:

He started by covering his body from head to toe with a coat of dark stain, over which went a layer of greasy black make-up, which he and his dresser then polished vigorously with a chiffon cloth, to achieve a shiny finish . . . The palms of his hands, the soles of his feet, his specially thickened lips and even his tongue were then dyed with incarnadine; a course of drops added a penetrating sheen to the whites of his eyes; he even varnished his fingernails to give them a pallid blue lustre. The wig was of crinkly, matted curls, flecked with grey at the temples, and the final touch was a thin, surly-looking moustache. Most backstage anecdotes about this production concern people of either gender walking in on a naked Olivier, of various hues between Brighton white and Caribbean black, because it all had to dry before he could don Othello's pristine white robe.

Once this visual effect had been achieved, Olivier added "the walk" – "a gently rolling, loose-limbed gait, swaying from the hips on naked feet, prowling around the stage with the easy, flowing movements of a giant cat."[28] To prepare for the role, Olivier worked out regularly, using weights to develop his muscles and jogging along the Brighton seashore. He also used vocal training to lower his voice an octave.[29] Some accounts say he based

---

[26] Charles Dickens, *Nicholas Nickleby* (New York: Books, Inc., n.d.), p. 594.
[27] "The Great Sir Laurence," *Life*, 1 May 1964, 88.
[28] Anthony Holden, *Laurence Olivier* (New York: Atheneum, 1988), p. 378.
[29] See Cottrell, *Laurence Olivier*, p. 337, and Holden, *Laurence Olivier*, p. 379.

7 A close-up of Sir Laurence Olivier as Othello in the 1964–65 Royal National Theatre production. Angus McBean.

his speech patterns on West Indians he encountered in London pubs,[30] but Holden suggests another origin: Sammy Davis Jr. proudly boasted on a David Frost television show that Sir Laurence had come to watch his song-and-dance routine. "The devastating opening to Olivier's performance, when he brushed Iago's cheek lightly with his red rose, was modelled, it transpired, on the way Davis played with the microphone . . . at the opening of *his* performance. Davis also helped Olivier with sundry bodily rhythms and movements."[31]

[30] See Foster Hirsch, *Laurence Olivier* (Boston: Twayne, 1979), p. 127.
[31] Holden, *Laurence Olivier*, p. 381.

Whatever its source, Olivier's Othello was a masterful impersonation, and although the performance's racial implications were hotly debated at the time and remain a source of disagreement to this day, his interest was not in public policy but in acting. Olivier claimed his ambition was "to lead the public towards an appreciation of acting – to watch acting for acting's sake."[32] In this he succeeded. The National Theatre could not accommodate all who thronged to see his stellar performance, and the majority of reviewers were stunned by Olivier's achievement.

Philip Hope-Wallace of the *Guardian* is typical: "[I]t was the inventiveness of it above all, the sheer variety and range of the actor's art which made it an experience in the theatre altogether unforgettable by anyone who saw it." Bernard Levin of the *Daily Mail* wrote that "Sir Laurence Olivier's Othello is great acting of a kind that we see more and more rarely today, larger than life, bloodier than death, more piteous than pity. He is stupendous." Alexander Anikst marvelled in *Sovetskaya Kultura*, "Such complete immersion in the character is rare on the stage. The smallest details in Olivier's gestures and movements contribute to his idea of Othello."[33]

A critical ingredient in the pleasure viewers took in Olivier's performance was the double consciousness I have described above. Bamber Gascoigne states it best: "Watching him, you can blink between two fascinating viewpoints. Either, with some difficulty, you peer through the pretence and just manage to make out the familiar figure of Sir Laurence Olivier at work. Or you happily relax and see, as if for ever, Othello himself." The physical transformation itself evoked amazement. Gascoigne exclaims, "he walks like a Negro, talks like a Negro: from his hairless shins, drooping eye-lids, the stipulated 'thick lips' of the text and a loose hip-rolling walk . . . to the uncanny inflections in his voice or the deep-throated chuckle with which he parries Iago's preliminary thrusts."[34] Throughout there is an awareness that this "Negro" is not real, but a performance. Hope-Wallace reports being surprised "at first sight that this Othello compels you to accept him, not merely as a coloured man, but as a Negro, with negroid speech and easy, generous, frank and easily articulated gait, and physically imposed authority."[35] Robert Kee notes that "Olivier's Othello is not exactly a representational Negro; he's a hybrid, though with a coal black face, someone who could only be the figment of a white man's imagination."[36]

---

[32] "The Great Sir Laurence," 88.
[33] Quotations are taken from Kenneth Tynan, *Othello: The National Theatre Production* (New York: Stein and Day, 1966), pp. 101–10.
[34] From Tynan, *Othello*, p. 108.   [35] From Tynan, *Othello*, p. 101.
[36] From Tynan, *Othello*, p. 106.

To many this impersonation was inherently racist, in the same way that minstrel shows caricatured the American "darky." But as Eric Lott has shown, the simple label "racist" does not do justice to the complex cultural dynamics inherent in white impersonation of black Africans. Just as Lott finds "symbolic crossings of racial boundaries" in American blackface performances that "paradoxically engage and absorb the culture being mocked or mimicked" (the mixture of love and theft suggested by his book's title),[37] at least one critic found love in Olivier's imitation of West Indians. "For obviously it was done with love; with the main purpose of substituting for the dead grandeur of the Moorish empire one modern audiences could respond to: the grandeur of Africa. He was the continent, like a figure of Rubens allegory."[38] Known for his skill as a mimic, Olivier loved absorbing himself in the fictional Other. And audiences took as much pleasure watching this transformation as anything else in the production.

III

To be sure, audiences enjoy seeing a "star," a figure they recognize pretending to be someone else. There is pleasure in watching Laurence Fishburne impersonate Shakespeare's Othello. But because Fishburne does not have to pretend to be black, metatheatrical elements that are embedded in the role – "sooty bosom," for example – lose their impact. The different effect of Olivier's "impersonation" of Othello as opposed to a performance of the role by a man of African descent is perhaps best expressed by Margaret Webster, who described the actor who played Othello in her 1944–45 production for New York's Theatre Guild in this way:

When Paul Robeson stepped onto the stage for the very first time, when he spoke his very first line, he immediately, by his very presence, brought an incalculable sense of reality to the entire play. Here was a great man, a man of simplicity and strength; here also was a black man. We believed that he could command the armies of Venice; we knew that he would always be alien to its society.[39]

Looking back at this pronouncement from the early twenty-first century, we can see that for all its seeming liberalism, Webster's courageous casting decision was tinged with the racism of her time. Paul Robeson excelled in the role because he was "real," bringing the natural "simplicity and strength"

---

[37] Eric Lott, *Love and Theft: Blackface Minstrelsy and the American Working Class* (New York: Oxford University Press, 1993), p. 29.
[38] Ronald Bryden, *New Statesman*, quoted from Tynan, *Othello*, p. 105.
[39] Margaret Webster, *Shakespeare Without Tears* (New York: Capricorn Books, 1975; orig. pub. 1955), pp. 178–79.

of the African to the role. As the African-Anglo actor Hugh Quarshie asks, "if a black actor plays Othello does he not risk making racial stereotypes seem legitimate and even true? When a black actor plays a role written for a white actor in black make-up and for a predominantly white audience, does he not encourage the white way, or rather the wrong way, of looking at black men."[40] Elise Marks reminds us that Robeson's performance stunned audiences because it was "grounded in specific, lived experience – that of being a black man in twentieth-century America – and it is the pain of that experience . . . that drives his embodiment of Othello."[41] In and of itself, this is a good thing. But it essentializes what was originally an actor's role. When we remember that Othello is a wife murderer, there is danger in making the Moor stand for all black males.

That danger is palpable in Oliver Parker's 1995 feature film in which Laurence Fishburne portrayed a very sultry Moor. "Throughout the film," observes Francesca T. Royster, "we see much of Fishburne's body either open shirted, shirtless, or nude." This Othello is characterized by a combination of physical power – an attractively displayed athletic male body – and reticence. "More often than not, Othello's responses to the characters around him are glares, grunts, or lapses into feverish sexual fantasy . . . Fishburne's Othello is most evocative of a cultural figuration of the American black male in the 1990s."[42] Fishburne takes the play's sexual violence and adjusts it to the post-O. J. Simpson image of black male behavior circulating in American culture. (It is intriguing to think that Fishburne's performance might have been a black man's impersonation of the cultural stereotype of blackness, just as Eddie Murphy "acts black" in many of his comic routines.) In any event, despite the appearance of a black actor in the title role, the film substitutes a more subtle kind of racism for Olivier's old-fashioned image of black primitivism.

Fishburne's portrayal suggests the danger of restricting the role of Othello to black actors as is currently the case. Yes, there should be opportunities for black actors to play Shakespeare, but because so often Othello and Aaron are the *only* roles allotted to them, when they appear in the Moor's garb, they close down the metatheatricality of Othello's blackness. Some might argue that in the Senate scene the character of Othello "acts white" in ways calculated to ingratiate himself with his Venetian audience, but by the

---

[40] Hugh Quarshie, *Second Thoughts About Othello*, Occasional Paper no. 7 (Chipping Camden: International Shakespeare Association, 1999), p. 5.
[41] Marks, "'Othello/Me,'" 112.
[42] Francesca T. Royster, "The 'End of Race' and the Future of Early Modern Cultural Studies," *Shakespeare Studies* 26 (1998), 59–69, quote from 66.

murder scene he is deadly serious. Conceivably, a black actor could convey that he is really impersonating a white man who is, in turn, impersonating blackness, but I think this would be incredibly difficult. The danger with a black actor in the title role is that with the loss of the reminders that this is *not* real but an impersonation, the enactment of Othello's jealous rage and murder of his wife can strike audiences as the embodiment of their own stereotypes of black pathology rather than an actorly performance. Black British playwright Kwame Kwei-Armah confesses in a review of The Blue Mountain adaptation of *Othello, The Perfect Black Man*, "I feel I am yet to see or read a version of Othello in which the character is not inextricably linked to the notion of a[n] unacceptably weak and intellectually vulnerable black male."[43] Elise Marks is helpful here, too. She suggests that *Othello's* "tricky combination of 'strangeness' and 'kinship' is best achieved not by a black actor, someone likely to imagine for his Othello a subjectivity formed of the particular experiences of a black man, but by an actor in what could usefully be called 'racial drag.'" The reason for this is that "only a non-African knows how to be the perfect African, at least for the emotional fantasy-use of a thrill-seeking white audience."[44]

Edward Pechter ruefully notes in the conclusion to *Othello and Interpretive Traditions* that "Working on *Othello* means inhabiting a contaminated site; you want to say the right thing, but it comes out sounding terribly wrong."[45] Yet, the more I study the text of *Othello*, the more I see Shakespeare exploiting attitudes that circulated in his culture about blackness and black men for theatrical effect. When it was originally written, *Othello* was not racist in our contemporary sense because "race" was not a fully developed mode of thought for early modern Englishmen. It did, however, embody stereotypes about black people that were circulating in the culture at that time. And as *Othello* has been reenacted again and again over the years, its text has accumulated racial resonances like barnacles attach to a ship. Or, one might argue that like the process of "calcification" or congealment that Judith Butler describes in the performance of gender, the role of Othello has accrued significations that were not necessarily part of the original conception but which have solidified in contemporary readings.

After all the ink I have spilt on *Othello*, I currently find myself in agreement with Quarshie. If the play is performed as written, I am not sure Othello's part should be portrayed by a black actor at all, and it should

[43] Kwame Kwei-Armah, "My Problem with the Moor," *Guardian*, 7 April 2004, G 2.
[44] Marks, "'Othello/Me,'" 116.   [45] Pechter, *Othello and Interpretive Traditions*, p. 181.

not be seen as the pinnacle of a black actor's career, as it so often is. After all, as Dympna Callaghan insists, "Othello was a white man,"[46] and Shakespeare's tragedy is not about Africanness, but the white man's *idea* of Africanness.

---

[46] See her "'Othello Was a White Man': Properties of Race on Shakespeare's Stage," in *Alternative Shakespeares 2*, ed. Terence Hawkes (London: Routledge, 1996), pp. 192–213.

CHAPTER 7

Europeans disguised as black Moors

The first quarto of *The White Devil* includes "*little* Iaques *the Moore*" in stage directions at the beginning of act 2, scene 1.[1] Editor J. R. Mulryne contends that this call for a character who has no lines and never appears elsewhere indicates that the copytext was Webster's foul papers; theatrical transcriptions would not include such a ghost character.[2] If this stage direction was indeed part of Webster's draft, it shows how he imagined the scene, even if it was not performed that way: Isabella should be accompanied by a little black boy, a servant like the "Pompey" of William Hogarth's eighteenth-century engravings.[3] Little Jaques would add a touch of exotic Italian color and indicate Isabella's high social position as a duke's wife. His black skin would highlight her "white hands" (2.1.65) even as her virtue contrasted with Vittoria and Zanche's vice.

If a young black boy had been available to Queen Anne's Company to enhance this scene, he would have become what Dympna Callaghan terms an "exhibition," appearing "before the active scrutiny of the spectator, without any control over, or even necessarily consent to, the representational apparatus in which" he was placed.[4] Without language to express himself, he would have been a decorative figure.

Even more striking, little Jaques would have appeared in the same play that features two impersonations of blackfaced characters: Zanche, Vittoria's Moorish waiting woman and Flamineo's mistress, a role portrayed by a boy actor in black make-up; and Mulinassar, a Moorish general

---

[1] John Webster, *The White Devil* (London, 1612), sig. C2v.

[2] John Webster, *The White Devil*, ed. J. R. Mulryne (Lincoln: University of Nebraska Press, 1969), p. xi. Citations will be taken from this edition and noted by act, scene, and line numbers.

[3] Peter Fryer notes that although the total black population was very small during the first half of the seventeenth century, young black slaves were "used as household servants and status symbols in the mansions of English noblemen and gentry." See *Staying Power: The History of Black People in Britain* (London: Pluto Press, 1984), p. 14.

[4] Dympna Callaghan, *Shakespeare Without Women: Representing Gender and Race on the Renaissance Stage* (London: Routledge, 2000), p. 77.

who appears late in the play and is known to the audience to be the Duke of Florence in blackfaced disguise. Here are three levels of mimesis: a hypothetical little Jaques, a black boy being a black boy; Zanche, an English boy actor impersonating a black woman; and Mulinassar, an adult English male actor impersonating a powerful European male who disguises himself as a black Moor. Zanche demonstrates how "mimesis and exhibition" overlap, because she is both; her blackness constructs her as an exhibition – the stereotyped lascivious Moorish waiting woman – but her speaking voice and the actor's actions are mimetic. Mulinassar resides on the other extreme of the representational spectrum from Jaques because his role is palpably controlled by the English actor who draws the audience's attention to his impersonation as a performance by the European character he represents.

Webster's tragedy is a fruitful starting point for a discussion of a stage practice that flourished in the late Jacobean and Caroline theatre, the appearance of characters known to the audience to be "white" Europeans who blacken their faces. Such disguises sometimes overlap with the bedtricks discussed in chapter five, but here I focus on the mechanics of the disguise itself and its impact on the audience. The disguised Moor is a trickster who deliberately adopts blackface to get what he or she wants. In comedies, the trickster may be a wronged wife who, as we have seen, is policing a delinquent husband. In tragedies such as *The White Devil* and Harding's *Sicily and Naples* the goal is revenge.

Moorish disguise adds another layer to the audience's double consciousness, for it knows that the persona under the blackface – not simply the actor – is "white." Like costume changes that signify a crossing of gender or class barriers, these disguises are generally impenetrable to the characters on stage but clear to the audience.[5] Two disguised Moors keep their identity secret from the other characters and the audience (*The Lost Lady* and *The Fatal Contract*), another is revealed by a character in the play (*Sicily and Naples*), but the remaining disguised Moors make their deceptions known, inviting the audience, in a sense, to be co-conspirators in deceiving the other characters. Anthony Gerard Barthelemy rightly observes that "Because blackness itself is an overdetermined symbol, the character who disguises himself as black brings into the play all the various meanings that blackness itself conveys."[6] Even so, the audience's complex

---

[5] Stephen Orgel notes that "there are scarcely a handful of instances in which anyone sees through a disguise in English Renaissance drama." See *Impersonations: The Performance of Gender in Shakespeare's England* (Cambridge: Cambridge University Press, 1996), p. 102.

[6] Anthony Gerard Barthelemy, *Black Face, Maligned Race: The Representation of Blacks in English Drama from Shakespeare to Southerne* (Baton Rouge: Louisiana State University Press, 1987), p. 144.

awareness that blackface is only a façade represses fears of racial contamination (the production of mulattoes who are neither black nor white) by creating a double vision of a person who is white and black at the same time.

Peter Stallybrass argues that transvestite drama's emphasis on clothing and body parts suggests "that gender itself is a fetish, the production of an identity through the fixation upon specific 'parts.'"[7] Similarly, dramas that call attention to the actor's "blackness" fetishize black pigmentation as a marker of racial difference, constructing categories of blackness and whiteness even as they conflate them. The characters who don Moorish disguises, for example, reiterate the two proverbial tropes we heard from Aaron and Eleazar: that they feel no shame because they cannot blush, and that the Ethiop can never be washed white.[8] Both sayings call attention to what the audience and they know, that their black make-up will come off before the end of the play in a seemingly miraculous transformation. The flamboyant doffing of blackface becomes a sort of *deus ex machina*, solving the plot's complications and, in comedy, assuring a happy ending. The sudden transformation of the character from black to white – a change that can shock and, in a tragedy, horrify – sets up the miraculous moment when the Ethiopian is at last washed white, a metamorphosis that allows audience and players alike to expunge the darkened alien. Thus the *application* of black make-up is not nearly so important as the moment of its removal. Like Rosalind's many-layered disguise which culminates in the assertion of traditional gender roles, the temporary nature of these characters' blackness and their flamboyant transformation from black to white mark "whiteness" all the more dramatically as a normative state.

The plays discussed here were written for the elite audiences of the indoor playhouses, such as the Blackfriars and the Salisbury Court Theatre. Particularly in the Caroline period, the plot device of the disguised Moor must have suited audiences with a penchant for improbable and romantic endings. In many ways the disguised Moor is akin to what Alfred Harbage terms the "Child Recovered" theme, whereby a "chief character in the play is discovered to be the son of illustrious parents, lost to them as a babe." When his true identity is at last discovered, the happy outcome – his inheritance

---

[7] Peter Stallybrass, "Transvestism and the 'Body Beneath': Speculating on the Boy Actor," in *Erotic Politics: Desire on the Renaissance Stage*, ed. Susan Zimmerman (New York: Routledge, 1992), pp. 64–83; quotation from p. 77. See also Barthelemy, *Black Face*, p. 144.

[8] See Karen Newman, "'And wash the Ethiop white': Femininity and the Monstrous in *Othello*," in *Shakespeare Re-Produced: The Text in History and Ideology*, ed. Jean E. Howard and Marion F. O'Connor (New York: Methuen, 1987), pp. 141–62, for a discussion of the proverb and its resonance in *Othello*.

or marriage to an heiress – is assured.[9] But the disguised Moor is more than a convenient mechanical plot device. When the European character adopts the role of a black servant, the disguise insures his or her ability to maintain a kind of invisibility while participating in complicated sexual intrigues. Indeed, the pattern of the disguised Moor may reflect growing anxiety among aristocratic Londoners about the black servants in their own households, including fears that when masters and servants lived in such close quarters, the boundaries between "white" and "black" might become permeable.

I

The White Devil's disguised Moor, Webster's Francisco, exemplifies another characteristic of later seventeenth-century stage Moors, Othellofication. Francisco passes as black by imitating Shakespeare's Othello. He comes to Bracciano's court as a mercenary general, renowned for "honorable service 'gainst the Turk" (5.1.43). Flamineo reports

> I have not seen a goodlier personage,
> Nor ever talk'd with man better experience'd
> In state affairs or rudiments of war.
> He hath, by report, serv'd the Venetian
> In Candy these twice seven years, and been chief
> In many a bold design.   (5.1.6–11)

Like Othello, Mulinassar stands apart from the "wealthy, curled darlings" of the Italian court. Flamineo praises his "stern bold look" and his "deep contempt / Of our slight airy courtiers" (5.1.32–35). But unlike Othello, he is taciturn about his military career, telling Marcello, "'Tis a ridiculous thing for a man to be his own chronicle; I did never wash my mouth with mine own praise for fear of getting a stinking breath" (5.1.98–100). Whether or not Webster's audience would see Francisco's impersonation as a self-conscious imitation of Shakespeare's Moor and perhaps even as an ironic critique of Othello's bombastic language, its knowledge of his originary whiteness creates a metatheatrical awareness of blackness as a dramatic role.

Vittoria's waiting woman Zanche falls in love with the handsome Francisco/Mulinassar as soon as she sees him and makes a fetish of black skin in her sexual pursuit. She confesses, "I ne'er lov'd my complexion till

---

[9] See Alfred Harbage's discussion of the plot devices of Caroline drama in *Cavalier Drama* (New York: Modern Language Association, 1936), pp. 32–35; quotation from p. 33.

now, / 'Cause I may boldly say without a blush / I love you" (5.1.206–08).
Later, when she steals from Vittoria and plans to run away with Mulinassar,
Zanche claims to have "a dowry [that] . . . should make that sunburnt
proverb false, / And wash the Ethiop white" (5.3.257–59). Before dying
Zanche reiterates the theme of skin color: "I am proud / Death cannot alter
my complexion, / For I shal ne'er look pale" (5.6.229–31). Zanche's repetition of these tired tropes underscores the link between her sexuality and
her skin color. At the same time, like Viola's cry that "A little thing would
make me tell them how much I lack of a man" (3.4.307–08), the proverbial
phrases create fissures in the mimesis that assert the ineluctable nature of
pigmentation even as they remind the audience that blackness is a disguise.

Webster's title reflects his exploitation of a slippery white/black binary.
Ineffectual and poverty-stricken virtue is figured white, as in Flamineo's
angry outburst to his mother Cornelia: "shall I . . . still retain your milk /
In my pale forehead? No, this face of mine / I'll arm and fortify with lusty
wine / 'Gainst shame and blushing" (1.2.320–25). To rise in the court world,
he must gain some "color" so that like the Ethiop, he cannot blush.

Francisco/Mulinassar does not appear in the last scene of Webster's
tragedy. Perhaps Webster thought it would be too difficult to remove
the actor's black make-up in time for an appearance; instead, Lodovico
and Gasparo throw off their Capuchin disguises (a much easier unveiling) and report that the "Moor the duke gave pension to / Was the great
Duke of Florence" (5.6.173–74). This news is sufficient to strike terror
into Vittoria and Flamineo, however, and their violent deaths quickly end
the play. In his final moments Flamineo proclaims that his life "was a
black charnel" (5.6.270) and his sister describes the play's Italian setting as
"hell."

Webster makes more dramatic use of the disguised Moor's unveiling at
the finale of his tragicomedy, *The Devil's Law-Case*. After being introduced
as a "black one," the "fair" Jolenta reveals her true identity and asserts her
virtue:

> Like or dislike me, choose you whether:
> The down upon the raven's feather
> Is as gentle and as sleek
> As the mole on Venus' cheek.
> Hence, vain show! I only care
> To preserve my soul most fair;
> Never mind the outward skin,
> But the jewel that's within . . .
> Which of us now judge you whiter,

> Her whose credit proves the lighter,
> Or this black and ebon hue,
> That, unstain'd, keeps fresh and true?
> For I proclaim't without control,
> There's no true beauty but i'th' soul.[10]

Although Jolenta's reputation has been blackened by her greedy brother, she insists here on her essential whiteness, a whiteness of soul that outshines the black paint she wears. Still, the delivery of these sing-song tetrameter couplets by an English boy actor impersonating a female impersonating a black person undermines the legitimacy of the sentiment even as it is spoken.

Jolenta's disguise is a last ditch effort to preserve her reputation and escape her brother's plans to slander her publicly. The sudden exposure of her black make-up no doubt contributes to the play's comic resolution, but because it occurs with so little development, it is an arbitrary way of solving Jolenta's difficulties. The sudden transformation instantaneously and miraculously solves the character's problems. Webster exploits blackface disguise in *The Devil's Law-Case* (as well as *The White Devil*) to make the denouement astonishing to the characters on stage. The discovery of the disguised Moor also reassures the audience that its exposure to blackness was temporary. The play ends with white privilege restored and the boundaries between black and white reestablished.

II

Dramatists of the 1620s and 1630s develop Webster's comic pattern of the besieged female protecting herself – or seeking revenge against a predatory male – through a black disguise that is simultaneously attractive and repulsive to the European male gaze. The serving maid's blackness is read by the male character as a sign of her sexual availability; her disguise, and the freedom it gives her for sexual badinage forbidden to chaste European women, enables her to confront the man on his own terms. Even as it moves her from the aristocracy into the position of a slave, it paradoxically empowers her to change an unbearable situation.

The earliest play to use this device is Philip Massinger's *The Parliament of Love* (1624), discussed in chapter five. Calista's Moorish disguise warrants further discussion, however. Since much of the play's comic effect depends

---

[10] John Webster, *The Devil's Law-Case*, ed. Frances A. Shirley (Lincoln: University of Nebraska Press, 1972), p. 135.

VERGINE
MORA.

8 A Moorish girl from Cesare Vecellio's *Degli habiti* (Venice, 1590).

upon our knowing that Calista the Moor is really Clarindor's estranged wife, Beaupre, editors have assumed that the audience would have been told of this disguise in the first scene, which is missing from the manuscript. The first extant scene depicts the avuncular nobleman Chamont offering a "present" to his ward, the virtuous but independent-minded Bellisant. Chamont commands, "come in *Caliste*," and the stage directions that follow read, "*Enter* BEAUPRE *like a More*" (1.a.91).[11] Bellisant's reaction to Calista's appearance sets up the dramatic irony: "Tis the hansomest / I ere saw of her cuntry; shee hath neither / Thick lips nor rough curld haire" (1.a.92–94). Calista lacks, in other words, the other traditional signifiers of negritude – thick lips and woolly hair – but because her skin is painted black, she can pass as a Moor.

Chamont believes that he has to account for Calista's language, which is not some sort of pidgin-English, but the same as everyone else's:

> Her manners lady
> Vppon my honnor better her good shape;
> Shee speakes our language to, for beinge surprisd
> In *Barbarie*, shee was bestowd vppon
> A pirat of *Marselles*, with whose wife
> She liu'd five yeares and learnt it; there I bought her
> As pittyinge her hard vsage; yf you please
> To make her yours, you maie.   (1.a.94–101)

Later in the play, Clarindor reinforces the notion that Moors should speak a special language: "I desird / To heare her speake in the morisco tongue; / Troath, tis a pritty language" (2.3.30–32).[12] It seems likely that London's newly-imported African house servants did not arrive speaking perfect English, so their "morisco tongue" probably served as another signifier of difference, particularly servant status.

Calista's status as a chattel slave to be bought, sold, and possessed is underscored by the terms the other characters use in their relationships with her. Chamont *gives* her to Bellisant as a present. Later, in order to get her to cooperate with his plan to seduce Bellisant, Clarindor offers Calista her freedom as a reward: "Thou shalt liue / To bee the mistress of thie self and others / If that my proiects hitt" (3.3.19–21).

I have discussed *The Parliament of Love*'s exploitation of the bedtrick in chapter five. More pertinent here is the removal of Calisto's blackface

---

[11] Quotations from *The Parliament of Love* are taken from *The Plays and Poems of Philip Massinger*, ed. Philip Edwards and Colin Gibson (Oxford: Clarendon Press, 1976), and will be cited by act, scene, and line numbers within the text.

[12] Ian Smith discusses the association between linguistic inadequacy and barbarism in "Those 'slippery customers': Rethinking Race in *Titus Andronicus*," *Journal of Theatre and Drama* 3 (1997), 45–58.

at the play's conclusion, which serves as the mechanism for a seemingly miraculous transformation. Charles, King of France (perhaps a stand-in for another King Charles?) presides over a "court of love" in the final scene where Clarindor is tried for his abuses. Because *The Parliament of Love* is a comedy and must have a happy conclusion, once Beaupre's identity is revealed and the "varnish from her face washd of[f]" (5.1.68), Clarindor claims to be reformed and escapes punishment. Although his realization that he had sexual relations with a black Moor is only fleeting, the very thought of such a coupling – and his wife's cleverness in discovering and exploiting his lust – may be, the play optimistically suggests, sufficient to curb his libidinous appetites in future.

The Parliament of Love was performed by Lady Elizabeth's Men at the Cockpit,[13] and might well have influenced later versions of the disguised Moor plot device in plays performed at court. William Berkeley's *The Lost Lady* (1637–38) was a King's Company play that survives in a printed text and in a manuscript that was intended for Queen Henrietta Maria herself; it, too, was performed at the Cockpit, and on 26 March 1638, it was produced before the King and Queen.[14] Like *The Parliament of Love*, *The Lost Lady* features a white heroine, Milesia, who disguises herself as a Moor, Acanthe. Perhaps because Berkeley envisioned his play as a "Tragy Comedy" – akin perhaps to Shakespeare's *The Winter's Tale* – that would keep the audience in suspense until a dramatic reversal could spark the happy ending, Acanthe's real identity is kept secret until late in the play, when water applied to her face washes off some of her make-up.

Acanthe, like Calista, needs some explaining, particularly with regard to her speech. She is described as a fortune teller, an Egyptian lady,[15] who "speakes our Language."

> Her father was of Greece, a wealthy Marchant,
> And his businesse enforcing him to leave his
> Country, he married a Lady of that place where he liv'd,
> Who excellent in the Mystery of devination,
> Hath left that knowledge to her daughter,
> Enricht with thousand other modest vertues,
> As is deliver'd to me by those are frequent with her.[16]

[13] See G. E. Bentley, *The Jacobean and Caroline Stage*, 7 vols. (Oxford: Clarendon Press, 1941–68), vol. IV, p. 806.

[14] Bentley, *Jacobean and Caroline Stage*, vol. III, pp. 24–25.

[15] Possibly Berkeley was influenced by Othello's description of the Egyptian who gave his mother the handkerchief: "She was a charmer and could almost read / The thoughts of people" (3:4.59–60).

[16] William Berkeley, *The Lost Lady: A Tragy Comedy* (London: John Okes, 1638), p. 14. Quotations will be cited by page numbers within the text. See also the Malone Society edition of Berkeley's manuscript, ed. John Pitcher (Oxford: Oxford University Press, 1987).

Acanthe's facility with European language is attributed to her Greek father, her knowledge of sorcery to her Egyptian mother.

The court ladies frequently attest to Acanthe's virtue, but despite their high regard for her, the Moor soon becomes an object of lust for the predatory male. The libertine Phormio physically accosts her in act 3. Berkeley's stage direction reads, "*After a long whisper, the* Moore *strives to goe from* Phormio, *he holds her.*" He calls the audience's attention to her color: "In the name of darknesses, d'ee thinke I am not / In earnest that you coy it thus?" When Acanthe "*goes from him,*" Phormio's companion Cleon urges him to kiss her:

> Do'st thou not see that all the fire is out of the coale?
> If thou would'st have it burne, lay thy lips
> To the sparke that's left, and blow it into flame.

Phormio refuses, "Not for five hundred Crownes." Cleon wonders, "Wouldst lye with her, and not kisse her?" Phormio explains that it would enhance his reputation for sexual prowess with elderly rich widows if they knew of his "resolute / Incounter" with a black Moor (32–33). As Barthelemy rightly notes, this comic interlude acknowledges "sexual myths" about Moors' lascivious appetites that circulated in Berkeley's culture.[17] It also directs the audience's gaze to Acanthe's blackness, as does Irene's more favorable comment that Acanthe "is secret as the night she resembles" (29).

Secrecy gets Acanthe into trouble when her lover Lysicles suspects her betrayal of his dead mistress Milesia. To obtain revenge he poisons the Moor, or so he thinks. Act 5 begins with the Moor writhing in anguish on her bed. Everyone, including the audience, assumes that the poison is fatal and that she will soon die. Hermione and Irene, the women who have introduced her to court and supported her, try to comfort her, patting her face with water after she swoons. Suddenly "her blacknesse falls away." Irene exclaims:

> This Miracle, doth not Heaven instruct us in pitty
> Of her wrongs, that the opinion which prejudice
> Her vertue, should thus be wash't away with the
> Blacke clouds that hide her purer forme?

Soon "all the blacknesse of her face is gone" and Lysicles finally recognizes his lost love Milesia who had been disguised all the while (43).

The miracle – the *deus ex machina* that assures a happy ending – is the seeming impossibility that in this case the Ethiop can be washed white.

---

[17] Barthelemy, *Black Face*, p. 140.

Milesia's whiteness, as Barthelemy notes, "redeems both her reputation and her life."[18] More important, the sudden creation of whiteness out of blackness provides the miraculous theatrical spectacle required to resolve the complicated plot of a tragicomedy. Once the blackness is washed off, she becomes "white as Lillies, as the Snow / That falls upon PARNASSVS" (44). As the audience watches whiteness miraculously appearing out of blackness, the ineluctable connection between whiteness and virtue is reified before its eyes.

The English Moor's exploitation of blackface disguise is even more theatrical. Richard Brome's comedy, discussed in chapter five, was also written for an elite Caroline audience; it was produced under contract for the Salisbury Court Theatre where Queen Henrietta Maria's Company performed from 1637–42.[19] Phillis, as I noted earlier, substitutes herself for her mistress Millicent in Nathaniel's bed. But Brome also portrays the characters' use of blackface as a form of theatrical legerdemain.

When the old miser Quicksilver produces his "*box of black painting*" and begins to cover his wife's face, he describes it as "the quaint devise / Of a *Venetian* Merchant."[20] Kim F. Hall relates the rhetoric he uses in this scene to the language of the Petrarchan lover who sings in praise of blackness.[21] But in addition to fashioning himself as a Petrarchan lover, Quicksilver fantasizes himself here as a theatrical impresario. The black paint is a "quaint device," a phrase used in the Folio text of Shakespeare's *Tempest* to describe how Ariel makes a banquet vanish (3.3.52sd); Alden Vaughan and I note in our Arden edition of Shakespeare's play that "quaint device" is "a vague reference to stage machinery by someone who knows little about theatre mechanics."[22] Quicksilver, an amateur producer/director, sees his black paint as a way to create a theatrical spectacle, his own version of *The Masque of Blackness* in which the Ethiopian will literally turn white. He imagines that the removal of Millicent's black pigmentation will strike his enemies with wonder, making her whiteness shine all the brighter and affirming his own power and status within the community. He conceives the scene:

---

[18] Barthelemy, *Black Face*, p. 141.   [19] Bentley, *Jacobean and Caroline Stage*, vol. III, pp. 67–69.
[20] Richard Brome, *The English Moor, or the Mock-Marriage* (London, 1658), 37. Quotations will be cited by page numbers within the text.
[21] See Kim F. Hall's insightful discussion of *The English Moor* in *Things of Darkness: Economies of Race and Gender in Early Modern England* (Ithaca: Cornell University Press, 1995), pp. 166–75, esp. p. 168.
[22] William Shakespeare, *The Tempest*, ed., Virginia Mason Vaughan and Alden T. Vaughan, Arden Third Series (London: Thomson Learning, 2000), p. 129.

> It shall be such a night;
> In which I mean thy beauty shall break forth
> And dazzle with amazement even to death
> Those my malicious enemies, that rejoyc'd
> In thy suppos'd escape, and my vexation.
> I will envite 'hem all to such a feast
> As shall fetch blushes from the boldest guest.
>
> (52)

Like Ben Jonson's *Masque of Blackness* and *Masque of Beauty*, Quicksilver's scenario is intended to display Millicent's miraculous transformation from blackness to beauty as an affirmation of patriarchal power – in this case the husband's. But Brome shows this fantasy as the stuff that dreams are made on in act 4, scene 5. Quicksilver's plans are thwarted when his wife arranges for her servant Phillis to don black make-up and appear in her place, and by the young gallants' interruption of his carefully planned masque with a charivari scenario of their own.

Brome's stage directions show how this scene should be staged. The masque begins as Quicksilver directed, except that unbeknownst to him it features Phillis as the Ethiopian princess instead of his wife: "*Florish enter* Inductor *like a* Moor *leading* Phillis *black and gorgeously deck't with jewels*" (65). After Quicksilver takes some pleasure in taunting his young enemies, the stage directions continue: "*Enter the rest of the Moors. They Dance an Antique in which they use action of Mockery and derision to the three Gentle-men*" (67). In a parody of the conclusion of a court masque, the audience joins the dancers – the wastrel and philanderer Nathaniel grabs Phillis (thinking she's Quicksilver's wife) and rushes her off stage (presumably to bed her) while the music plays on. Meanwhile, the young gallants counter with their theatrical production: "*Enter* Arnold *like a Countrey man, and* Buz. *like a changling, and as they enter, exit* Nat. *with* Phil. *The Musick still playing. He* [Buzzard] *sings and dances and spins with a rock & Spindle*" (67). Here, in an antimasque that resembles the folk charivari, the old pantaloon is humiliated before the community for making an inappropriate marriage.

Quicksilver's onstage application of blackface to Millicent's fair cheeks graphically demonstrates that her Moorishness is a disguise. But Brome uses other comic tactics to remind the audience that she is role-playing. Unlike Massinger and Berkeley, who explain the disguised Moor's use of standard English by fabricating a phony biography, Brome has his Moor use a phony accent. When Nathaniel tries to court the blackfaced Millicent, she responds in the way she imagines a Moorish woman would speak, in pidgin English:

No see, o no, I darea notta . . .
O no de fine white Zentilmanna
Cannot a love a the black a thing a . . .
O take – a heed – a my mastra see – a.
(61)

Language that marks the Moor's otherness is dropped when it is no longer needed. After Phillis (disguised as the blackened Millicent) has succeeded in entrapping Nathaniel into a public profession of love (70), he notes a change in her language: "Thou speakest good English now" (71). These language references highlight Millicent and Phillis's impersonation as a burlesque of African dialects.

In contradiction to Quicksilver's expectation that Millicent's blackness will make her unattractive to the town gallants and cool his own lust (37), the sight of Cataline (Millicent in blackface disguise), the "black coney-berry" (60), fires Nathaniel's desire. Far from finding her "foul," Nathaniel marvels:

It is the handsom'st Rogue,
I have ere seen yet of a deed of darkness;
Tawney and russet faces I have dealt with,
But never came so deep in blackness yet.
(60)

Later, when Phillis has taken over the blackface disguise from Millicent, Nathaniel marvels, "How I am taken with the elevation of her nostrils" (67), an aside that is especially comic to an audience who knows that the woman he addresses is his cast-off mistress.

For Nathaniel, the Moor's blackness is a sexual enticement that evokes exotic and unfamiliar pleasures. When he sees her (or so he thinks) adorned with jewels in Quicksilver's masque, he calls her his "little Princess of dark-nesse," and promises "if / I rub her not as white as another can / Let me be hung up with her for a new / Sign of the labour in vain" (66). This double entendre refers to the painted head of a Moor, used on a tavern to symbolize its name, the "Labor in Vain," which in turn denotes the impossibility of washing the Ethiop white. Nathaniel's humor underscores the dramatic irony in the audience's awareness that she can indeed be washed white.

And so she is in act 5, scene 3. In the complicated unraveling of Brome's plot, Phillis (by now Nathaniel has had sex with her and has promised to marry her, still thinking she is Millicent) is told to leave the stage and to "let instant tryal be made / To take the blackness off" (81). When she returns some thirty lines later, the stage direction reads: "*Enter* Phillis *white*" (82).

Nathaniel, who has promised to take this woman and all her faults, exclaims, "The devil looks ten times worse with a white face, / Give me it black again" (82). *The English Moor* is a comedy, however, so Nathaniel resigns himself to matrimony, Millicent is rescued from marriage to a miserly old man, and the feuding families of the subplot are reconciled.

Ironically, the marvelous scenario that Quicksilver had hoped for actually occurs, but not as he had planned. Phillis's sudden transformation from black to white, a tour de force for the make-up artist, is so quick as to seem miraculous. Her new appearance marks her transition from the blackened character of a fallen woman to the whitened status of gentle wife. But, combined with the other unveilings that occur in the play's final scene, it also suggests a slipperiness of identity that permeates the play. *The English Moor*, like *The Parliament of Love* and *The Lost Lady*, uses the Moorish disguise to set up, in other words, a black–white binary and then, in a climactic moment, seemingly dissolve it, erasing blackness and constructing thereby a harmonious, homogeneous white community.

III

Blackface disguise is an ingenious device to insure a happy, homogeneous ending for comedy, but in tragedy it aids the revenger, making the bloody denouement especially grotesque. As we have seen, Francisco uses Moorish disguise to gain ascendancy over Bracciano in *The White Devil*, and in Samuel Harding's unperformed *Sicily and Naples* (discussed in chapter five), Frederico disguises himself as Zisco, a dependable Moorish servant. As noted earlier, Ursini describes Zisco as a man "that's fit to kill a King, / A thing, whose soule is but a spot / Transmitted from foule parracides, / whose thoughts / Weare a more deep and horrid blacke, than that / Which spread upon his body."[23] The reference to "spotted souls" links Moorish blackness with horrendous deeds and recalls the sixteenth-century association between blackness and damnation so evident in Shakespeare's Aaron. Zisco's villainy is more complicated than Aaron's, however, because early in the play Ursini sees through Zisco's disguise and makes the audience aware of his true identity as a European nobleman. At the tragedy's bloody conclusion, there is little shock effect when Zisco pulls off his disguise. Zisco, the revenger who rapes and kills his own sister, cannot be redeemed. Whatever astonishment the audience feels must come from a rapid succession of stabbings that litters the stage with bodies.

---

[23] Samuel Harding, *Sicily and Naples, or the Fatall Vnion: A Tragedy* (Oxford, 1640), p. 11.

Harding's *Sicily and Naples, or, The Fatal Vnion* may have influenced the most graphic Caroline revenge tragedy, *The Fatal Contract*. This relatively unknown drama demonstrates that the trickster/servant disguised as a Moor can be especially disturbing.[24] Written by William Hemings, a graduate of Oxford, between 1638 and 1639, *The Fatal Contract* was performed by Queen Henrietta Maria's Men at the Cockpit.[25] Hemings's drama exploits language, character types, and plot elements from at least three Shakespearean tragedies: *Hamlet*, *Othello*, and *King Lear*. This indebtedness is not surprising when we realize that Hemings was the son of Shakespeare's colleague, John Hemings (Hemminge), co-compiler of the 1623 First Folio. Anthony à Wood explains why the play was printed: after *The Fatal Contract* had "justly gained an esteem with men of excellent judgments, by several copies of it that flew abroad in MS, [it] was therefore published for the satisfaction of all persons, especially such who had lighted upon imperfect copies."[26] Gerard Langbaine confirmed in 1691 that "This Play was published after the Author's Death, having pass'd thro' many Hands, as a Curiosity of Wit and Language,"[27] an observation that attests to its appeal to an educated, elite audience.

The subtitle of *The Fatal Contract* is *A French Tragedy*, which suggests the primary source, Jean de Serres's *General Inventorie of the History of France*, an exposé of French monarchs from the beginnings to 1598, that was translated into English in 1607. Hemings's drama of sexual and political intrigue taken from events in the sixth-century French court may have been of interest to the company's patron, Queen Henrietta Maria, a French princess and the daughter of Marie de Médicis and Henry IV, but its version of French history is highly sensationalized. Hemings's play includes as much, if not more, intrigue and violence as any revenge tragedy by Cyril Tourneur or John Webster. At the risk of tediousness, the analysis that follows will include as much plot summary as seems necessary to convey how blackface performance was exploited in Hemings's script.

Hemings tops his predecessors' grotesque art by creating a female character, Chrotilda, who disguises herself as a black Moorish eunuch, Castrato

[24] Neither Elliot H. Tokson's *The Popular Image of the Black Man in English Drama, 1550–1688* (Boston: G. K. Hall, 1982) nor Barthelemy's *Black Face* include *The Fatal Contract* in their inventories of plays with black characters. Arthur L. Little, Jr. first drew my attention to this fascinating play in *Shakespeare Jungle Fever: National-Imperial Re-visions of Race, Rape, and Sacrifice* (Stanford: Stanford University Press, 2000) pp. 60–62, 100, and 164–65.

[25] Bentley, *Jacobean and Caroline Stage*, vol. IV, pp. 539–47.

[26] Anthony à Wood, *Athenae Oxoniensis*, ed. Philip Bliss, vol. III (Hildesheim: Georg Olms, 1969), pp. 277–78.

[27] Gerard Langbaine, *An Account of the English Dramatick Poets* (London, 1691), p. 247.

(also referred to as Eunuch), and instigates most of the play's murder and mayhem.[28] In *The Fatal Contract*, the disguised black servant's trickster role permeates the play, insuring violence and degradation rather than a happy unveiling at the end. Moreover, Castrato's black skin is repeatedly associated with sexual perversion in eroticized images of cross-racial, cross-gender coupling.

Hemings saves the revelation of Castrato's identity for the play's final scene when the eunuch is unmasked: "no *Eunuch* she; / No sun-burnt vagabond of Aethiope, / Though entertain'd for such."[29] This Iago-like figure who haunts the play and directs much of the action turns out to be the fair Chrotilda, daughter to the nobleman Brissac. She was raped by King Childerick's son, Clotair, before the play began, an action that sparks a series of murderous intrigues and revenges. Although the eunuch has frequent asides that signal her/his hatred for the Queen and her son Clotair, Castrato never directly reveals his/her true identity until the very end.

It may well be that the actor performing the role was able to convey the truth through facial expressions or body language.[30] By 1638 the disguised Moor had become a theatrical convention. Castrato's asides and soliloquies directly inform the audience that s/he is playing a role, and conventional references to her/his blackness may also remind the audience that the figure before them is a European in black make-up. The Queen addresses Castrato as "my black Genius" (C1v) and, in phrasing reminiscent of Emilia's description of Othello as a "dull Moor," "My dul Aethioppe" (F2v); Clotair calls Castrato "my black Saint" (G2v), and as the plot begins to unravel, the eunuch reiterates the conventional trope that a Moor has no shame: "lend me impudence, / I'm sure I cannot blush" (H2r). It is impossible to prove what an audience might have thought of this impersonation, but I believe Hemings intended his viewers to suspect that the mysterious eunuch was a European character using blackface disguise – perhaps even female – long before the conclusion.

---

[28] *A General Inventorie* briefly mentions a page who was with King Chilperic the night he was murdered, but otherwise the character of Chrotilda, the disguised black eunuch, is Hemings's invention. See Edward Grimeston's translation (London, 1607), p. 30.

[29] William Hemings, *The Fatal Contract, a French Tragedy* (London, 1653), sig. K1v. Quotations from this play will be cited by signature numbers within the text.

[30] When Elkanah Settle adapted this play in the Restoration as *Love and Revenge*, he added passages to act 1, scene 2, that clarify the crimes committed before the play begins and make the eunuch's identity much more obvious through repeated asides. See Elkanah Settle, *Love and Revenge: A Tragedy* (London: William Cademan, 1675) and my discussion in chapter eight.

Without this dramatic irony, Castrato's interview with Queen Fredigond in act 1, scene 2, loses much of its force. The Queen draws the curtain on a picture of the murderer of her brother, Clodimer, and describes past events that spawned her hatred for Chrotilda's family. Fredigond explains that, except for the younger Dumain, Lamot, and Chrotilda, she has killed the entire family – grandmother, parents, and infant baby – and in a frenzy of hatred she stabs the painting.[31] Castrato implies but does not declare her true identity in her response:

> Were but *Chrotilda* here, and these two youngsters,
> It were a pastime for the Gods to gaze on.
> Oh were I but a man as others are,
> As kind and open-handed nature made me,
> With Organs apt and fit for womans service.

The Queen asks, "What if thou wert?" to which Castrato replies:

> What if I were Great queene?
> I'd search the Deserts, Mountaines, Vallies, Plaines,
> Till I had met *Chrotilda*, whom by force
> I'd make to mingle with these sootie limbs,
> Till I had got on her one like to me,
> Whom I would nourish for the *Dumaine* line:
> That time to come might story to the world,
> They had the Devil to their Grand-father.   (B4r)

The dramatic irony here is hardly subtle, but it would be lost if the audience did not know the speaker's true identity. Moreover, this intriguing passage (which was deleted from Elkanah Settle's 1674 adaptation and from the 1687 printing of Hemings's play under a new title, *The Eunuch*) draws on the myth of the black male rapist[32] and fantasizes a cross-racial coupling that would take revenge on the Dumain family by polluting its line. A mulatto baby would broadcast to the world that "They had the Devil to their Grand-father." Castrato's speech veers toward the pornographic by describing the sexual act – "sootie limbs" covering the female body – and

---

[31] De Serres claims that Queen Fredegond "possessed her husband so absolutely, as she commanded imperiously, under the cloake of his authority." As a result, "insolency rageth against the poore people, by taxes, impositions and insupportable exactions: and report imputes all to the devises of the same workewoman." However, Fredegond was not as bad as Brunehault, another scheming royal: "this old bitch, even in the fury of war, found still means to follow her beastly lechery." See *A General Inventorie*, pp. 30–33.
[32] See Little, *Shakespeare Jungle Fever*, pp. 58–61.

signals a preoccupation through the rest of the play – the voyeuristic imagination of rape, unnatural sexual coupling, and monstrous births.[33]

The Queen's response to this visual image is telling, too. She confides, "I find thee Eunuch apt for my imployments, / Therefore I will unclaspe my soul to thee, / I've alwaies found thee trusty, and I love thee" (B4r). Then she unveils her plan to murder her husband Childerick and blame it on Dumain and Lamot, simultaneously ridding herself of a doddering husband and the remainder of the Dumain family. Her delight in this scheme, added to the excitement of Castrato's image of cross-racial coupling, seems to rouse her sexually:

> Now by this light I'm taken strangely with thee,
> Come kiss me, kiss me sirra, tremble not.
> Fie, what a January lip thou hast,
> A paire of Iscicles, sure thou hast bought
> A paire of cast lips of the chaste *Diana's*,
> Thy blood's meere snow-broth, kiss me again.
>
> (B4v)

Accompanied by the stage direction, "*Queene kisses him,*" this interchange acts out the picture of interracial coupling, which Castrato had only imagined. The kiss and the eunuch's reaction to it suggest the Queen's voracious sexual appetite, fed by images of death and the monstrous, and Castrato's underlying nature – white and chaste like icicles and snow-broth.

Like Iago, who obviously inspired Hemings, Castrato frequently addresses the audience and explains his/her plans for the rest of the characters. After the King has been murdered by poison, the eunuch considers ways to get even with Queen Fredigond:

> And now bethink thee *Eunuch*, all thy plots
> Find fruitlesse issues . . . my hate extends
> To the whole family, I must root them up,
> And beldam first with you: but how? but how?
> If (in her proud desire) I do prevent
> Her lust this second time, before the third
> She may repent and save her loathed soul,
> Which my revenge would damn; yet were she crost,
> Her lust being now at full flood in her,

---

[33] Michael Neill's construction of *Othello's* audience as offstage voyeurs seems apropos here. See "'Unproper Beds': Race, Adultery, and the Hideous in *Othello*," in *Putting History to the Question: Power, Politics, and Society in English Renaissance Drama* (New York: Columbia University Press, 2000), pp. 237–68.

And no way left to quench her burning flame,
Her dryer bones would make a bonfire,
Fit for the Devill to warm his hands by:
Stay, stay, *Castrato*; no, this must not be,
                    . . . I must set
Some mischief instantly on foot to stop it;
If I miscarry in it story shall tell,
I did attempt it bravely though I fell.

(F3r–v)

Castrato's methods are as metadramatic as Iago's; s/he creates scenarios and then scripts them for the other characters. In act 2, scene 2, for example, s/he plots a quarrel between the Queen's two sons, Clotair (who is now King) and Clovis. Knowing that both men are in love with the fair Aphelia (clearly derived from Shakespeare's Desdemona, with some Ophelia thrown in), Castrato leads her into a chamber, and while she reads a book (appropriately the story of Philomel), Castrato plans to bring in Queen Fredigond to interrupt the ensuing fight, promising "Thus on all sides the eunuch will play foul, / And as his face is black he'l have his soul" (C4v–D1r). Here Castrato recalls Shakespeare's Aaron who linked his black face with a blackened soul. Later, Aphelia repeats the familiar trope of washing the Ethiop white: "here I see / One bath'd in Virgins tears, whose puritie / Might blanch a Blackmore, turn natures stream / Back on it's self" (D1r). But Aphelia's goodness is powerless to change Castrato's color and her villainy.

Hemings's plot moves from one melodramatic spectacle to another. Clotair becomes king, wounds, then banishes his brother, and accuses Aphelia of unchastity. Then he astonishes everyone by declaring that he will marry Aphelia rather than execute her. Act 4, scene 1, is set in Aphelia's bedchamber where her ladies are preparing her for the consummation of her marriage. In this scene Hemings's debt to Shakespeare's *Othello* is palpable. While Clotair reads, according to the stage directions, "*The bed thrust forth with* Aphe. asleep." (G1r). Aphelia lies prone in the bed (similar to Desdemona's sleeping posture at the beginning of Shakespeare's murder scene), as Clotair and Castrato have an interchange similar to conversations between Othello and Iago. When the eunuch protests that he is just trying to protect the honor of Clotair's house, the King shouts:

Truth! Hence and avoid my sight, fly where the world
Promiscuously combines without distinction;
Where every man is every womans husband,
Or where it's thought a curtesie to have

> A fellow labourer in the marriage bed.
> These were a people that might bear with thee,
> And fit for thee to dwell with.   (GIv–G2r)

Although Africa is never mentioned here, Clotair implies that the black eunuch should go back to where he came from, a place of polygamy, sexual promiscuity, and perversion.

After Clotair exits in a rage, Aphelia wakens and leaves the room. The young king returns a few lines later, resolved to be cruel: "And rise black vengeance from the depth of hell, / And fate me her destruction" (G2v). He draws his dagger to strike, but finds that Aphelia has escaped. This bedroom scene is a tease, offering the audience the prospect of a helpless woman slain in her bed as was Shakespeare's Desdemona.

But Hemings has an even more sensational denouement in mind. As the play concludes, Queen Fredigond is finally caught in her illicit relationship with Landrey, and Castrato devises a ghoulish punishment for them. The eunuch conceives another perverse play-within-the play, and again the central prop will be a bed. The stage directions for act 4, scene 2, read *Enter the* Eunuch, *whilst the waits play softly, and solemn'y drawes the Canopie, where the* Queen *sits at one end bound with* Landrey *at the other, both as asleep*" (H3r). Castrato offers meat and wine to assuage their hunger and thirst and then withdraws them. At last, s/he lets them eat and drink, then laughs: "Ha, ha, ha, y'have both eat and drunk abominable poyson" (H4v). When Landrey pulls a knife to attack Castrato, the stage direction reads, "*The Eunuch tript up his heels in scuffle and sits on him*" (H4v). Castrato stabs Landrey, gags the dying Queen so she can not cry out, and then props her up next to Landrey, leaving a "peeping hole" through which she can see. The dying Fredigond and Landrey's corpse – adulterous lovers caught in the "honeying sty" – thus form an audience for the next grisly spectacle.

Castrato, much like Iago, next whips Clotair into a jealous frenzy against Aphelia by repeating the play's leitmotif, images of monstrous coition:

> You are her husband sir, and now must own
> Her doubtfull issue, and her lawlesse lust;
> Although a Bull should leap her, you must father,
> And have a drove of forked Animals,
> Shall have their horns born with them to the sound,
> 'Twill save their prodigall wives the reacky labour.
>   (I1v)[34]

---

[34] See Neill, "'Unproper Beds,'" p. 264, for a discussion of the link in *Othello* between adultery and monstrosity.

At the threat of bastardy, the text directs Aphelia to enter, *"drag'd by two Ruffins in her petticoat & hair."* She describes herself as a lamb led to slaughter, and so she is. Further stage directions instruct a man *"with pan and irons"* to enter, and when Aphelia refuses to confess her guilt, Clotair drags her by the hair. Then *"they bind her to the Chair, the* Eu. *much sears her breast"* (I3r). (The 1687 version clarifies this stage direction as *"they sear one of her breasts."*)[35] Here Hemings converts the last scene of *Othello* when Desdemona is strangled in her bed into a more overtly pornographic spectacle that caters to the audience's scopophilic desire to see the female body spread out and tortured.

At this moment the guard enters with news that the castle is beseiged by Chrotilda's brother Dumain, who seeks vengeance for his father's death and his sister's rape, and by Clovis, who leads an army against his brother. The despairing Clotair begs Castrato to shoot him. In an aside, the eunuch steels himself to the task: "do not betray me tears, / The *Eunuchs* nature must be harsh and cruell" (I4r). Ignoring Aphelia's pleas that he spare Clotair, Castrato opens the curtain, displays Landrey and the Queen (who finally dies),[36] and cries:

> hear me King,
> Thy Mother was a foul adulteress,
> A cruel butcherer of innocents . . .
> You ravisht fair *Chrotilda*; *Clodimir*
> Your valiant Uncle, brother to this Queen,
> Was for the foul fact slain; for which mistake,
> *Dumain, Lamot, Maria, Isabel,*
> And the abus'd *Chrotilda*, if by flight
> She had not sav'd her life, had fall'n with them.
> I knowing this, and ever pittying
> The wrongs that they indur'd,
> Have found it time thus to revenge them.
> (I4v)

But Castrato cannot bring himself to strike because "[her] relenting heart / Yerns on his Princely person." Like many tragic heroines, Chrotilda has fallen in love with her ravisher.[37] Rather than killing Clotair, Castrato/ Chrotilda incenses him to strike her. Instead of a miraculous transformation, the revelation of Castrato's identity comes almost as an afterthought

---

[35] William Hemings, *The Eunuch: A Tragedy* (London: J.B., 1687), p. 49.
[36] According to de Serres, Queen Fredegonde died peacefully in her bed, presumably of natural causes. See *A General Inventorie*, p. 33.
[37] See Suzanne Gossett, "'Best Men Are Molded Out of Faults': Marrying the Rapist in Jacobean Drama," *English Literary Renaissance* 14 (1984), 305–27.

in the exhausting litany of crimes he/she has committed. When her brother asks, "who ha's done these fatall deeds[?]" Castrato responds, "*Chrotilda* and a woman" (K1r). Clotair is stricken with remorse when he realizes that the blackfaced eunuch is really the woman he had raped before the play began. He exclaims: "no *Eunuch* she; / No sun-burnt vagabond of Aethiope . . . here lies thy ravisht sister slain / By me the ravisher" (K1v). Castrato lives long enough to present Clotair with a letter that reveals her true identity as the wronged Chrotilda, and to explain:

> I should have kill'd thee King, and had put on
> A masculine spirit to perform the deed;
> Alas how frail our resolutions are!
> A womans weakness conquer'd my revenge:
> I'd spirit enough to quit my Fathers wrongs;
> And they which should have seen me act that part,
> Would not believe I should so soon prove haggard:
> But there is something dwels upon thy brow
> Which did perswade me to humanitie;
> Thou injurd'st me, yet I spar'd thy life;
> Thou injurd'st me, yet I would fall by thee;
> And like to my soft sex, I fall and perish.   (K1v)

Like the black paint and male garb she wears, Chrotilda's vengeful spirit is a theatrical role, an impersonation that belies her inner nature. The black disguise of an androgyne offers Chrotilda opportunities for agency; working slyly from the margins, she can obtain revenge. A perverse trickster, she works like a spider, imbricating the evil characters around her in a fatal net. In the end her womanly nature wins out, and she cannot take the bloody revenge she had sought against her ravisher.

The Fatal Contract's inept design should be obvious by now. The plot moves from one sensationalized tableau to another without clarifying the action or the characters' motivations to the audience. Yet however botched this play may seem, its exploitation of the disguised Moor plot is revealing. Hemings's appropriation of *Othello* discards Shakespeare's ironic fashioning of a Venetian villain who bedevils a noble black man to make the Iago-like villain Castrato into a blackened monstrosity. Portrayed by an English male actor pretending to be a French female impersonating an African male who has been castrated, Castrato embodies racial and sexual perversion. S/he serves as a purveyor of grotesque scenarios – to the audience as well as the characters on stage. That so many of these scenarios enact or imply miscegenation suggests that by the time Hemings wrote *The Fatal Contract*, the idea of a sexual union between black Moor and white European had assumed a conventional, albeit pornographic, power.

IV

The White Devil, the Jacobean tragedy that begins this chapter, uses disguise to fashion a Moorish general who is akin in some respects to Shakespeare's Othello. In sharp contrast, *The Fatal Contract*, written twenty-six years later, contains a black villain inspired by Iago. It is too easy to read this shift as a hardening of racial stereotypes during the intervening years, but the plays' disparate treatment of the disguised Moor does demonstrate, I believe, the degeneration of what had become a theatrical convention. In comedies of the same period, audiences were conditioned to expect the sudden doffing of the racial disguise as a key mechanism in the plot's unraveling. When William Hemings wrote his tragedy in the late 1630s, he tried to make the device of the disguised heroine as shocking as possible, stretching the convention grotesquely.

The Lost Lady, *The English Moor*, and *The Fatal Contract* were performed during 1637–38, a period of religious controversy leading up to Charles I's invasion of Scotland that, by hindsight at least, signaled the coming of the Civil War.[38] All three plays were associated in one way or another with Queen Henrietta Maria through her acting company or performance at court. Of course, it is possible to read too much into this curious circumstance. The popularity of the disguised Moor plot device at this critical moment could stem from the availability of a talented boy actor who specialized in such roles. Yet, might it also reflect anxieties about threats to patriarchal and royal authority in a nation shortly to be embroiled in civil war, fears that are embodied in these plays in the painted image of a black Moor and the figure of a slave who seems to serve her European masters even as she betrays them?

[38] See, for example, Kevin Sharpe's discussion of 1637 as a critical year in *The Personal Rule of Charles I* (New Haven: Yale University Press, 1992), pp. 769–802.

CHAPTER 8

Avenging villains

The signifying power of the actor's blackened face, as earlier chapters attest, stems from the codes that circulate within society at large during a particular cultural moment. Previous studies of blackfaced characters on the English stage have often conflated Restoration plays with dramas written before the closing of the theatre in 1642.[1] Yet the vastly different social and cultural contexts of the 1660s to 1690s affected what playwrights and actors conveyed through blackfaced characters and how the audience responded. This chapter will test this hypothesis by a close examination of three tragedies written and performed in the 1670s that reworked old plays for Restoration audiences: Elkanah Settle's *Love and Revenge* (1675), based on Hemings's *Fatal Contract*; Aphra Behn's *Abdelazer: The Moor's Revenge* (1676) adapted from *Lust's Dominion*; and Edward Ravenscroft's 1678 adaptation of *Titus Andronicus*.[2]

By the 1670s England's overseas empire was flourishing. Colonies in the Caribbean and North America were rapidly expanding, and, as historian Robin Blackburn contends, by this time "any lingering reservations about slavery or slave trading" had been discarded.[3] The Royal African Company was founded in 1672, and among the shareholders were the Duke of York, Prince Rupert, members of the royal family, and prominent figures from

---

[1] Anthony Gerard Barthelemy and Elliot Tokson frequently discuss characters and plots from both periods, but they include little discussion of the different circumstances of production or changing cultural contexts. See *Black Face, Maligned Race: The Representation of Blacks in English Drama from Shakespeare to Southerne* (Baton Rouge: Louisiana State University Press, 1987) and *The Popular Image of the Black Man in English Drama, 1550–1688* (Boston: G. K. Hall, 1982).

[2] I discuss *Love and Revenge* in chapter seven, *Lust's Dominion* and *Titus Andronicus* in chapter three. For a detailed comparison of *Lust's Dominion* and *Abdelazer*, see Susie Thomas, "'This Thing of Darkness I Acknowledge Mine': Aphra Behn's *Abdelazer, or The Moor's Revenge*," *Restoration* 22 (1998), 18–39. For comparisons of Shakespeare's and Ravenscroft's versions of *Titus Andronicus*, see Barbara A. Murray, *Restoring Shakespeare: Viewing the Voice* (Madison: Fairleigh Dickinson Press, 2001), pp. 111–21 and Hazelton Spencer, *Shakespeare Improved: The Restoration Versions in Quarto and on the Stage* (Cambridge, MA: Harvard University Press, 1927), pp. 287–92.

[3] Robin Blackburn, *The Making of New World Slavery* (London: Verso, 1997), p. 250.

the city, including lord mayors, sheriffs, and aldermen. Between 1672 and 1713, this trading company "was responsible for buying 125,000 slaves on the African coast, losing a fifth of them on the 'Middle Passage' and selling the remainder, about 100,000 to the English West Indian planters."[4] English men and women's burgeoning taste for consumer goods, particularly chocolate and coffee sweetened with sugar, made investments in human capital enormously profitable. From 1660 to 1700 the English consumption of sugar increased fourfold.[5] The trade in black bodies that supported English consumption began to be a way of life in the 1670s.

The expansion of England's sugar colonies also spawned a growing black presence in London. Planters who had made their fortunes in the colonies would often return and bring slaves with them. By the 1670s approximately 300 sons of West Indian planters were coming to England for their education, often accompanied by personal slaves. Black servants also accompanied the officers on slave ships, and some Africans served as free seamen. Newspapers of the 1680s and 1690s contained reports of runaway slaves wearing metal collars. The largest concentration of black people remained in London, the capital of slave-trading ventures, but, as Peter Fryer observes, "black people were scattered all over England in the second half of the [seventeenth] century."[6] Audiences at the Restoration's theatres were used to seeing "blackamoors" on London's city streets and a black face was no longer a spectacle of strangeness.

Despite the prosperity generated by overseas investments, political unrest ran rampant in the 1670s. Early in the decade it had become clear that Charles II's wife, Catherine of Braganza, was barren and that his brother James would inherit the throne after his death. James's public avowal of his conversion to Catholicism in 1672 raised the specter of a return to the religious turmoil of earlier reigns. Whigs and Royalists were both fearful of the future, and according to theatre historian Derek Hughes, "The increasing political gloom of drama reflects the national mood. There was growing mistrust of the King's aims in the Third Dutch War and fear of his brother's religion and character, which was to be compounded by James's marriage in September 1673 to the Catholic Princess Mary of Modena."[7]

Concerns about the future of the monarchy are refracted in tragedies of this period, which frequently portrayed tyrannical kings and royal

---

[4] Blackburn, *Making of New World Slavery*, p. 255.
[5] Peter Fryer, *Staying Power: The History of Black People in Britain* (London: Pluto Press, 1984) provides an overview of the black presence in England during this period. See p. 14 in particular.
[6] Fryer, *Staying Power*, p. 32.
[7] Derek Hughes, *English Drama, 1660–1700* (Oxford: Clarendon Press, 1996), p. 95.

families beset by problems of legitimacy and succession. Performed by acting companies that were underwritten by King Charles II (The King's Company) and his brother James (The Duke's Company), Restoration tragedies reaffirmed the values of the ruling class. In plays such as Elkanah Settle's *The Empress of Morocco* or John Dryden's *Conquest of Granada*, aristocrats came under attack from alien figures drawn from the New World, Spain, northern Africa, the Far East, and the Mediterranean. Improbable plots set in exotic locales contained multiple significations, as Bridget Orr eloquently argues, and alien cultures served as "a screen for the projection of local anxieties."[8] Machiavellian villains reveled in court intrigues, revenge, and murder, opposing deceit and inconstancy against ideals of loyalty and constancy. They were allowed to "strut and fret openly," as Douglas Canfield puts it, "and at their best, they represent formidable, nominalistic threats to the established order. It is hard to get some of these genies back into their bottles. But that is how an ideology creates bogeymen."[9]

The three tragic adaptations examined in this chapter could all be described as "villain plays," a genre that flourished in the 1670s and is notable for its "blood-and-thunder" scenes of gore and horror.[10] In each a villain seeks revenge on those who have wronged him before the play begins. Settle, Behn, and Ravenscroft changed their source plays with Restoration notions of decorum in mind. They eliminated characters to suit a smaller acting company, conflated scenes, and exploited the special effects that were now possible at the Dorset Garden Theatre. All wrote in blank verse rather than the heroic couplets that dominated Restoration tragedy. Most important to my purposes is a consideration of the villains they recycled from earlier dramas, who were figured black.

I

Like their antecedents in medieval morality plays, the blackfaced villains of the 1670s have a special relationship to the audience. By this time, the "vengeful Moor," as Joyce Green MacDonald observes, had become a stage device with "a kind of theatrical and cultural vitality of its own, regardless

---

[8] Bridget Orr, *The Empire on the English Stage, 1660–1714* (Cambridge: Cambridge University Press, 2001), p. 11.
[9] Douglas J. Canfield, *Heroes and States: On the Ideology of Restoration Tragedy* (Lexington: University Press of Kentucky, 2000), p. 1.
[10] This term comes from Robert D. Hume's *The Development of English Drama in the Late Seventeenth Century* (Oxford: Clarendon Press, 1976), pp. 199–202.

of the specific dramatic actions . . . designed to contain it."[11] In asides and soliloquies, the black villains inform the audience of their hatred for the other characters, their plans for revenge, and their delight when the revenge is accomplished. As these intimate exchanges with the audience increase in number, the characters become more complex, less one-dimensional. Changes in the texts also suggest that the Restoration revisers tried to humanize the villains, adding emotions and motivations that were missing in the originals.

Chrotilda, Hemings's rape victim who blackened her face and disguised herself as Castrato in *The Fatal Contract*, is reincarnated in Settle's *Love and Revenge* as Chlotilda. Disguised as "a Moor, and Favourite to the Queen," Chlotilda takes the telling name Nigrello. While Castrato's status as a sexless eunuch was her most salient feature, Settle's Nigrello is a "little Negro." Castrato was enacted by a boy actor impersonating a young woman impersonating a castrated male Moor; Nigrello was performed by Mary Lee, a female member of the Duke's Company, known for her skill at creating pathos in romance and tragedy, but also known for playing "breeches parts," which allowed her to expose her legs as she appeared in male disguise.[12] She delivered the Epilogue "in a Mans Habit, but in a white Wig, and her face discover'd,"[13] lines that suggest that Nigrello's blackness was conveyed by a mask rather than black face paint. Nigrello could have removed the mask during her frequent asides to the audience, adding piquancy to her role as white, female rape victim.

For most of the play Nigrello frames the action. She is on stage more often than Castrato was, interspersing the action with asides and beginning and ending each scene with soliloquies that highlight the evil nature of Queen Fredigond and suggest her own victimization and understandable desire for revenge. In 1.2, for example, when the Queen reveals her secret plans to Nigrello, the black servant comments sotto voce: "Now for the greatest Rancour of her Soul," followed later by the shocked "Was ever such a Bawd, or such a Mother." She whispers in surprise, "Her husbands death!" after Fredigond tells Nigrello of her plans to poison the King. Later she editorializes,

[11] Joyce Green MacDonald, *Women and Race in Early Modern Texts* (Cambridge: Cambridge University Press, 2002), p. 146. MacDonald's reading of Aphra Behn's *Abdelazer* complements my own.

[12] See Philip H. Highfill, Jr., Kalman A. Burnim, and Edward A. Langhans, eds. *A Biographical Dictionary of Actors, Actresses, Musicians, Dancers, Managers & Other Stage Personnel in London, 1660–1800*, 16 vols. (Carbondale: Southern Illinois University Press, 1973–93), vol. IX, pp. 200–01.

[13] Elkanah Settle, *Love and Revenge: A Tragedy* (London: William Cademan, 1675), pp. 6–9. Quotations will be cited by page numbers within the text.

> I defie thy pow'r
> The pow'r of Woman damn'd in Lust, whose Breast
> Harbours more Hell then Zealots Feats, or Poets Fables ever framed,
> Furies are Tame, and burning Lakes are coole
> To thy Insatiate Lust and monstrous Villanies.   (6–9)

Such direct addresses to the audience coupled with Mary Lee's obvious disguise make Nigrello's role overtly metatheatrical. They also invite the audience to sympathize with her point of view; no matter what horrendous crimes she commits, pathos permeates her position as a wronged maiden.

Aphra Behn's Abdelazer, portrayed by one of the Restoration's finest heroic actors, Thomas Betterton, is less a devil figure than his antecedent Eleazar, more a hero in the mode of heroic tragedy. His exotic stature is underscored by the Moorish costume he insists on wearing, an outfit that includes, according to the stage directions, a "*Helmet of Feathers.*"[14] He is also a loner. Often acting as an observer or an intruder "in the great scenes of ceremonial power," Abdelazer never enters "along with a white person of importance: not even his wife or mistress . . . The stage directions reiterate the fundamental point: he comes from somewhere else."[15]

Betterton's Moor is also humanized. The play's opening scene exemplifies the kinds of changes Behn makes. Whereas Eleazar suddenly appeared "*sitting on a chair*" in *Lust's Dominion*, Abdelazer is described as "*sullenly leaning his head on his hands*" (248) while musicians play a song describing Love's tyrannic power.[16] World weary, Abdelazer regrets "those mighty graces" he has purchased,

> My blooming Youth, my healthful vigorous Youth,
> Which Nature gave me for more Noble Actions
> Then to lie fawning at a woman's feet,
> And pass my hours in idleness and Love.   (250)

Then he exploits the blushing trope, but this time in a way that reiterates what Thomas Wright had argued in *The Passions of the Mind*, that blushing is a sign of shame: "If I cou'd blush, I shou'd through all this Cloud / Send forth my sence of shame into my Cheeks" (250).

Behn frequently (but not always) omits or alters the homiletic epithets of her source – devil, fiend, Lucifer – in one instance substituting "Prince of

---

[14] Aphra Behn, *Abdelazer* in *The Works of Aphra Behn*, ed. Janet Todd, vol. v (Columbus: Ohio State University Press, 1996), p. 284. Quotations will be cited by page number within the text.
[15] Derek Hughes, *The Theatre of Aphra Behn* (London: Palgrave, 2001), p. 59.
[16] See *Lust's Dominion* in *The Dramatic Works of Thomas Dekker*, ed. Fredson Bowers, vol. iv, (Cambridge: Cambridge University Press, 1961), p. 133. Quotations will be cited by page number within the text.

Fate" for "Prince of Hell" (286 and 181 respectively). She also "Othellofies"
Abdelazer, giving him passages that express his anguish, as in this speech
to his wife, Florella. Torn by love and jealousy, the Moor cries:

> Oh wonderfully! y'ave learnt the art to move;
> Go, leave me. –
> Flor. Still out of humour, thoughtful, and displeas'd!
>   And why at me, my *Abdelazer*, what have I done?
> Abd. Rarely! You cannot do amiss you are so beautiful,
>   So very fair – Go, get you in, I say –
>   She has the art of dallying with my soul,
>   Teaching a lazie softness from her looks. –
>   But now a nobler passion's enter'd there,
>   And blows it thus, – to air.   (258–59)

While giving Betterton an opportunity to enact the passions he later portrayed so well in his rendition of Othello,[17] Behn undemonized the black
man.[18] To be sure he is a "subtle Villain / Yet of such Power, we scarce dare
think him such" (304), but he is not a devil in disguise.[19]

Aaron remains "black and Loathsome" in Ravenscroft's *Titus Andronicus*,
and the carnivalesque qualities of his make-up are suggested by Lucius'
exclamation, "Behold the Hellish dog: / See how he Rowls his eyes and
grins."[20] Nevertheless, he is less devilish in Ravenscroft's text. In a major
change Aaron speaks lines originally assigned to Demetrius after the sacrifice
of Alarbus:

> No, Madam stand resolv'd, but hope withall,
> That the same Gods that Arm'd the Queen of *Troy*
> With opportunity of Sharp revenge
> Upon the *Thracian* Tyrant in his Tent,
> May favour *Tamora* the queen of *Goths*
> With like successful minutes to requite
> Thee Bloody wrongs and *Romans* Injuries.   (5)

After she is chosen Empress, Tamora commends Aaron to Saturninus, who
responds, "Dark is the Case, but there's noble light / There Shines" (10–11).

---

[17] See my *Othello: A Contextual History* (Cambridge: Cambridge University Press, 1994), pp. 96–99.
[18] Hughes uses this expression in his discussion of Behn's presentation of the black body. See *The
Theatre of Aphra Behn*, p. 62.
[19] Thomas argues that Abdelazer differs from Eleazar in that he is "not evil because he is black. Behn's
play does not insist that Moors are by nature lustful, scheming, and bloodthirsty; it suggests that
Abdelazer chooses the path of chaos and destruction, or rather, that this is the only course of action
he can pursue because he is a slave." See "'This Thing of Darkness,'" 26.
[20] Edward Ravenscroft, *Titus Andronicus, or the Rape of Lavinia* (London, 1686), p. 52. Quotations will
be cited by page number within the text.

Saturninus, unlike his predecessor, admits the possibility of a virtuous and noble Moor. Aaron's role as advisor to royalty is underscored when he takes over Tamora's advice to the newly planted emperor later in the same scene (13).

Ravenscroft expands Aaron's act 2 soliloquy with lines that provide the motivation for his hatred of the Romans:

> Hence abject thoughts that I am black and foul,
> And all the Taunts of Whites that call me Fiend,
> I still am Lovely in an Empress eyes,
> Lifted on high in Power, I'le hang above
> Like a black threatning Cloud o're all their heads;
> That dare look up to me with Envious Eyes.   (15)

Aaron's hatred, it seems, was born in the taunts of whites who criticize his color, but it is also rooted in a quest for status and power.

All three black villains are granted more agency than they had in the pre-Restoration originals. Nigrello, as we have seen, is constantly on stage, sharing her plots with the audience. In act 3, she saves Lewis's life, an action performed by Lamot in *The Fatal Contract*. She also masterminds a rebellion against the King, something planned by Clovis in the earlier play. As the tragedy draws to its bloody conclusion, stage directions show her control over what happens: "Nigrello *stamps, and immediately a Company of Villains rush in with drawn Swords, and massacre the* Queen *and* Clarmount" (74). Later, she stamps her foot again, and the "*former Villains rush in, seize, and disarm*" the King (79). Proud of her success, Nigrello admonishes him:

> You are too rash: Kings may be Kings in Pallaces,
> But not in Dungeons. 'Tis I am Monarch here.
> *Clotair*, it would be Charity to kill you,
> For you've outliv'd your pow'r. This day your Brother
> By my Conspiracy, converts that force
> You lent him to assist the Rebels cause.
> And you shall live to see him crowned.   (80)

Mortally wounded, the King expresses his admiration: "thy glorious Villany, thy Wit. / Thy Courage, and thy Conduct" attest that "blackness hides some noble blood" (81). Nigrello dies with a request that she be remembered not as a traitor, but for "Revenge, / A satisfaction due to an Injur'd Lady. / Call me an honourable Murderer" (82). *Love and Revenge* establishes that epitaph as essentially correct, and Nigrello's expanded role makes her the most important character in Settle's potboiler, the one responsible for the play's multiple intrigues and murders.

While Eleazar certainly had agency in *Lust's Dominion*, Abdelazer is stronger. His words and deeds are marked by machismo.[21] John Genest, an early nineteenth-century reader of Restoration plays, observed that we may detest Abdelazer, "but cannot despise him; and must feel some sort of respect for his courage."[22] Abdelazer relishes his martial prowess; he brandishes his sword in the public, ceremonial scenes and his dagger in private. He stabs the Queen without compunction. In *Lust's Dominion* the Queen lives and promises to repent; in Behn, the Queen's villainy is so monstrous that she has to be dispatched.

Particularly telling is Abdelazer's death scene. Instead of foolishly play-acting in his dungeon as Eleazar did, the Moor walks into a trap. He is surprised by his enemies, who gang up on him and run him through: Philip *"Runs on him, all the rest do the like in the same minute. Abdelazer aims at the Prince, and kills Osmin: and falls dead himself"* (314). This "busy tableau" presents, as MacDonald suggests, "a kind of corporate revenge" against the Moor, "one in which the particular injuries he has done to any individual lose significance in comparison to the harm his sexual crimes have done against the social order."[23] Although he has been a villain for most of the play, Abdelazer is at the end the victim of a gang killing.

Aaron, too, is credited with agency. As mentioned above, Tamora and the Emperor defer to him in the opening scenes. Later Demetrius offers to hide Bassianus' body in a cave "As *Aron* did direct" (21); and after Lavinia's rape Tamora seeks him out to "know what farther mischiefs are in store" (23). Aaron lures Martius and Quintus to the fatal pit with the expectation of an assignation with two ladies. Then, when Titus discovers that two of his remaining sons are charged with Bassianus' murder, Aaron can hardly contain himself. In words added by Ravenscroft, he exclaims:

> Ha, ha, ha, Poor easy loving fools,
> How is their Armorous Expectation cross'd,
> Death wayted for their coming here, not Love,
> Woman's a sure bait to draw to ruine.
> How Easily men are to confusion hurl'd,
> 'Tis gold and women that undo the world.
>
> (26)

Ravenscroft's spectacular ending shows Aaron tortured on the rack. Asked to confess his crimes, the stage directions indicate he chooses not to speak:

---

[21] Hughes, *Aphra Behn*, argues that Abdelazer's machismo is more sinister than his blackness. See p. 57.
[22] John Genest, *Some Account of the English Stage from the Restoration in 1660 to 1830*, 10 vols. (Bath: H. E. Carrington, 1832), vol. 1, p. 216.
[23] MacDonald, *Women and Race*, p. 162.

"Aron *shakes his head, in sign he will not.*" "Aron *shakes his head again*" (53). Only when the fire licks around him does he fall to cursing. From the beginning, when Tamora introduces him to the Emperor as a man to be trusted, to his final curses, Aaron makes choices, speaks, and acts from clearly defined motives.

By the 1670s Londoners were probably more familiar with the products of cross-racial liaisons than their forebears, and not surprisingly these dramas portray anxieties about miscegenation. *Love and Revenge* mutes the issue, eliminating Hemings's speech describing Castrato covering the Queen with his "sootie limbs." The speech may have been too overtly sexual for the "chaste" lips of Mary Lee, or perhaps Nigrello's obvious female form made it seem inappropriate.

Settle does raise the issue of sexual misalliances, however, in the King's lengthy speech on the dangers of lust. Cuckoldry is perilous to the state because the "issue" of a woman's Groom,

> Or Page, is made her cousen'd Husband Heir:
> And thus not only her own blood's defiled,
> But the base Canker spreads through Families;
> And so one minutes sin leaves stains to Ages.
> (78)

Sexual activity outside of marriage, particularly between an aristocrat and a member of the lower orders, inevitably leads to pollution, not just in the people involved but to families, the building block of the body politic.

Interracial sex is more prominent in *The Moor's Revenge*. Philip castigates his mother for wantoning in "yon sooty Leacher's arms" (255), a change from *Lust's Dominion*'s "that leachers armes" (143). But the most graphic representation of Abdelazer's sexuality occurs in act 5, scene 2, a scene expanded from *Lust's Dominion*, when he nearly rapes Leonora. When she protests she will not violate her engagement to Alonzo, Abdelazer insists, "His Birth! His glorious Actions! Are they like mine?" Leonora's response does not mention color, per se, but her reference to "those advantages, / Which Nature has laid out in Beauty on his Person" provokes Abdelazer to respond:

> Aye! There's your cause of hate! Curst be my Birth,
> And curst be Nature, that has dy'd my skin
> With this ungrateful colour! Could not the Gods
> Have given me equal Beauty with *Alonzo*! . . .
> The Lights put out! Thou in my naked arms
> Wilt find me soft and smooth as polisht Ebony:

> And all my kisses on thy balmy lip as sweet,
> As are the Breezes, breath'd amidst the Groves,
> Of ripening Spices in the height of day:
> As vigorous too
> As if each Night were the first happy moment
> I laid thy panting body to my bosom.   (307)

There are no suggestions of monstrosity in this speech; black skin is now as smooth as ebony, a black man's kisses like the exotic spices of the East.

Tamora begs just such a kiss in Ravenscroft's *Titus Andronicus*. Aaron pulls from her embrace, however, when he notices that Bassianus "starts / To see our fondness." The young Roman responds to the sight of white Tamora kissing black Aaron: "Hell – Kiss a Moor. / Believe me Madam, your Swarthy *Cymerian* / Has made your Honour of his bodies hue, / Black, Loathsome, and Detested" (20). Aaron also raises the specter of miscegenation when he refers to his child in words added to the final scene; he claims that Tamora's embraces were sweet, "When we were acting Pleasures, which produc'd / That Little thing, where *Moor* and *Goths* combin'd" (55). At the same time, Ravenscroft omits Shakespeare's references to Aaron's plan to take his infant son to stay with Muliteus, a countryman who has a white baby of the same age. During the Restoration, when the results of interracial sex were more readily observed, audiences might have skoffed at Muliteus' white son as being genetically impossible. At any rate, Ravenscroft's version recognizes interracial sex as a reality rather than a monstrosity.

Love and Revenge ends much the way Hemings's original concluded. The final scene reviews the revenges and counter-revenges that have been committed and Nigrello is finally unveiled. Stabbed by the king, Chlotilda reveals her identity:

> And though I had worne so long a masculine shape
> For all my other Scenes of Cruelty,
> I put on my own Sex agen to dye.   (82)

Like Othello her namesake, Nigrello asks to be recalled as "an honourable Murderer." Her dying words reveal more clearly than Castrato's had the pathos of her situation.

Unlike his precursor, Abdelazer defiantly fights to the end. The man "Whose Sword reapt Victory, / As oft as 'twas unsheathed" (283) fittingly dies by the sword, but not after "enacting" many scenes of revenge. Surrounded by his enemies, he compares himself to the hunted lion:

> Now thou dar'st see me lash my sides, and roar,
> And bite my snare in vain; who with one look,
> (Had I been free) hast shrunk into the Earth
> For shelter from my Rage:
> And like that noble Beast, though thus betray'd,
> I've yet an awfull fierceness in my looks,
> Which makes thee fear't approach.   (313–14)

This is quite a change from Eleazar's call for "Devills" to come and claim him in *Lust's Dominion* (216). The angry lion suggests that Abdelazer dies a proud prince of Africa, not a devil from Hell.

The ending to Ravenscroft's *Titus Andronicus* is more drastically altered. Aaron, as mentioned earlier, is *"discover'd on a Rack"* (53). He is silent until Marcus threatens to kill his son, "the Hellish Infant"; if he remains silent, "the young Kid goes after the Old Goat." Tamora warns him not to speak against her honor, but when he recounts the murderous deeds he has committed, she asks to hold the infant so that she can give it a parting kiss. The stage direction reads: *"The Child is brought to the Empress, she Stabs it"*; as she performs this action, Tamora cries, "Dye thou off-spring of that Blab-tongu'd Moor" (55). In one of the most remarkable turnabouts in all literature, Aaron marvels:

> She has out-done me in my own Art –
> Out-done me in Murder – Kill'd her own Child,
> Give it me – I'le eat it.   (55)

Spectators are then treated to this spectacle: *"The Fire flames about the Moor."* Lucius pronounces that Aaron shall be "burnt and Rack'd to death." Aaron dies cursing, and Marcus' parting shot – "Snarle on, and like a curs'd fell dog, / In howling end thy Life" (56) – indicates that the actor playing Aaron writhed, cursed, and howled to the bitter end.

In a tragedy that repeatedly features the murder of children – Alarbus, Mutius, Quintus, Lavinia, Chiron, Demetrius, and finally the mulatto baby – Tamora's desire to kill her child seems entirely consistent. Aaron's attempt to eat his own offspring parallels Tamora's consumption of her sons in a pie and invokes the racialized trope of African anthropophagi. It may suggest, as Jonathan Bate argues, Aaron's desire to compete with Tamora for control of the child.[24] Or it may be an exercise in autonomy, the desire to incorporate the baby into himself and keep it from anyone else. In any event, the spectacular scene of Aaron's demise reinforces his responsibility

---

[24] See the Introduction to *Titus Andronicus*, Third Arden Series (London: Routledge, 1995), p. 53. Bate wryly notes that in Ravenscroft, "Aaron has a truly consuming love for his baby."

for the carnage that has destroyed Rome, and Lucius' assumption of the Emperorship is brief and half-hearted.

Large generalizations from a mere three plays performed during the 1670s are inherently fragile, but the changes made in these blackfaced characters from their pre-Restoration originals are highly suggestive. From them we can tease out some changes in the cultural landscape. The plays' language, for example, suggests a paradigm shift in the ways stage Moors were imagined – from "devil" to "slave." In the sixteenth and early seventeenth centuries, as Gary Taylor persuasively argues, there was no particular association between slavery and blackness. When slave markets were depicted in plays such as *The Jew of Malta*, the people bought and sold were mostly Europeans and Turks rather than black Africans. By the 1670s, however, when England was fully involved in the Atlantic slave trade, the word "slave" had become indelibly connected to blackness.[25] "Slave" is the most frequent sobriquet for Nigrello. Toward *Love and Revenge*'s conclusion, he is frequently addressed as such (61, 62, 71, 79, 80), and the eunuch describes himself as "Your loyal faithful Slave" (63) and "your poor humble slave" (74). Abdelazer complains that even though he was born the son of the Moorish king Abdela, after his father's defeat his "Slavery" began (252). And at the finale Behn gives Philip the exclamation: "Poor angry Slave, how I contemn thee now" (313). Aaron is the exception. Ravenscroft promotes him to the rank of General, perhaps in an allusion to Othello or possibly because of his expanded role in the early scenes.

During the 1670s the average Londoner was exposed frequently to people of color, and it stands to reason that black people would no longer be thought of as devils or bogeymen but human beings who, whatever their legal or social status, were biologically similar to white English men and women. Unlike the servants to be seen on London's streets, Restoration stage Moors were highly involved in the imperial courts of France, Spain, and Rome, but their liaisons with powerful white women that destabilized the body politic reflect unease about the black presence in everyday life.

II

The three villains discussed here function as dark shadows around the throne – whether France, Spain, or ancient Rome. And sharing that throne is the figure of the lascivious Queen. Like Lyndaraxa in John Dryden's *The Conquest of Granada by the Spaniards*, each is the "Dread Maternal Anarch, who threatens all the bonds of patriarchal society."[26] As she plots

[25] See Gary Taylor, *Buying Whiteness: Race, Culture and Identity from Columbus to Hip Hop* (New York: Palgrave, 2005).
[26] Canfield, *Heroes and States*, p. 13.

her children's murder, her perversion of maternity reflects concerns about legitimacy and succession.

Settle's Fredigond, a role acted by Margaret Osborne,[27] is a bold adulteress, even more so than her predecessor in *The Fatal Contract*. In words added by Settle to act 1, she confesses to Nigrello:

> I once was a Kind Wife and Pious Mother.
> But now my Husband, and my Sons must dye,
> And I must be the Traytor . . .
> Almighty Love this wondrous Change has made,
> A Love that has my hopes of Heav'n betray'd:
> And yet I can't resist it.   (8)

Fredigond poisons her husband and plans the death of her sons in hopes of planting her lover, Clarmount, on the French throne. She tells him that "The Kingdoms Heir shall be a Child of thine, / And Kings and Queens shall follow in thy Line" (9). Settle thus underscores the theme of legitimacy and inheritance so important to his audience.

Fredigond's pernicious influence on the court and body politic is construed as effeminizing. A loyal courtier, Lamot, recalls that in King Childrick's reign (he is poisoned at the beginning of the play),

> before his Queen
> Had taught him Revels, and untaught him War,
> Before her wanton Lust had sheathed his Sword,
> To give her treacherous Poyson, pow'r of death:
> I knew that they [the nobles] had valour, and a cause
> To shew it in.   (53)

The Queen epitomizes the corruption at the heart of the French court, a corruption that is figured by darkness and femininity. When her son Lewis (renamed for Hemings's Clovis, perhaps in homage to France's Louis XIV) traps her in a grotto where she has taken her lover, he exclaims:

> Thou glorious Light, that in thy natural Orbe
> Didst comfortably shine upon this Kingdom,
> How is thy worth Ecclips'd? what a dull darkness
> Hangs round about thy Fame? In all this piece
> To every limb whereof, I once owed duty:
> I know not now where to find out my Mother.

The discovery of his mother's insatiate sexuality forces Lewis to question his own paternity:

---

[27] *Biographical Dictionary*, vol. XI, pp. 119–20.

> Whilst I reflect upon thy tainted blood,
> I doubt the pureness of my own. The spring head
> Defiled, who know but the under stream may be
> Corrupted. (69–70)

And, as in so many revenge plays, the state can only be purged through a spectacle of retribution. After sending her "villains" to massacre the Queen and Clarmount, Nigrello hides their bodies behind a curtain. Later, in the final scene, the stage direction reads "*A Curtain drawn,* Clarmount *and* Fredigond *appear dead*" (80). Only after the "wicked Queen" is dead can Chlotilda/Nigrello unveil the twisted conspiracies she has fostered in her quest for vengeance.

The Queen of Spain in Behn's *Abdelazer*, renamed Eugenia from the original's Isabella, was portrayed by Mary Lee, the same actress who personated Nigrello. As Susie Thomas contends in her comparison of *Abdelazer* and *Lust's Dominion*, Behn strengthened the Queen's role in her version, making her Abdelazer's equal in villainy.[28] She insists on being heard in the tragedy's opening scene, and she uses her maid Elvira, a character added by Behn, to assist in her Machiavellian plots against Abdelazer's wife Florella. Like Nigrello, Eugenia is given soliloquies to explain her evil stratagems. At the beginning of act 3, for example, she has arranged for her son Ferdinand to find his way to Florella's bed, where she hopes he will stay until Abdelazer returns:

> Where in her Lodgings he shall find his Wife,
> Amidst her Amorous dalliance with my Son. –
> My watchful Spyes are waiting for the knowledge;
> Which when to me imparted, I'le improve,
> Till my Revenge be equal to my Love. (275)

Mary Lee likely delivered this speech from the forestage to the audience with the same intimacy she used as Nigrello in Settle's *Love and Revenge*, but here the motivation for her malignancy is lust and jealousy rather than violated chastity.

Eugenia's lust pollutes the state and undermines legitimacy. When her second son Philip learns that she plans to marry Abdelazer, he cries:

> Oh, I cou'd curse my Birth! –
> This will confirm the world in their opinion,
> That she's the worst of women.
> That I am basely born too. (285)

---

[28] Thomas, "'This Thing of Darkness,'" 20–22.

Like *Lust Dominion's* Isabella, Eugenia publicly proclaims herself an adulteress to keep her son Philip from inheriting the throne. But unlike her precursor, Eugenia is too steeped in evil plots to repent at the play's conclusion. "In *Abdelazer*," Thomas argues, "the Queen never sees the error of her ways; nor does she ever proclaim herself a silly woman with a naturally weak mind. She is Abdelazer's equal in villainy and a far more powerful and domineering presence than her counterpart in *Lust's Dominion*."[29] In her role as Queen and Queen Mother, she thus represents a more formidable threat to the political order than did her predecessor.

Tamora, in contrast, is weaker in Ravenscroft's version of *Titus Andronicus* than in Shakespeare's. She recommends Aaron to Saturninus as a wise counselor and repeatedly defers to his judgment. For example, her aside warning Saturninus to dissemble his anger in act 1, scene 1, lines 448–53 is given to Aaron. Later, as she leaves Chiron and Demetrius who are about to rape Lavinia, Tamora says, "Now will I hence and seek my lovely Moor, / To know what farther mischiefs are in store" (23). Until the final scenes of the play, when Aaron is absent from Saturninus' court and Tamora takes over as advisor, she is consistently subordinated to him. Like Fredigond and Eugenia, Tamora perverts maternity. Her piteous plea for Alarbus is undercut by Ravenscroft's additions to Titus' and Lucius' speeches; the Romans explain that their sacrifice of a prisoner of the Goths is in retribution for a similar murder committed by Tamora before the play begins. Lucius recalls

> Deaf like the Gods when Thunder fills the Air,
> Were you to all our suppliant *Romans* then;
> Unmov'd beheld him made a Sacrifice
> T'appease your Angry Gods; What Gods are they
> Are pleas'd with Humane Blood and Cruelty?

And Titus remembers his vow that "If any of the Cruel *Tamora's* Race / Should fall in *Roman* hands, him I wou'd give / To their Revenging Piety." Ravenscroft's Tamora thus begs for mercy that she had previously denied Titus when her "Priestly Butchers Murder'd" his son (4). Tamora's association with this barbarous practice makes her abrupt request to kiss her mulatto infant in the play's final moments only to stab it seem entirely consistent. Once again, a mother murders her own child.

Ravenscroft also provides a motive for the Goths to abandon their Queen that is lacking in Shakespeare. The Goth who brings the captured baby and Aaron to Titus exudes disgust at Tamora's act of miscegenation:

---

[29] Thomas, "'This Thing of Darkness,'" 21.

> Behold this *Moor* the Sire of this Squob toad.
> For he and *Tamora* club'd together,
> The Queen of *Goths* Tup'd by a Goat.

Aaron is the "old black ram" who has tupped the Goths' "white ewe," and the result, according to the Goth, is "*Romes* dishonour / In a polluted Empress" (51). Tamora's adultery with a barbarous Moor undermines the polity of Goth and Roman alike.

These lascivious queens, so closely intertwined with figures of blackness, signal the crisis of legitimacy and succession that haunted Restoration England in the 1670s. It is not hard to read the queens figured in these plays as projections of English anxiety. Their "promiscuous sexuality," concludes Canfield, "threatened the patrilineality upon which the succession of property – and the very kingdom itself – rested." This "uppity-woman type symbolized the rebellious aspects of England."[30] Embedded in her sexuality was the fear that the English race would become polluted by "intercourse" with the alien other. On stage the lascivious Queen could be stabbed – as all three described here were – and expunged from the body politic. The anxieties she embodied, however, were less easily assuaged.

III

Opposed to the lascivious Queen was "the virtuous woman, constant as lover, wife, queen." As Canfield observes, the concept of constancy she embodied was crucial to "aristocratic monarchal ideology."[31] In our three tragedies, the chaste heroine is beset by predatory males who threaten rape and torture. Lavinia, like her predecessor in Shakespeare, is raped, mutilated, and finally murdered by her father. The other two heroines are somewhat changed from their pre-Restoration originals and their roles expanded, perhaps because the beleaguered but virtuous female was a mainstay of Restoration tragedy, perhaps because actresses asked that the roles be expanded. In any event, both Settle's Aphelia and Behn's Leonora are formidable women.

Aphelia was portrayed by Mrs. Betterton who was known for her skill in tragedy. In a major change from the original – presumably required by the dictates of poetic justice – Aphelia is not tortured or killed in *Love and Revenge*, but lives to marry Lewis, the heir to the throne, and help restore legitimacy to France. Up to that point, she is a threat to legitimacy because she is the object of illicit desire. Clotair, Lewis's older brother, desperately

---

[30] Canfield, *Heroes and States*, p. 7.   [31] Canfield, *Heroes and States*, p. 7.

wishes to bed her, and as Nigrello tells Aphelia at the beginning of act 2, that desire threatens to interfere with "Designs to match him with th'Infanta of *Spain*" (13). Aphelia refuses all of Clotair's demands, however, even when he locks her in a dungeon.

Part of Nigrello's strategy to save Aphelia from a fate worse than death is to slander her in hopes that Clotair will find her less attractive if she is unfaithful. The resulting change in Clotair's rhetoric makes it clear that Aphelia and Nigrello (remember, Nigrello, the young woman Chlotilda in disguise, was raped by Clotair before the play begins) are mirror images. Clotair excoriates Aphelia:

> She's no Saint now:
> All her Divinity's expired; she's turn'd
> A Monster, as deform'd, as chang'd, and black
> As Angels when they fell.   (46)

Like Nigrello's suspect sexuality, Aphelia's character is now blackened and monstrous. Of course, the slander is just a device to keep Aphelia from Clotair's dastardly clutches, and the maiden remains true to Lewis through a host of perilous adventures. Her virtue is rewarded at the conclusion when she is finally united with Lewis; his investment in her, the chaste and loyal woman, then effects a restoration in the state. Aphelia's charms, Lewis proclaims, and her love will afford him "leisure to be just" (83).

The chaste heroine of *Abdelazer*, Leonora, is Eugenia's daughter and a princess of Spain. Her role was performed by Elizabeth Barry early in her career. Barry, who was for a time the Earl of Rochester's mistress, was acclaimed for exciting pity in spectators when she acted tragic roles.[32] Leonora is engaged early in the play to Florella's brother Alonzo, a Spanish noble beneath her in birth but equal in virtue. She has little to say for the first half of the play, but once Abdelazer's wife Florella is safely dispatched, the Moor is beset by a consuming passion for her. This aspect of the tortuous plot comes to a head in act 5, scene 2, when Abdelazer first asks for her love and then threatens to rape her.

> Coy Mistress, you must yield, and quickly too:
> Were you devout as Vestals, pure as their Fire,
> Yet I wou'd wanton in the rifled spoils
> Of all that sacred Innocence and Beauty.
> Oh my desires grow high!   (308)

---

[32] Highfill et al., *Biographical Dictionary*, vol. 1, p. 316.

Fortunately for Leonora, Abdelazer's Moorish servant Osmin interrupts; Abdelazer is so angry he stabs Osmin in the arm, and Leonora rises to his defense. Her pity inspires Osmin to help her, and through his efforts Leonora is freed and Abdelazer defeated. In *Lust's Dominion* the heroine is saved because she persuades Zarack, Osmin's counterpart, to help her. Here her kindness moves the Moorish servant to assist her.

She is no shrinking violet, however. She is on stage when Abdelazer is surrounded and stabbed, and she might well have joined the fray when the stage direction calls for "*all the rest*" to run on him with their weapons (314). When the Cardinal pronounces that this day has "restor'd you / To all the Glories of your birth and merits" and has "restored all Spain," Leonora is right by her brother's side urging him to assume his kingly role. Again, the chaste female restores the trust and constancy that enable the monarchy, in turn, to restore itself.

IV

Although the black Moor who appears in the revenge tragedies examined here is humanized in comparison to the "talking devils" of the 1580s and 1590s, that humanity in some ways makes him a more threatening figure. He is biologically compatible with white women and capable of producing mixed-race offspring. Bridget Orr contends that Restoration tragedies used Spain to figure English concerns about the dangers of "polluted blood." If the Spanish lost their empire partly as a result of intermarriage with Moors (as was suggested in plays of the period), what might happen to England, which aspired to its own mercantile empire in the late seventeenth century?[33] While these plays were being performed, laws against miscegenation were being enacted in England's American colonies.[34] The black people who appeared on London's streets signaled England's growing investment in a slave economy, but they were also visual reminders of the danger of biological pollution that accompanied overseas ventures.

These tragedies also feature dark underground spaces – grottos, tombs, dungeons, caves – hellish holes conducive to rapes, mutilations, and murders. Such spaces served as mirror images of the throne rooms where power is displayed. As Barbara A. Murray notes of Ravenscroft's *Titus Andronicus*,

---

[33] Orr, *Empire on the English Stage*, pp. 138–39.
[34] In 1664 Maryland banned interracial marriages and by 1691 Virginia had prohibited all interracial liaisons, whose fruits the Assembly described as "that abominable mixture and spurious issue." See Winthrop D. Jordan, *White Over Black: American Attitudes Toward the Negro, 1550–1812* (Chapel Hill: University of North Carolina Press, 1968), pp. 79–80.

such spaces further "the sense of a desperate people whose gaze has become fixed on what is dark below."[35] This darkness is multivalent. Morally, it suggests the forbidden sexuality that lies below the characters' waists; geographically, it suggests the dark continent where the Moorish figure originated; and psychologically, it represents the repressed desires that lurk in the unconscious mind.[36] What is dark below is terrifying, and it is also embodied in all three plays in the black figure who hovers around a white female sovereign, visually signifying the danger of racial pollution.

These plays thus illustrate how by the 1670s the Moor's black face had come to signify racial and sexual taboos. It is tempting to argue that the dramas' "blood-and thunder" violence is so extreme because the emotional stakes are so high. Whether they realized it or not, when Settle, Behn, and Ravenscroft recycled a black Moor from a pre-Restoration tragedy, they fashioned figures who embodied the fears and anxieties of a new and deeply conflicted age.

[35] Murray, *Restoring Shakespeare*, p. 117.
[36] These resonances were pointed out to me by James Bulman.

CHAPTER 9

Royal slaves

Oroonoko, the hero of Thomas Southerne's adaptation of Aphra Behn's novel, and Zanga, the villain in Edward Young's *The Revenge*, were popular with English audiences throughout the eighteenth century. Following in the path of Behn's Abedelazer, both were "Othellofied," but in different ways. As the sons of African kings who had been sold into slavery, they were paradoxically labeled "royal slaves," and their behavior – for good or evil – was cast as grandly heroic, even sublime. Wylie Sypher describes the "Oroonoko pattern" for royal slaves, as opposed to ordinary field workers: "The African appears . . . as a thoroughly noble figure, idealized out of all semblance of reality, and living in a pastoral Africa – a pseudo-African in a pseudo-Africa. This august Negro is then betrayed into slavery, and with this betrayal comes the pathos essential to propaganda. Retaining only his simple austerity, he endures the brutality of West-Indian life and may die with the grand gesture."[1]

Although Zanga does not fit this pattern because of his self-confessed villainy, both he and Oroonoko bear the marks of the slave-owning white culture that created them; at the same time, their pathos catered to the age of sensibility and evoked sympathetic responses from many in their predominantly white audiences. At least some audience members apparently saw in these fictional figures, performed by white actors in blackface, support for the growing abolitionist sentiments in the second half of the century.

I

Both tragedies were regular offerings in the London repertories during the eighteenth century, but *Oroonoko* was more popular. Southerne's play was

---

[1] Wylie Sypher, *Guinea's Captive Kings: British Anti-Slavery Literature of the Eighteenth Century* (Chapel Hill: University of North Carolina Press, 1942), p. 9.

first performed at Drury Lane in 1695 and published soon after. According to *The London Stage*, it immediately became a stock play that was performed nearly every year, over 300 times between 1695 and 1800.[2] Although it started at Drury Lane, competing productions sometimes alternated between Covent Garden and Drury Lane as the century progressed, and *Oroonoko* was also produced frequently at the marginal theatres at Lincoln's Inn Fields and Goodman's Fields. Often performed at the request of "Persons of Quality" and for benefits, *Oroonoko* also was used to introduce new actors to the stage in the relative anonymity of blackface.

Southerne's main plot presented Aphra Behn's tragic story of the African prince Oroonoko, who was tricked by an unscrupulous sea captain, enticed onto his ship, and later sold into slavery. The tragedy opens with Oroonoko's arrival in Surinam where, as in Behn's novel, he is befriended by several white settlers. But unlike Behn, Southerne made Oroonoko's wife Imoinda a white woman, a change that added to the tragedy's resonance with *Othello*.[3] Oroonoko demonstrates his heroism by defending the white settlers against the Indians, and he never rejects slavery per se. His fellow slave Aboan convinces him to participate in a slave revolt only by pointing out that no matter how well Oroonoko and his pregnant wife Imoinda are treated, their children will be born slaves. As a man of feeling, Oroonoko cannot bear the thought that the child Imoinda carries would suffer such indignity. During the rebellion Oroonoko kills the captain who had betrayed him, and he submits after its unsuccessful conclusion only to save his wife. The Governor, who embodies all the cruelty and corruption attributed to West Indian planters in literature of the time,[4] breaks his promise to treat Oroonoko fairly and tries to rape Imoinda. Although the actual rape is prevented by the "good" white Blandford, the attempt indicates that

---

[2] See *The London Stage, 1660–1800*, ed. George Winchester Stone et al. (Carbondale: Southern Illinois University Press, 1962–72), passim.

[3] Recent discussions of *Oroonoko* have pondered the significance of this decision. Perhaps the Restoration's leading actresses did not want to wear blackface, and as Laura J. Rosenthal points out, the success of Southerne's comic subplot depends on the absence of black African women to satisfy the settlers' desires. See "Owning *Oroonoko*: Behn, Southerne, and the Contingencies of Property," *Renaissance Drama* 23 (1992), 24–58. Joyce Green MacDonald argues that Imoinda's whiteness is "the product of a cult of sensibility as it confronted that most ungenteel of human institutions, slavery." See *Women and Race in Early Modern Texts* (Cambridge: Cambridge University Press, 2002), pp. 87–107; quote from p. 100. See also Margaret Ferguson's "Juggling the Categories of Race, Class and Gender: Aphra Behn's *Oroonoko*," in *Women, "Race," & Writing in the Early Modern Period*, ed. Margo Hendricks and Patricia Parker (London: Routledge, 1994), pp. 209–24.

[4] See, for example, Richard Ligon, *A True and Exact History of the Island of Barbados* (London, 1657); Morgan Godwyn, *The Negro's and Indians Advocate, Suing for their Admission into the Church* (London, 1680; and Thomas Tryon, *A Discourse in Way of Dialogue, Between an Ethiopean or Negro-Slave and a Christian* (London, 1684).

there is no room for Oroonoko and Imoinda's love in Surinam. Just before he dies, Aboan informs Oroonoko of the torture he has received, which makes Oroonoko and Imoinda choose suicide as the only escape from their predicament. Torn between despair and tender passion for his wife, Oroonoko cannot bring himself to kill her. He is successful only when Imoinda puts her own hand on his and pushes the knife into her breast. In a final act of defiance, Oroonoko stabs the corrupt Governor and then himself.

To this tragic plot Southerne added a comic subplot in which two sisters who were unsuccessful in finding marriage partners in London intrigue their way to prosperous husbands in Surinam. One sister disguises herself as a man and uses a bedtrick (substituting a "real" man in the bed for herself after she "marries" a lusty widow) as part of her stratagem. This subplot was widely criticized during the eighteenth and early nineteenth centuries as an excrescence on the text. Mid-eighteenth-century adaptations of *Oroonoko* by John Hawkesworth, by an anonymous writer, and by theatre devotee Francis Gentleman dropped it altogether.[5] David Baker wrote in *Biographica Dramatica* (1812) that while "the love of Oroonoko to Imoinda" was possibly "the tenderest and at the same time most manly, noble, and unpolluted, that we find in any of our dramatic pieces," the "intermixture of the low, trivial and loose comedy of the Widow Lacket and her son Daniel . . . are so greatly below, and indeed so much empoisons the merit of the other parts, that nothing but the corrupt taste of the period" (i.e. the Restoration) can excuse it.[6] Modern editors are more tolerant of the subplot's cuckolding farce, often finding thematic links between its commodification of women and the buying and selling of slaves in the main plot.[7] Certainly, as Laura Rosenthal contends, both plots center on issues of ownership.[8] But the effects of the subplot are even more complicated, and as Joyce Green MacDonald persuasively argues, "the rowdy Welldons and the imperiled Imoinda are both products of the appropriation of their female English spectators to the racial and sexual imperatives of colonialism."[9] To

[5] John Hawkesworth's adaptation was printed in 1759 and was used by David Garrick at Drury Lane. The version published in 1760 anonymously added some six hundred lines in place of the comic scenes but was never acted. Francis Gentleman's version of 1760 was published in Glasgow and acted in Edinburgh.
[6] David Baker, *Biographica Dramatica*, vol. III (London, 1812), p. 103.
[7] Maximillian E. Novak and David Stuart Rodes argue that "Southerne needed a contrast to Oroonoko's tragic love," the resulting blend of farce and tragedy "succeeded very well." See the introduction to their edition of *Oroonoko* for the Regents Restoration Drama Series (Lincoln: University of Nebraska Press, 1976), esp. p. xxvii.
[8] See Rosenthal, "Owning *Oroonoko*," passim.   [9] MacDonald, *Women and Race*, p. 109.

audiences in the eighteenth century however, Southerne's satire on wooing and wedding in the Welldon plot was perceived as a sign of bad taste.

Edward Young's *The Revenge* has no subplot and was not subject to the same kinds of criticism, although its protracted passages of melodramatic rant gave some commentators pause. The tragedy premiered at Drury Lane on 18 April 1721 and soon became a standard in theatrical repertoires. According to *The London Stage*, it was performed over ninety times in London between 1721 and 1800.[10] Edward Young, a poet and cleric who is better known today for his brooding proto-romantic poems, *Night-Thoughts*, was educated at Oxford and became a protégé of the Duke of Wharton, to whom the first edition of *The Revenge* is dedicated.

Young's Zanga was no doubt influenced by Aphra Behn's Abdelazer. But the dramatist also borrowed freely from Shakespeare's *Othello* to craft a tragedy about a villainous slave who poisons his master's imagination with the fantasy that his wife is unfaithful. *The Revenge* differs from its Shakespearean predecessor, however, in that this time the villain, Zanga, is a black Moor while the master is a white European. His motivation, unlike Iago's, is made clear from the beginning. In the plot summary that follows, I will try to convey the melodramatic qualities of this adaptation of Shakespeare's tragedy.

As the tragedy opens, Zanga explains to his mistress Isabella why he bears such a grudge against his master Don Alonzo:

> 'Tis twice three Years since that Great Man,
> (Great let me call him; for he conquer'd Me,)
> Made me the Captive of his Arm in Fight.
> He slew my Father, and threw Chain's o'er me,
> While I with pious Rage pursu'd Revenge.
> I then was young, he plac'd me near his Person,
> And thought me not dishonour'd by his Service.
> One Day (may that returning Day be Night,
> The Stain, the Curse of each succeeding Year)
> For something, or for nothing, in his Pride
> He struck me. While I tell it, do I live?
> He smote me on the Cheek – I did not stab him;
> For that were poor Revenge – E'er since, his Folly
> Has strove to bury it beneath a heap
> Of Kindnesses, and thinks it is forgot . . .
> Proud *Spaniard*, thou shalt feel me![11]

---

[10]   *The London Stage*, passim.
[11]   Edward Young, *The Revenge: A Tragedy* (London, 1721), 2–3. Further quotations will be cited by page numbers within the text.

At first Zanga tries to attain his revenge by subverting the Spanish campaign against the Moors; but despite his treachery, Don Alonzo succeeds in battle and comes home triumphant. Alonzo has also freed his best friend Don Carlos from imprisonment by the Moors, a generous act of friendship considering that while Don Carlos was away, Alonzo has fallen in love with his friend's amour, Leonora. Her father, Don Alvarez, is now anxious for a marriage between his daughter and the wealthy Don Carlos, but she loves Don Alonzo instead. After Alonzo confides his passion for Leonora to Zanga, the Moor decides on a more personal form of revenge and the plot is hatched.

When word comes that Don Carlos's ships have been lost at sea and he is no longer wealthy, Leonora's father breaks off the match. Zanga then encourages Alonzo in his suit and suggests that he ask his friend, who now has no hope of marriage with Leonora, to relinquish his claim. Carlos reluctantly agrees, and Leonora and Alonzo are married. Meanwhile, Zanga has forged a letter from Carlos to Leonora and has Isabella drop it in the bride's chamber. Alonzo finds it there, and although he is too honourable to read it, he is smitten with jealousy. Zanga tears the letter up, and in scenes reminiscent of act 3, scene 3 (the temptation scene) in Shakespeare's *Othello*, the Moor plays his master as Iago plays Othello. He insinuates that Carlos resigned Leonora to his friend because he had already enjoyed her, and without any evidence, Alonzo concludes that the letter is "Proof equivalent to Sight" that Leonora is unfaithful (34). Zanga prevents Alonzo from confronting his wife, arguing that she would only lie. Then he applies the final touch, a description of Don Carlos and Leonora in each other's arms in the Jessamin Bower the night before, when Carlos cried, "O Night of Ecstasie!" (39).

Even after this "Proof," Alonzo is reluctant to act. After all, this is the afternoon of his wedding day and his marriage has not yet been consummated. When Leonora asks that he come and join the festivities, he challenges her love. Leonora demands:

> Am I not your Wife?
> Have not I just Authority to know
> That Heart, which I have purchas'd with my own?
> (43)

This response only fuels Alonzo's jealousy, so he sends her to her chamber. After she exits, Zanga reprimands Alonzo for not killing Leonora, and the frustrated Spaniard commands Zanga to murder Carlos. Then, Iago-like, Zanga suggests that Alonzo might as well forgive his wife:

> If you forgive, the World will call you Good;
> If you forget, the World will call you Wise;
> If you receive her to your Grace again,
> The World will call you, very, very Kind.
>
> (47)

This is too much for Alonzo. He resolves to murder his wife on her nuptial bed.

The tragedy concludes on a melodramatic note. Zanga reports that Don Carlos is dead, and Alonzo seeks Leonora out in the Jessamin Bower, the place that she had "polluted." Zanga paints the scene:

> Sisters of *Acheron*, go hand in hand,
> Go dance around the Bow'r, and close them in;
> And tell them that I sent you to salute them.
> Profane the Ground, and for th' Ambrosial Rose,
> And Breath of Jessamin, let Hemlock blacken,
> And deadly Nightshade poyson all the Air.
> For the sweet Nightingale may Ravens croak,
> Toads pant, and Adders rustle thro' the Leaves;
> May Serpents winding up the Trees, let fall
> Their hissing Necks upon them from above,
> And mingle Kisses – such as I should give them.
>
> (50)

The bower is another dark place; like the forest in Shakespeare's *Titus Andronicus*, it is made more horrific by the ravens, toads, adders, and serpents that inhabit it. Alonzo approaches the sleeping Leonora, kisses her, and like Desdemona, she awakes. At first Alonzo cannot go through with the murder, so he leaves. Zanga then informs Leonora that her husband is jealous. When husband and wife are alone again, Leonora angrily protests her husband's jealousy, which makes him turn on her. To prove her innocence, she stabs herself. Alonzo seeks out Zanga, who confesses that Leonora is indeed guiltless and that he was lying. When Alonzo falls into a trance in one of the play's most celebrated "points," Zanga stands over the Spaniard's prostrate body and exults in his victory. Don Alvarez and the gentlemen of the palace enter, seize Zanga, and order his torture. When Alonzo learns that Leonora is dead, he stabs himself. The play ends with the Moor carried off, but not until he expresses some remorse for what he has done: "Oh Vengeance! I have follow'd thee too far, / And to receive me, Hell blows all her Fires" (63).

Like many speeches in *The Revenge*, this plot summary has undoubtedly lasted too long, but it demonstrates the play's most salient qualities. As melodramatic as Young's tragedy may seem to us today, it was highly respected in the eighteenth century (although Henry Carey and Thomas Chatterton both wrote burlesques that exaggerated its absurdities, especially Zanga's furor over "the blow"). Francis Gentleman praised it in his *Dramatic Censor* for "indisputable marks of a powerful genius; the versification is flowing and nervous; the sentiments noble and comprehensive; the moral, a warning against that hydra of calamities, jealousy." At the same time, Gentleman noted the "wearisome length of laboured dialogue."[12] Writing four decades later, David Baker went so far as to argue that *The Revenge* was superior to Shakespeare's *Othello* because the villain was more clearly motivated, the hero less credulous, and the heroine more assertive of her innocence; Young's tragedy should be assigned, he argued, "a place in the very first rank of our dramatic writing."[13] However strange it may seem, *The Revenge* remained a popular play throughout the eighteenth century and well into the nineteenth.

II

Aboan and Oroonoko in Southerne's tragedy and Zanga in Young's were blackface roles. *A Biographical Dictionary of Actors, Actresses, Musicians, Dancers, Managers and Other Stage Personnel* includes a telling anecdote regarding the make-up used by Barton Booth, a leading actor at Drury Lane for most of his career. He made his debut in blackface as Oroonoko at the Smock Alley Theatre in Dublin during the summer of 1698.

It being very warm Weather, in his last Scene of the Play, as he waited to go on, he inadvertantly wip'd his Face, that when he enter'd he had the Appearance of a Chimney-Sweep (his own Words). At his Entrance, he was surpriz'd at the Variety of Noises he heard in the audience (for he knew not what he had done) that a little confounded him till he receiv'd an extraordinary Clap of Applause, which settl'd his Mind. The Play was desir'd for the next Night of Acting, when an Actress fitted a Crape to his Face with an Opening proper for the Mouth, and shap'd in form for the Nose; But in the first Scene, one Part of the Crape slip'd off. And "Zounds!" said he, (he was a little apt to swear) "I look'd like a Magpie! When I came off they Lampblack'd me for the Rest of the Night, that I was flead before it could be got off again."[14]

[12] Francis Gentleman, *The Dramatic Censor, or Critical Companion*, 2 vols. (London: J. Bell, 1770), vol. II, p. 331.
[13] Baker, *Biographica Dramatica*, p. 203.
[14] Philip H. Highfill, Jr., Kalman A. Burnim, and Edward A. Langhans, *A Biographical Dictionary of Actors. Actresses, Musicians, Dancers, Managers and Other Stage Personnel in London, 1660–1800*, 16 vols. (Carbondale: Southern Illinois University Press, 1973–93), vol. X, pp. 211–12. Restoration and eighteenth-century actors were used to elaborate make-up; the use of a prosthetic device for Shylock's nose had been standard practice in productions of *The Merchant of Venice* since the early modern period.

Black paint might be used for the face, but some costume notes suggest that fabrics were used to cover the arms and legs. For example, an 1831 edition of *Oroonoko* describes a rich costume for the hero when he first appears, including "black silk arms & leggings, red sandals, cream coloured shirt and cloak handsomely ornamented – rich belt – bracelet – gold band for the head." Aboan, who is Oroonoko's slave and of much lower social status, wears "black cotton arms and leggings."[15]

Reviews are more difficult to find for eighteenth-century performances than later, but it is possible to tease out from extant records some sense of how the characters of Oroonoko and Zanga were performed. Anecdotes and memories of particular productions are, of course, selective, but it is particularly telling that these accounts seldom discuss Oroonoko and Zanga as blackface roles or the characters' status as slaves. Apparently by the eighteenth century the appearance of a performer as a black African was taken for granted. Commentators focused instead on the quality of the acting.

The first impersonator of Southerne's hero was John Verbruggen, who, according to the *Biographical Dictionary*, was best at "rough hewn characters" who were wild and untaught. Verbruggen had a shambling gait, and as one commentator noted, he "had a Roughness in his Manner, and a negligent Wildness in his Action and his Mein [sic], which became him well."[16] He often played the hero torn between passions of love and honor.[17] Verbruggen was succeeded by Barton Booth, who was naturally graceful and "had the deportment of a nobleman, and so well became a Star and Garter, he seemed born to it." According to Colley Cibber, Booth's countenance "had a manly sweetness, so happily formed for expression, that he could mark every passion with a strength to meet the eye of the most distant spectator."[18]

John Wilks followed in the role at Drury Lane, and it was said of him, "To beseech gracefully, to approach respectfully, to pity, to mourn, to love, are the places wherein Wilks may be made to shine with the utmost beauty."[19] David Garrick played Oroonoko briefly in the middle of the eighteenth century (in Hawkesworth's version), but soon yielded the role to Spranger Barry, who was six feet tall and very handsome. Barry, who excelled as Othello as well as Oroonoko, was recognized for his skill in personating

---

[15] Cited from Novak and Rodes, *Oroonoko*, p. xxix.
[16] Highfill et al., *Biographical Dictionary*, vol. xv, p. 136.
[17] Novak and Rodes, *Oroonoko*, p. xviii.
[18] Highfill et al., *Biographical Dictionary*, vol. ii, pp. 220–21.
[19] Highfill et al., *Biographical Dictionary*, vol. xvi, p. 121.

pathos. It was said that "he gave dignity to the hero and passion to the lover as few others."[20] Oroonoko also became a standard role for Edmund Kean in the early nineteenth century. One early biographer claimed that the "unlooked for strokes of passion which seemed to well up spontaneously from his heart, moved the audience to tears," and "in his fine transition to tenderness and love the feelings of Oroonoko, as conveyed by Edmund Kean, seemed to gush from his heart, as if its inmost veins had been laid open."[21]

Two qualities stand out in these recollections. First, regardless of his blackness Oroonoko was a prince, and the actor who personated him in the eighteenth century was expected to bear himself with nobility. Second, he was a lover, and his tender regard for his wife, especially in the lengthy final scene before they die, had to seem genuine. It is not surprising that the most successful Oroonokos of the period – Booth, Barry, and Kean – also excelled as Othello, for nobility and tenderness are the qualities that were most often identified with Shakespeare's Moor.[22]

Nor is it surprising that actors who excelled as Oroonoko did not generally personate Young's Zanga. Records indicate few overlaps. A supporting actor, Edmund Burton, acted Zanga on 27 October 1746, and Oroonoko on 16 December at Goodman's Fields;[23] Charles Holland, who had a manly figure and a deep-toned voice, debuted as Oroonoko on 13 October 1755, and later performed Zanga at Drury Lane;[24] and Edmund Kean excelled in both roles. Actors were more likely to play both Aboan and Zanga. Though his role in *Oroonoko* is comparatively minor, Aboan, like Zanga, seethes with resentment at the way he and his people are treated. Aboan is the one who subtly persuades Oroonoko to join the slave revolt, and, like Zanga, he is full of anger and hatred, not romantic love.

In the Remarks appended to her edition of *The Revenge*, Elizabeth Inchbald argued that the actor who performs Zanga must be the play's sole support. "This character is of such magnitude, and so unprotected by those which surround him, that few performers will undertake to represent it: a less number still have succeeded in braving the danger."[25] At the first

[20] Highfill et al., *Biographical Dictionary*, vol. I, p. 338.
[21] F. W. Hawkins, *The Life of Edmund Kean*, vol. 1 (London: Tinsley Brothers, 1869), pp. 408–10.
[22] See my *Othello: A Contextual History* (Cambridge: Cambridge University Press, 1994), chaps. 5 and 6 for discussion of *Othello* on the Restoration and eighteenth-century stage.
[23] Highfill et al., *Biographical Dictionary*, vol. II, p. 435.
[24] Highfill et al., *Biographical Dictionary*, vol. VII, p. 367.
[25] Elizabeth Inchbald, ed., *The British Theatre, or A Collection of Plays*, 25 vols. (London: Longman, ca. 1825), vol. XII, p. 4.

performance, the role of Don Alonzo was taken by Barton Booth, Drury Lane's leading actor, while Zanga was listed last in the "Dramatis Personae" as being performed by the utility actor John Mills. As the eighteenth century progressed, however, Zanga became a preferred role for London's leading performers.

James Quin, who also claimed Aboan as one of his parts, began performing Zanga in 1744, and it became a staple. Quin was a large, hulking man who tended to declaim his lines. Charles Churchill described his rendition of Zanga: "His eyes, in gloomy socket taught to roll, / Proclaim'd the sullen habit of his soul."[26] Francis Gentleman claimed that Quin "wanted ease of insinuation" in the role and that he was "heavy," although he did acquit himself with "great ability."[27] The most celebrated Zanga of the eighteenth century, however, was Quin's protégé, Henry Mossop, who debuted as Zanga at Smock Alley on 30 November 1749 (and also later played Aboan). Gentleman described Mossop as standing alone in the role because he possessed "an unequalled spirit, extent, and propriety of expression."[28] Another commentator wrote: "*See Mossop appears, though ungraceful his mien, / A better performer scarce ever was seen . . . The Turbulent passions he nobly expressed / And stormed the fierce feelings which live in the breast.*"[29] An extant sketch in the Harvard Theatre Collection shows the actor as Zanga, clad in a flowing robe and wearing a turban with lofty feathers; his arms are akimbo, signaling his burning resentment. The anonymous pamphlet *An Epistle to Henry Mossop* singles out Mossop's gloomy Zanga for praise, especially the moment when he stands over Alonzo's inert body and cries: "Oh my dear Countrymen, look down and see / How I bestride your haughty conqueror." To this commentator, Mossop's Zanga was an exquisite piece of acting.[30]

John Philip Kemble, London's leading actor at the end of the eighteenth century, also won high praise as Zanga. He first assayed the role in 1789 at Drury Lane, and Zanga became a mainstay for the rest of his career. Leigh Hunt praised the same "point" so admired in Mossop's interpretation as an unforgettable highlight of Kemble's rendition: "there is always something sublime in the sudden completion of great objects, and perhaps there is not a

---

[26] Cited from George D. Parker, "The Moor's Progress: A Study of Edward Young's Tragedy, *The Revenge*," *Theatre Research International* 6, no 3 (1981), 172–95, n. 28.

[27] Gentleman, *The Dramatic Censor*, p. 333.   [28] Gentleman, *The Dramatic Censor*, p. 333.

[29] Highfill et al., *Biographical Dictionary*, vol. x, p. 343.

[30] *An Epistle to Henry Mossop, Esq; on the Institution and End of the Drama and the Present State of the Irish Stage* (Dublin, 1750), pp. 29–30.

sublimer action on the stage than the stride of Mr. KEMBLE as *Zanga*, over the body of his victim, and his majestic exultation of revenge."[31] Kemble's early biographer James Boaden also singled out this moment, but added that the actor conveyed a sensibility of "the *blow* throughout, and the dismission of enmity at the offender's death – 'a lion preys not upon carcasses.'"[32] Known for his Coriolanus, Kemble successfully conveyed Zanga's sense of his own great place as the son of a king and his haughty resentment at any sign of disrespect.

The early years of the nineteenth century brought the most notable and the most flamboyant Zanga to London's theatres in Edmund Kean. William Hazlitt thought Kean was the definitive Zanga:

He had all the wild impetuosity of barbarous revenge, the glowing energy of the untamed children of the sun, whose blood drinks up the radiance of the fiercer skies. He was like a man stung with rage, and bursting out with stifled passions. His hurried motions had the restlessness of the panther's: his wily caution, his cruel eye, his quivering visage, his violent gestures, his hollow pauses, his abrupt transitions were all in character.[33]

When Kean's Zanga revealed to Alonzo that he was the author of these calamities, "Know then, 'twas I," his biographer F. W. Hawkins writes: "His eye lit up with a preternatural brilliance; the long-smothered hate blazed forth with fearful intensity . . . towering over the prostrate body with terrific energy and power, he trampled upon it in an attitude which Hazlitt regarded as not the less dreadful from its being perfectly beautiful." Another observer found the effect "appalling, beyond anything we have ever witnessed. Rae, who played Alonzo, seemed to wither and shrink into half his size . . . As we ourselves contemplated the dark and exulting Moor standing over his victim, with his flashing eyes and arms thrown upwards . . . we thought that we never beheld anything so like the 'archangel ruined.'"[34] Hawkins likewise claimed that Kean's Zanga recalled Milton's Lucifer, suggesting that in his Zanga, the actor imbued the resentful Moor with the titanic passion of romanticism's Satanic hero.[35]

[31] Leigh Hunt, *Critical Essays on the Performers of the London Theatres* (London, 1807), p. 7.
[32] James Boaden, *Memoirs of the Life of John Philip Kemble, Esq.*, 2 vols. (London: Longman, 1825), vol. 1, p. 424.
[33] William Hazlitt, *Collected Works*, ed. A. R. Waller and Arnold Glover, 12 vols. (London: J. M. Dent, 1903), vol. VIII, pp. 27–28.
[34] Cited from Harold Newcomb Hillebrand, *Edmund Kean* (New York: Columbia University Press, 1933), p. 149.
[35] Hawkins, *Edmund Kean*, vol. I, p. 302.

III

Iago and Othello were Zanga's and Oroonoko's forebears. Eighteenth-century audiences familiar with Shakespeare's texts would have recognized the resonances. Oroonoko frequently recalls Othello's words and phrasing. His joyful speech at being reunited with his beloved Imoinda at the conclusion of act 2, for example, echoes the sentiments, if not the words, of Othello's joy on the Cyprus quay in Shakespeare's act 2, scene 2:

> This little spot of Earth you stand upon,
> Is more to me, than the extended Plains
> Of my great Father's Kingdom. Here I reign
> In full delights, in Joys to Pow'r unknown;
> Your love my Empire, and your Heart my Throne.[36]

When Aboan suggests they steal the sea captain's ship to return to Africa, Oroonoko replies in Othello's words, "There is a justice in it pleases me." When he is cornered by the Governor's soldiers in the final scene, he cries, "Put up your Swords." His final words before he kills himself – "the Deed was mine; / Bloody I know it is" (84) – suggests Othello's last words as well. Such echoes clearly were meant to signal that Oroonoko, like Othello, was a noble figure of pathos.

The Othellofication of *The Revenge* is less in words and phrases than in the plot structure. All the elements of Shakespeare's last three acts are there: the villain's manipulative plot and temptation of the hero, the hero's reluctance to believe his wife is false, the production of artificial "proof," the murder of the supposed lover, and the hero's suicide. Young, however, has his heroine kill herself rather than be murdered, an obeisance perhaps to eighteenth-century standards of decorum that decree noble heroes do not murder their wives or to the actresses' desire to control their onstage demise.

Although both Oroonoko and Zanga are black slaves, they seize the audience's attention because they are also princes. Neither ever forgets his pedigree. Although he enters in chains, Oroonoko proudly proclaims that "there's another, Nobler part of Me, / Out of your reach, which you can never tame" (16). The Governor aptly names him Caesar, which reflects both the irony of the white settlers' naming practices (Pompey, Scipio, Caesar, etc.) and Oroonoko's leadership qualities. Thus, after Oroonoko successfully defends the settlers against the Indians, the Governor

---

[36] Citations from *Oroonoko* are taken from the first edition (London, 1696) and noted by page numbers within the text. Quotation from p. 34.

proclaims, "Thou glorious Man! thou something greater sure: / Than *Caesar* ever was!" (31). Aboan reminds Oroonoko and the audience that he is "A Prince" (40) with princely obligations to help his people.

Zanga informs Isabella and the audience of his birth in the opening scene of *The Revenge*, but his claim to royal status is stated most emphatically in the play's final scenes. In the famous "point," as he stands astride Alonzo's body, the villain cries:

> Let *Europe* and her palid Sons go weep,
> Let *Africk* and her Hundred Thrones rejoyce.
> O my dear Countrymen! Look down, and see
> How I bestride your prostrate Conqueror!
> I tread on Haughty *Spain*, and all her Kings . . .
> Look on me. Who am I? I know, thou say'st
> The *Moor*, a Slave, an abject beaten Slave . . .
> But look again. Has six Years cruel Bondage
> Extinguish'd Majesty so far, that nought
> Shines here, to give an Awe of one above thee?
> When the great *Moorish* King *Abdalla* fell,
> Fell by thy Hand accurst, I fought fast by him,
> His Son . . .
> Thou see'st a Prince, whose Father thou hast Slain,
> Whose Native Country thou hast laid in Blood,
> Whose Sacred Person, Oh, thou hast prophan'd!
> Whose Reign extinguish'd; What was left to me
> So highly born! No Kingdom, but Revenge;
> No Treasure, but thy Tortures, and thy Groans.
>
> (60–61)

In these exultant cries, Zanga establishes himself as a representative of his people in ways that Oroonoko – whose attention centers for the most part on his love for Imoinda – never does. Alonzo seems to recognize this, too, when in his dying words he exclaims, "*Africk*, Thou art reveng'd" (63). Zanga is Africa, and, while the injustices he has suffered certainly do not warrant the villainy he perpetrates, his anger sweeps every other consideration away.

Audiences also seem to have been moved by the pathos of Oroonoko's enslavement. Whether it is based on fact or not, the anecdote that circulated in the 1749 *Gentleman's Magazine* indicates how Southerne's tragedy was appropriated in the anti-slavery debates of that period. The Earl of Halifax, it seems, rescued a young African slave whose story was much the same as Oroonoko's. A Moorish king had been betrayed by an English Captain who enticed his son on board. The captain received the prince and his friend "with great joy, and fair treatment, but basely sold them for slaves." After his rescue, the prince was brought to England, dressed like a European, introduced into polite society, and even presented to the King. One night he and his friend were taken to Covent Garden to see a production of *Oroonoko*:

> The seeing [sic] persons of their own colour on the stage, apparently in the same distress from which they had been so lately delivered, the tender interview between *Imoinda* and *Oroonoko*, who was betrayed by the treachery of a captain, his account of his sufferings, and the repeated abuse of his placability and confidence, strongly affected them with that generous grief which pure nature always feels, and which art had not yet taught them to suppress; the young prince was so far overcome that he was obliged to retire at the end of the fourth act. His companion remained, but wept the whole time; a circumstance which affected the audience yet more than the play, and doubled the tears which were shed for *Oroonoko* and *Imoinda*.[37]

It is hard to see how audiences would not be moved by Oroonoko's plight. Stage directions in act 2, scene 5, describe what they saw: "*The Scene drawn shews* Oroonoko *upon his Back, his Legs and Arms stretch out, and chain'd to the Ground*" (70). Later, Aboan "*enters bloody*" after having been tortured. Oroonoko commiserates, "I see thee gasht, and mangled" (75). No wonder, then, that Ignatius Sancho, a freed slave turned grocer and literary savant, wished he could perform the role.[38]

No wonder, too, that when John Ferriar wanted to arouse abolitionist sentiment, he revised Southerne's text to emphasize Oroonoko's abjection. "It is my wish," his Preface insists, "that the reader should not consider these additions to the Play of Oroonoko, merely as a poetical effort, but that he should view the Tragedy thus alter'd, as designed to communicate and extend those impressions of the African Slave Trade."[39] By adding new speeches for Aboan and Oroonoko that describe the sufferings of a typical slave, Ferriar pleads "*For each poor* African *that toils and bleeds.*"[40]

From his inception, Oroonoko was a figure of pathos that moved audiences by his "most tender and exquisite Distress,"[41] a dynamic that intensified during the eighteenth century. As Wylie Sypher notes, in the context of anti-slavery debates in the 1780s, "the meaning of the play changed: it was not so much amusement as homily."[42] That audiences were

[37] *Gentleman's Magazine* 19 (1749), 89–90.
[38] See *The Letters of Ignatius Sancho*, ed. Paul Edwards and Polly Rewt (Edinburgh: Edinburgh University Press, 1994), p. 23.
[39] John Ferriar, *The Prince of Angola, a Tragedy, Altered from the Play of Oroonoko and Adapted to the Circumstances of the Present Times* (Manchester: J. Harrop, 1788), pp. vii–viii.
[40] Ferriar, *Prince of Angola*, p. 1.   [41] Hawkesworth's Preface to *Oroonoko*, sig. A2r.
[42] Sypher, *Guinea's Captive Kings*, p. 116.

10 The Frontispiece to the 1791 British Library Edition illustrates the staging of act 5, scene 3, of *Oroonoko* and indicates the kind of costumes worn in production.

increasingly affected by Zanga is perhaps more difficult to understand. *The Stage* observed in an 1815 review of Kean's villain: "The character is an anomaly; there is no connection between the respect we are seduced to pay to Zanga, and the detestation that we ought to feel for his conduct; the principle of revenge might influence the noblest minds, but it could never sway them to such malignant and unworthy means. His language bespeaks a lofty mind, his conduct betrays the meanest spirit; but we lose his moral guilt in his poetical elevation."[43] Zanga is a creature of extremes. Like the fate of Imoinda and Oroonoko, his Fortune must, as Imoinda explains, "Be wonderfull, above the common Size / of Good or ill; it must be in extreams: / Extreamly happy, or extreamly wretched" (36).

In this, Zanga is akin to Milton's Lucifer, and it is not surprising that both Edward Young, the Moor's creator, and James Quin, his first impersonator of any note, both loved Milton. Early on the figure of Zanga was associated with the "sublime," the eighteenth-century aesthetic that favored vistas of power experienced through extremes of passion that could transport the reader (or audience member) to a higher plane.[44] Zanga came to be seen as a terrifying natural force that went beyond ordinary considerations of morality. The stage directions for Zanga's entrance in Mrs. Inchbald's edition reflect the standard staging practice: Zanga was to appear on the battlements, *"with a Sea Prospect. A Storm, with Thunder and Lightning"* can be heard and seen. Zanga's mood smacks of the pathetic fallacy:

> Whether first Nature, or long want of Peace
> Has wrought my Mind to this, I cannot tell;
> But Horrors now are not displeasing to me:
> I like this Rocking of the Battlements.
> Rage on, ye Winds, Burst Clouds, and Waters Roar!
> You bear a just Resemblance to my Fortune,
> And suit the gloomy Habit of my Soul.   (1)

Zanga can be seen as a Byronic hero, not a villain. At the end of act 3, he emotes like the protagonist of a Gothic novel:

> Whither, my Soul! Ah! whither art thou sunk
> Beneath thy Sphere? E'er while, far, far above
> Such little Arts, Dissemblings, Falshoods, Frauds,
> The Trash of Villany it self, which falls

---

[43] *The Stage*, 2 (London, 1815), 169–70.
[44] For a definition of "the sublime," see *The Bedford Glossary of Critical and Literary Terms*, 2nd edn., ed. Ross Murfin and Supryia M. Ray (Boston: Bedford, 2003), 467–68. Parker notes that Zanga was associated with the sublime as early as 1747 in a review in the *London Chronicle*. See "The Moor's Progress," 193, n. 29.

To Cowards and poor Wretches wanting Bread.
Does this become a Soldier? this become
Whom Armies follow'd, and a People loved?
My Martial Glory withers at the Thought.
But Great my End; and since there are not other,
These Means are just, they shine with borrow'd Light
Illustrious from the Purpose they pursue.
          And greater sure my Merit, who to gain
          A Point Sublime, can such a Task sustain.

(35)

As Hazlitt noted in his review of Robert Campbell Maywood, "Zanga's blood is on fire; it boils in his veins; it should dilate, and agitate his whole frame with the fiercest rage and revenge." The actor must convey the "ungovernable passions that torment and goad on his mind."[45] Zanga seems to exist in a stormy world of his own, beyond good and evil, and his extremes of emotion apparently satisfied the audience's taste for the sublime. In the process, it is possible that his position as a "royal slave" evoked English audiences' sympathy, perhaps awakening their consciences to the injustices of slavery and the slave trade.[46]

IV

As should be evident by now, the surviving records of performance imply that complex and often contradictory responses to Zanga and Oroonoko arose from the synergistic interaction of audience expectation and actorly performance. Both blackface characters had the potential of arousing the spectators' pity, and neither was simply a figure of abjection. Southerne's transformation of the blushing trope that had been repeated so often by black characters in the sixteenth and early seventeenth centuries is symptomatic of changes in the culture at large. Aaron had insisted that his inability to blush came from a lack of shame, whereas Oroonoko uses the trope to stress his moral superiority to the corrupt whites around him. Surrounded by the men who have entrapped him, he cries:

Let 'em stare on. I am unfortunate, but not asham'd
Of being so: No, let the Guilty blush,
The White Man that betray'd me: Honest Black
Disdains to change its Colour.   (16)

---

[45] Hazlitt, *Collected Works*, vol. XI, p. 398.   [46] Parker suggests this in "The Moor's Progress," 190.

At this point Oroonoko feels innocent, but he invokes the trope again when the other slaves begin to beg their cruel masters for pardon:

> I own the Folly of my Enterprise,
> The Rashness of this Action, and must blush
> Quite thro' this Vail of Night, a whitely Shame,
> To think I cou'd design to make those free,
> Who were by Nature Slaves – Wretches design'd
> To be their Masters Dogs, and lick their Feet.
>
> (59)

Blushing is no longer a sign of innocence and modesty; instead, it signals shame and wrongdoing, and to Oroonoko, it is "whitely Shame." In Southerne's tragedy, the old proverb is reworked for a new audience who came into contact with black servants and knew they were human and whose feelings about them were complicated by personal experiences.

In addition, Oroonoko's speech sends mixed messages. His royal status, never far from his mind, differentiates him from the other slaves, who, he seems to indicate, deserve their condition because of their servile "Nature." Thus while *Oroonoko* might inspire an English audience with its depiction of a noble African hero, the protagonist hardly seems like an abolitionist, at least not for his fellow slaves.

Approximately 10,000 black people lived in late-eighteenth-century England, and despite the popular impression that there was no slavery in England in this period, slaves were bought and sold in London and the major trading cities of Bristol and Liverpool. The 1772 Somersett case had spurred vociferous public debate about the rights and wrongs of the slave system.[47] *Oroonoko* and *The Revenge* were performed within this social context, and while the evidence I have teased out here is more suggestive than conclusive, it seems reasonable to assume that the blackfaced figures of Oroonoko and Zanga both absorbed and reflected the contradictory feelings about black people that were circulating in the culture at large. Both Southerne's hero and Young's victim were sites of love and theft, desire and derision that showcased the double consciousness created by the white actor in blackface.

---

[47] See, for example, Jerome Nadelhaft, "The Somersett Case and Slavery: Myth, Reality, and Repercussions," *Journal of Negro History* 51 (1966), 193–208; Peter Fryer, *Staying Power: The History of Black People in Britain* (London: Pluto Press, 1984), esp. chaps. 3–8; Gretchen Gerzina, *Black London: Life Before Emancipation* (New Brunswick, NJ: Rutgers University Press, 1995); and my "Race Mattered: *Othello* in Late Eighteenth-Century England," *Shakespeare Survey* 51 (1998), 57–66.

v

By the middle of the nineteenth century, *Oroonoko* and *The Revenge* were out of fashion. In the waning years of their popularity, however, both plays were prominent in the repertoire of Ira Aldridge, the "African Roscius." The African-American actor was barred from Drury Lane and Covent Garden because of his race, but he nevertheless had a remarkably successful career in the provincial theatres of England and on European tours. When Aldridge opened at the Coburg Theatre in London, he played Oroonoko, a role that he continued to alternate with Othello and Zanga. A reviewer who saw Aldridge's Oroonoko in Brighton reported his surprise at the actor's competence and reflected that "It is really a curious and an interesting spectacle to behold a representation of such a character as Oroonoko by an African."[48] What is more surprising – or perhaps less when we consider how lighter skin was adopted for Edmund Kean's Othello in the belief that a noble Moor could not possibly have been coal black – is that Aldridge was deemed too dark for the role of the African prince. John Coleman, who played Aboan to Aldridge's Oroonoko, reports that "the Roscius, who was dark as ebony, toned his sable hue down to a copper tint; on the other hand, I was black as burnt cork and Indian ink could make me."[49] Instead of blacking up, Aldridge had to copper down to fit nineteenth-century expectations regarding royal status and skin color. Yet Aldridge could play Aboan without make-up when he supported Edmund Kean in 1829.[50] By the early nineteenth-century, it would seem, the connection between color and status had become entrenched; light-skinned Moors bespoke an aristocratic bearing, while black skin denoted the fieldworker. An actor's handbook of 1836 notes that it is customary to play Othello, Bajazet, and Zanga (royal Moors) as tawny; "Spanish brown is the best preparation for the purpose." But servile characters like Sambo and Mungo require burnt cork.[51]

Aldridge was a great success in Zanga and kept the role through much of his career. After a performance in 1848, *The Morning Post* of Surrey commented, "It was interesting to witness the acting of Mr. Ira Aldridge, a native of Africa, giving utterance to the wrongs of his race in his assumed

[48] Quoted from Herbert Marshall and Mildred Stock's biography, *Ira Aldridge: The Negro Tragedian*, 2nd edn. (Washington DC: Howard University Press, 1993), p. 66.
[49] James Coleman, *Fifty Years of an Actor's Life* (New York: James Pott, 1904), p. 402.
[50] Marshall and Stock, *Ira Aldridge*, p. 102.
[51] Leman Thomas Rede, *The Road to the Stage* (London: J. Onwhyn, 1836), p. 34.

character, and standing in an attitude of triumph over the body of one of his oppressors." Another review of a later performance noted,

Nothing could have been more admirably portrayed than the exultation of Zanga when he finds that his schemes for the destruction of Alonzo are ripening to success. There is a mad intoxication in his joy – and intensity in his savage delight that is scarcely less terrible than his rage . . . occasionally, however, we have touches of humanity gleaming athwart the dark picture, which was elicited with great effect by Mr. Aldridge. The remembrance of his father's death and his country's wrongs, and his own degradation, which had burned into his heart, is obliterated when he holds his enemy at his feet, and the late remorse of a noble heart was expressed with deep feeling.[52]

Aldridge seems to have succeeded in bringing out the Moor's humanity despite his palpable and melodramatic villainy.

But by the 1850s the popular appetite for Young's kind of tragedy had faded. London's theatres increasingly catered to the tastes of a growing urban population with burlettas and melodramas, and the African Roscius had to find new roles.[53] Shakespeare, to be sure, continued as a mainstay. Aldridge repeatedly performed Othello and, in addition, branched out to Lear (in whiteface) and Shylock. But the harbinger of future taste in entertainment was Aldridge's spectacularly successful Mungo, the Uncle Tom-like house slave in Isaac Bickerstaff's *The Padlock*. Reviewers repeatedly praised Aldridge in this role; one reports that he "is exceedingly funny. You see the veritable nigger, whose good nature, humour, and even wit, are so commonly ridiculed. As Mungo he is very amusing, giving way to his absurdity with all the zest of one of his colour. Mr. Aldridge sings, too, and his 'Opossum Up a Gum Tree' is one of the funniest things that can be imagined."[54] However dignified Aldridge's representation, Mungo pointed the way to what the working-class audiences of the late nineteenth century wanted, the humorous, singing "nigger" of the minstrel shows.

---

[52] Quoted from Marshall and Stock, *Ira Aldridge*, pp. 162–64.

[53] Marshall and Stock suggest this on p. 169. See also Joseph Donohue, *Theatre in the Age of Kean* (Totowa, NJ: Rowman and Littlefield, 1975), pp. 92–102, for a discussion of changing theatrical tastes.

[54] Marshall and Stock, *Ira Aldridge*, pp. 165–69.

CHAPTER 10

Afterthoughts

Until Ira Aldridge, the actors who impersonated black Moors on English stages were Europeans wearing black make-up. Their words and gestures say nothing about people of sub-Saharan ancestry, but they reveal much about European self-fashioning. Imagining the black Moor contributed to the white audience's own imagined communities[1] and to the dissemination of its social and cultural values. Moving from the middle ages to the early nineteenth century, I have tried to show how these performances contributed to the construction of the audience's identification of itself as white in opposition to others who were color-coded black. Impersonation is, of course, never static; it changes from performance to performance as audience dynamics, playing spaces, and cultural attitudes change. And by repetition impersonation builds on what has gone before, its reiterations and variations adding layers of meaning to the performance's signification with each new reenactment. Over time, such repetitions create what Judith Butler calls the "appearance of substance," the sense of "a natural sort of being."[2] From play to play, for example, characters allude to the proverb that Moors cannot blush, but with each repetition, new resonances are added, new meanings found, and over time, the truism that the black Moor cannot blush is accepted as a natural fact. From devil to slave to avenging villain to pathetic hero, the black Moor imagined by English audiences from the sixteenth to the nineteenth centuries accrued layers of signification that contributed, through the medium of popular entertainment, to the racial attitudes of the twentieth century.

Blackface roles from the late seventeenth and eighteenth centuries also demonstrate the pervasiveness of *Othello*'s influence on white imaginations.

---

[1] This widely circulated term was coined by Benedict Anderson in his study of the rise of nationalism, but it seems apropos here. See *Imagined Communities: Reflections on the Origin and Spread of Nationalism*, rev. edn. (London: Verso, 1991).

[2] Judith Butler, *Gender Trouble: Feminism and the Subversion of Identity*, 2nd edn. (New York: Routledge, 1999), p. 44.

By the beginning of the nineteenth century, non-Shakespearean tragedies had "Othellofied" their blackface characters in plots palpably reminiscent of Shakespeare's tragedy. When Ira Aldridge appeared in European productions of *Othello*, the racial composition of the cast and the plot of Shakespeare's tragedy had become well known to popular audiences. Nineteenth-century travesties of *Othello* also attest to widespread familiarity with the play's basic features even among lowbrow audiences. The history of Shakespeare's text is imbricated, as I have shown elsewhere,[3] in the history of English and American racial attitudes. In fact, more than any other Shakespearean drama, *Othello* is weighed down by cultural baggage. *Othello* is, consequently, a special case; a drama that has often been adopted by people of color throughout the world, it is more than the words that appear in the early seventeenth-century quarto and folio texts. Thus, at the risk of repeating myself, I want to return to it.

Contemporary audiences view *Othello* as a major work of Western literature, and the text is often used in classrooms as a touchstone for discussions of race relations. Even though my preference – as explained in chapter six – is for a white actor to take Othello's part, it is no longer acceptable for a white actor to portray a lead role – perhaps any role – in blackface. Ian McKellen explained in 1986: "every modern, white actor, taking on Othello, feels obliged to explain why he's not playing him black, which was surely Shakespeare's intention, when the unspoken reason is that to 'blackup' is as disgusting these days as a 'nigger minstrel show.'"[4] The Shakespeare Theatre in Washington DC tried to get around this widely shared sentiment in 1997 by casting a "photo-negative" *Othello*, with the Moor impersonated by the white actor Patrick Stewart and the rest of the cast by black actors. The experiment had mixed success, partly because Stewart's "star" power and his mastery of Shakespearean verse turned the play upside down. "Although it seemed to be shaking up racial stereotypes," concludes Lois Potter, "the visual coding of intellectual difference had been reversed only for the characters, not the actors: the white Othello was lean, cerebral and humorous, while the black Iago was heavy-set, obsessed with rules and a wife-abuser."[5] The production was symptomatic of the problems contemporary productions and adaptations of *Othello* face. Consumed largely by white audiences who are often unaware of their own privileged racial position, productions of *Othello* can reify racial stereotypes. When the role of

---

[3] See my *Othello: A Contextual History* (Cambridge: Cambridge University Press, 1994).
[4] Quoted in Lois Potter, *Othello*, Shakespeare in Performance Series (Manchester: Manchester University Press, 2002), p. 153.
[5] Potter, *Othello*, pp. 183–84.

Othello is restricted to black actors – and I think the critical reaction to Ira Aldridge's Othello reflects this – his characteristics become *essentialized*, as if he acts as he does simply because he is black.

There is, I believe, some danger in keeping Othello – and other roles described in this book such as Aaron and Oroonoko – restricted to actors of color. Celia Daileader has shown how "Othellophilia" – imposing the black male/white female pattern of Shakespeare's original onto other texts through casting decisions – "with its attendant opportunities for something approaching biracial porn, functions to exploit both white women *and* black men."[6] Fear of casting that is politically incorrect, in sum, may reinforce racial stereotypes that circulate so freely in contemporary life.

One may well ask, then what roles should black actors play? The well-publicized debate between Robert Brustein, who served for many years as the director of the American Repertory Theatre in Cambridge, Massachusetts, and award-winning playwright August Wilson on 27 January 1997 demonstrated that intelligent and progressive people can disagree vehemently on casting issues. Brustein has long been an advocate of color-blind casting, the practice of assigning actors to roles without regard to race. To Wilson, "Colorblind casting is an aberrant idea that has never had any validity other than as a tool of the Cultural Imperialists who view American culture, rooted in the icons of European culture, as beyond reproach in its perfection." Black actors, according to Wilson, should participate in a black theatre, perform in black plays, and express the black experience.[7]

To deny actors of African descent the opportunity of performing Shakespeare – the dramatist who dominates regional festivals throughout the United States, not to mention the Royal Shakespeare Company and other major theatres in England – is to deny them rewarding artistic and economic advancement. And surely there is room for multi-racial casting in Shakespeare. Kenneth Branagh's choice of Denzel Washington to play Don Pedro in his film of *Much Ado About Nothing* shows that having a major role – not just that of a servant or a subaltern – performed by a black actor does not detract from the drama's overall effect. White American audiences were probably more struck by Washington's star status than his race, but even if they noticed his blackness, what may have seemed strange in the opening scene soon became familiar. Hugh Quarshie's fiery Tybalt in the Royal Shakespeare Company's 1986 production of *Romeo and Juliet* lit up

[6] Celia R. Daileader, "Casting Black Actors: Beyond Othellophilia," in *Shakespeare and Race*, ed. Catherine M. S. Alexander and Stanley Wells (Cambridge: Cambridge University Press, 2000), pp. 177–202; quote from p. 179.
[7] August Wilson, "The Ground," *American Theatre* (September 1996), 72. See also Stephen Nunns, "Wilson, Brustein and the Press," *American Theatre* (March 1997).

the stage. Ray Fearon's 2002 appearance as Pericles in the RSC production was also particularly effective in a play whose hero travels throughout the Mediterranean and engages in a variety of international and intercultural exchanges.

Fearon's Bracciano in the RSC's 1996 production of John Webster's *The White Devil* is more troublesome, because the presence of a black actor in a role that was originally envisioned as white diminishes the tragedy's exploration of race in the roles of Zanche and Francisco/Mulinassar (discussed in chapter seven). Plays that focus on race per se are based on the assumption that the non-Moorish characters will be white. Casting a black actor in a role usually reserved for whites is not necessarily a bad decision, but it has repercussions. We do not live in a race neutral environment, alas, and when we attend the theatre we bring our racial attitudes and, perhaps more important, our color *perceptions* with us. The selection of a black woman as Bianca in Oliver Parker's 1995 *Othello*, for example, affected other aspects of the play. Othello was no longer the only black person on Cyprus, and Bianca's blackness and her sexual behavior were made to seem connected. When a Moor appeared on the early modern stage, the impersonation was a deliberate decision on the dramatist's part. Mixing up the casting in these plays can change their impact.

Some would argue that such changes are for the good, that audiences should be shielded from language and actions that most would now consider racist. The National Asian American Telecommunications Association (NAATA), for example, recently intervened to prevent Fox Television from screening *Charlie Chan's Mystery Tour*, a retrospective of films from the 1930s. They argued that Charlie Chan is both "demeaning" and "culturally inaccurate." The detective was portrayed by white actors in "yellow-face," while the films also featured Asian actors as Chan's children. But as Chris Fujiwara contends in the *Boston Globe*, although Charlie had a strong accent, he was portrayed as "diligent, intelligent, benevolent, and moral." To be sure, the Chan films were produced in a racist culture. Fujiwara notes that the studios were afraid that audiences would not come to see an Asian actor in the title role; indeed, the "popularity of the series may have depended on white audiences' awareness that the actor playing Chan was Caucasian." The white audience needed to know the actor was white because the films showed that Charlie Chan is better and smarter than the films' white characters.[8]

---

[8] Chris Fujiwara, "Charlie Chan and the Case of the Cancelled Film Festival," *Boston Globe*, 13 July 2003.

If the Charlie Chan films are presented as pure entertainment, NAATA might have a point, although few film audiences would confuse the fiction with the reality of life in the 1930s. Presented within their cultural context, however, the films can teach us about the production and dissemination of racial stereotypes in a popular media during an earlier period. We will not overcome twenty-first century racism if we do not understand how it permeated the lives of our forebears. And what is true of "yellowface" films in the 1930s is true of blackface performances in early modern England.

The reconstructed Globe Theatre on Bankside is an experimental theatre that, in selected productions, attempts to approximate the playing conditions of Shakespeare's own time. There were, of course, no noisy airplanes overhead or bathroom facilities at the original Globe, and we can never fully recuperate the original theatrical experience. At the same time, all-male productions of *Antony and Cleopatra* and *Twelfth Night* at the reconstructed Globe have shown how erotically charged cross-gender casting can be. Could we not have an experimental *Lust's Dominion* or *Oroonoko* that demonstrates blackface performance at work? Would the resulting impersonations be seen simply as derogatory racial slurs? Or would some other qualities – dignity and courage, perhaps – capture the audience's attention? Because the dynamics of performance are so volatile, so subject to changes in time, mood, and place, we can not pre-judge such a production. The risk, it seems to me, is worth taking. In a spirit of inquiry, the Globe, the reconstructed Blackfriars in Staunton, Virginia, and other experimental theatres should consider offering selected blackface performances, perhaps of some of the plays discussed in this book. If we can bring back flexibility to productions, particularly of non-canonical plays, we can imagine more clearly what they were like and how they contributed to early modern English self-construction.

Spike Lee's dismay at the negative critical reaction to *Bamboozled* suggests that even a gifted African-American director can not "play" with race and satirize its dynamics with impunity. But like Mantan, we're in a new millennium. Perhaps someday *Othello* and the other, lesser known blackface roles discussed here will be obsolete museum pieces, and their racial and gender dynamics will no longer move audiences because those dynamics have no connection to the audiences' experiences. Understanding the past, as I have tried to do here, may be a small step toward that millennial goal.

Bibliography

Aasand, Hardin, "'To Blanch an Ethiop, and Revive a Corse.' Queen Anne and *The Masque of Blackness*," *Studies in English Literature* 32 (1992): 271–85

Anderson, Benedict, *Imagined Communities: Reflections on the Origin and Spread of Nationalism*, rev. edn. (London: Verso, 1991).

Andrea, Bernadette, "Black Skin, the Queen's Masques: African Ambivalence and Feminine Author(ity) in the Masques of *Blackness* and *Beauty*," *English Literary Renaissance* 29 (1999): 246–81.

Appiah, Anthony, "Race," in *Critical Terms for Literary Study*, ed. Frank Lentricchia and Thomas McLaughlin (Chicago: University of Chicago Press, 1990), pp. 274–87.

Baker, David, *Biographica Dramatica*, vol. III (London, 1812).

Baker, Robert, "The First Voyage of Robert Baker to Gunie" and "The Second Voyage to Gunie," in *The Principall Navigations, Voiages, and Discoveries of the English Nation*, by Richard Hakluyt (London, 1589).

Bale, John, *King Johan*, ed. Barry B. Adams (San Marino: Huntington Library, 1969).

Bandello, Matteo, *The Novels of Matteo Bandello Bishop of Agen Now First Done into English Prose and Verse*, 6 vols. (London: Villon Society, 1890), vol. v.

Banton, Michael, *Racial Theories*, 2nd edn. (Cambridge: Cambridge University Press, 1998).

Barbour, Richmond, "Britain and the Great Beyond: *The Masque of Blackness* at Whitehall," in *Playing the Globe: Genre and Geography in English Renaissance Drama*, ed. John Gillies and Virginia Mason Vaughan (Madison: Fairleigh Dickinson University Press, 1998), pp. 129–53.

Barroll, Leeds, *Anna of Denmark, Queen of England* (Ithaca: Cornell University Press, 2001).

Barthelemy, Anthony Gerard, *Black Face, Maligned Race: The Representation of Blacks in English Drama from Shakespeare to Southerne* (Baton Rouge: Louisiana State University Press, 1987).

Bate, Jonathan, ed., *Titus Andronicus*, by William Shakespeare, Third Arden Series (London: Routledge, 1995).

Beaumont, Francis, and John Fletcher, *Four Plays or Moral Representations in One*, in *The Works of Francis Beaumont and John Fletcher*, ed. A. R. Waller, vol. x (Cambridge: Cambridge University Press, 1912).

Behn, Aphra, *Abdelazer*, in *The Works of Aphra Behn*, ed. Janet Todd, vol. v (Columbus: Ohio State University Press, 1996).

Bentley, G. E., *The Jacobean and Caroline Stage*, 7 vols. (Oxford: Clarendon Press, 1941–68).

Berkeley, William, *The Lost Lady: A Tragy Comedy* (London: John Oakes, 1638).

  The Lost Lady: A Tragy Comedy, ed. John Pitcher, Malone Society edition (Oxford: Oxford University Press, 1987).

Bernard, John, *Retrospections of the Stage*, 2 vols. (London: Henry Colburn and Richard Bentley, 1830), vol. i.

Berry, Herbert, "The Date on the 'Peacham' Manuscript," *Shakespeare Bulletin* 17 (Spring 1999): 5–6.

Best, George, *True Discourse of the Late Voyages of Discoverie*, in *The Principal Navigations, Voyages, Traffiques and Discoveries of the English Nation*, by Richard Hakluyt, vol. vii (Glasgow: James MacLehose and Sons, 1904).

Blackburn, Robin, *The Making of New World Slavery* (London: Verso, 1997).

Bland, Sheila Rose, "How I Would Direct *Othello*," in *Othello: New Essays by Black Writers*, ed. Mythili Kaul (Washington DC: Howard University Press, 1997), pp. 29–41.

Block, K. S., ed., *Ludus Coventriae, or The Plaie called Corpus Christi* (London: Early English Text Society, 1922).

Boaden, James, *Memoirs of the Life of John Philip Kemble, Esq*, 2 vols. (London: Longman, 1825), vol. i.

Boose, Lynda E, "'The Getting of a Lawful Race': Racial Discourse in Early Modern England and the Unrepresentable Black Woman," in *Women, "Race," and Writing in the Early Modern Period*, ed. Margo Hendricks and Patricia Parker (London: Routledge, 1994), pp. 35–54.

Bowden, William P., "The Bed Trick, 1603–1642: Its Mechanics, Ethics, and Effects," *Shakespeare Studies* 5 (1969): 112–23.

Braunmuller, A. R., *George Peele* (Boston: Twayne, 1983).

Bristol, Michael D., "Charivari and the Comedy of Abjection in *Othello*," *Renaissance Drama* 21 (1990): 3–21.

Brome, Richard, *Five New Playes* (London, 1653).

  The English Moor, or the Mock-Marriage (London, 1658).

  Five New Playes viz The English Moor, or the Mock-Marriage (London: A. Crook and H. Brome, 1659).

  Five New Playes viz The English Moor, or The Mock-Marriage, ed. Sara Jayne Steen (Columbia, MO: University of Missouri Press, 1983).

Brown, Horatio F., ed., *Calendar of State Papers Venetian*, vol. x (London, 1900).

Bullough, Geoffrey, *Narrative and Dramatic Sources of Shakespeare's Plays*, vol. vi (London: Routledge and Kegan Paul, 1966).

Butler, Judith, *Bodies That Matter: On the Discursive Limits of "Sex"* (New York: Routledge, 1993).

  Gender Trouble: Feminism and the Subversion of Identity, 2nd edn. (New York: Routledge, 1999).

Callaghan, Dympna, "'Othello Was a White Man': Properties of Race on Shakespeare's Stage," in *Alternative Shakespeares 2*, ed. Terence Hawkes (London: Routledge, 1996), 192–213.

Shakespeare Without Women: Representing Gender and Race on the Renaissance Stage (London: Routledge, 2000).

Campion, Thomas, *The Discription of a Maske in Honour of the Lord Hayes* (London, 1607).

Maske Presented in the Banqueting Room at Whitehall (London, 1614).

Canfield, Douglas J., *Heroes and States: On the Ideology of Restoration Tragedy* (Lexington: University Press of Kentucky, 1999).

Carlisle, Carol Jones, *Shakespeare from the Greenroom: Actors' Criticism of Four Major Tragedies* (Chapel Hill: University of North Carolina Press, 1969).

Chambers, E. K., *The Medieval Stage* (Oxford: Clarendon Press, 1903).

The English Folk-Play (Oxford: Clarendon Press, 1933).

The Elizabethan Stage, 4 vols. (Oxford: Clarendon Press, 1923), vol. II.

George Chapman, *The Blind Beggar of Alexandria*, ed. W. W. Greg, Malone Society Reprint Series (Oxford: Oxford University Press, 1928).

Cibber, Colley, *The History of the Stage* (London: J. Miller, 1742).

Clark, Robert L. A., and Claire Sponsler, "Othered Bodies: Racial Cross-Dressing in the *Mistere de la Sainte Hostie* and the Croxton *Play of the Sacrament*," *Journal of Medieval and Early Modern Studies* 29 (1999): 61–87.

Coleman, James, *Fifty Years of an Actor's Life* (New York: James Pott, 1904).

Cottrell, John, *Laurence Olivier* (Englewood Cliffs, NJ: Prentice Hall, 1975).

Cox, John D., *The Devil and the Sacred in English Drama, 1350–1642* (Cambridge: Cambridge University Press, 2000).

Cunliffe, John W., ed., *Early English Classical Tragedies* (Oxford: Clarendon Press, 1912).

Cushman, L. W., *The Devil and the Vice in the English Dramatic Literature Before Shakespeare* (Halle: Max Niemeyer, 1900).

Daileader, Celia R., "Casting Black Actors: Beyond Othellophilia," in *Shakespeare and Race*, ed. Catherine M. S. Alexander and Stanley Wells (Cambridge: Cambridge University Press, 2000), pp. 177–202.

D'Amico, Jack, *The Moor in English Renaissance Drama* (Tampa: University of South Florida Press, 1991).

Dasent, John Roche, ed., *Acts of the Privy Council of England*, vol. XXVI (London: Mackie and Co., 1902).

Dekker, Thomas, *Lust's Dominion*, in *The Dramatic Works of Thomas Dekker*, ed. Fredson Bowers, 4 vols. (Cambridge: Cambridge University Press, 1961), vol. IV.

Deimling, Hermann, ed., *The Chester Plays* (Oxford: Early English Text Society, 1892).

Desens, Marliss C., *The Bed-Trick in English Renaissance Drama: Explorations in Gender, Sexuality, and Power* (Newark: University of Delaware Press, 1994).

DeVisse, Jean and Michel Mollat, *The Image of the Black in Western Art, II: From the Early Christian Era to the 'Age of Discovery,'* Part 2: *Africans in the Christian*

Ordinance of the World (Fourteenth to the Sixteenth Century) (Cambridge: Harvard University Press, 1979).

Dickens, Charles, *Nicholas Nickleby* (New York: Books, Inc., n.d.).

Doniger, Wendy, *The Bedtrick: Tales of Sex and Masquerade* (Chicago: University of Chicago Press, 2000).

Donohue, Joseph, *Theatre in the Age of Kean* (Totowa, NJ: Rowman and Littlefield, 1975).

Drew-Bear, Annette, *Painted Faces on the Renaissance Stage: The Moral Significance of Face-Painting Conventions* (Lewisburg: Bucknell University Press, 1994).

Eden Richard, and Richard Willes, *The History of Travayle in the West and East Indies* (London, 1577).

Elam, Keir, *The Semiotics of Theatre and Drama* (London: Routledge, 1980).

Elliott, John R., Jr., "*Mr. Moore's Revels*: A 'Lost' Oxford Masque," *Renaissance Quarterly* 37 (1989): 411–20.

An Epistle to Henry Mossop, Esq; on the Institution and End of the Drama and the Present State of the Irish Stage (Dublin, 1750).

Erickson, Peter, "Representations of Blacks and Blackness in the Renaissance," *Criticism* 35 (1993): 499–527.

Ferguson, Margaret, "Juggling the Categories of Race, Class and Gender: Aphra Behn's *Oroonoko*," in *Women, "Race," and Writing in the Early Modern Period*, ed. Margo Hendricks and Patricia Parker (London: Routledge, 1994), pp. 209–24.

Ferriar, John, *The Prince of Angola, a Tragedy, Altered from the Play of Oroonoko and Adapted to the Circumstances of the Present Times* (Manchester: J. Harrop, 1788).

Feuillerat, Albert, ed., *Documents Relating to the Office of the Revels in the Time of Queen Elizabeth* (Louvain, 1908).

  Documents Relating to the Revels at Court in the Time of King Edward VI and Queen Mary (Louvain, 1914).

Fletcher, John, *A Critical Edition of John Fletcher's Comedy Monsieur Thomas or Father's Own Son*, ed. Nanette Cleri Clinch (New York: Garland, 1987).

Fletcher, John, and Philip Massinger, *Parliament of Love*, in *The Plays and Poems of Philip Massinger*, ed. Philip Edwards and Colin Gibson, 5 vols. (Oxford: Clarendon Press, 1976), vol. II.

Floyd-Wilson, Mary, "Temperature, Temperance, and Racial Difference in Ben Jonson's *The Masque of Blackness*," *English Literary Renaissance* 28 (1998): 183–209.

  English Ethnicity and Race in Early Modern Drama (Cambridge: Cambridge University Press, 2003).

Forbes, Curdella, "Shakespeare, Other Shakespeares and West Indian Popular Culture: A Reading of the Eroticized Errantry and Rebellion in *Troilus and Cressida*," *Small Axe* 9 (2001): 44–69.

Ford, John R., "'Words and Performances': Roderigo and the Mixed Dramaturgy of Race and Gender in *Othello*," in *Othello: New Critical Essays*, ed. Philip C. Kolin (New York and London: Routledge, 2002), pp. 147–67.

Forrest, John, *The History of Morris Dancing, 1458–1750* (Toronto: University of Toronto Press, 1999).

Fradenburg, Louise Olga, *City, Marriage, Tournament: Arts of Rule in Late Medieval Scotland* (Madison: University of Wisconsin Press, 1991).

Fredrickson, George M., *The Black Image in the White Mind* (Middletown, CT: Wesleyan University Press, 1987).

Fryer, Peter, *Staying Power: The History of Black People in Britain* (London: Pluto Press, 1984).

Fujiwara, Chris, "Charlie Chan and the Case of the Cancelled Film Festival," *Boston Globe*, 13 July 2003.

Furness, H. H., ed., *A New Variorium Edition of Othello* (Philadelphia: J. B. Lippincott, 1886).

Genest, John, *Some Account of the English Stage from the Restoration in 1660 to 1830* vol. 1 (Bath: H. E. Carrington, 1832).

Geneva Bible: A Facsimile of the 1560 Edition (Madison: University of Wisconsin Press, 1969).

Gentleman, Francis, *The Dramatic Censor, or Critical Companion*, 2 vols. (London: J. Bell, 1770).

Gentleman's Magazine 19 (1749): 89–90.

Gerzina, Gretchen, *Black London: Life Before Emancipation* (New Brunswick, NJ: Rutgers University Press, 1995).

Godwyn, Morgan, *The Negro's and Indians Advocate, Suing for their Admission into the Church* (London, 1680).

Goldberg, David Theo, *Racist Culture: Philosophy and the Politics of Meaning* (Oxford: Blackwell, 1993).

Golden, Frederick, trans., *The Song of Roland* (New York: Norton, 1978).

Gossett, Suzanne, "'Best Men Are Molded Out of Faults': Marrying the Rapist in Jacobean Drama," *English Literary Renaissance* 14 (1984): 305–27.

"The Great Sir Laurence," *Life*, 1 May 1964.

Gubar, Susan, *Racechanges: White Skin, Black Face in American Culture* (Oxford and New York: Oxford University Press, 1997).

Guilfoyle, Cherrell, "Othello, Otuel, and the English Charlemagne Romances," *Review of English Studies* n.s. 38 (1987): 50–55.

Gurr, Andrew, *Playgoing in Shakespeare's London*, 2nd edn. (Cambridge: Cambridge University Press, 1996).

Hakluyt, Richard, *The Principal Navigations, Voyages, Traffiques and Discoveries of the English Nation*, 12 vols. (Glasgow: James MacLehose and Sons, 1903–05), vol. 7.

Hall, Edward, *Henry VIII*, ed. Charles Whibley, 2 vols. (London: T. C. and E. C. Jack, 1904), vol. 1.

Hall, Kim F., *Things of Darkness: Economies of Race and Gender in Early Modern England* (Ithaca: Cornell University Press, 1995).

"'Troubling Doubles': Apes, Africans and Blackface in *Mr. Moore's Revels*," in *Race, Ethnicity, and Power in the Renaissance*, ed. Joyce Green MacDonald (Madison: Fairleigh Dickinson University Press, 1997), pp. 120–44.

Hankey, Julie, ed., *Othello, Plays in Performance* (Bristol: Bristol Classical Press, 1987).

Harbage, Alfred, *Cavalier Drama* (New York: Modern Language Association, 1936).

Harding, Samuel, *Sicily and Naples, or, the Fatall Vnion. A Tragoedy* (Oxford, 1640).

Harris, Bernard, "A Portrait of a Moor," *Shakespeare Survey* 11 (1958): 89–97.

Hawkins, F. W., *The Life of Edmund Kean*, vol. 1, (London: Tinsley Brothers, 1869).

Hazlitt, W. Carew, ed., *Pasquil's Jests, Mixed with Mother Bunches Merriments* (London, 1866).

Hazlitt, William, *Collected Works*, ed. A. R. Waller and Arnold Glover, 12 vols. (London: J. M. Dent, 1903).

Hemings, William, *The Fatal Contract, a French Tragedy* (London, 1653).

The Eunuch: A Tragedy (London: J.B., 1687).

Hendricks, Margo, and Patricia Parker, eds., *Women, "Race," and Writing in the Early Modern Period* (London: Routledge, 1994).

Herrtage, Sidney J. H., ed., *The English Charlemagne Romances, Part VI* (London: Early English Text Society, 1882).

Heywood, Thomas, *An Apology for Actors* (London, 1612).

The Fair Maid of the West, Parts I and II, ed. Robert K. Turner, Jr., Regents Renaissance Drama edition (Lincoln: University of Nebraska Press, 1967).

Highfill, Philip H., Jr., Kalman A. Burnim, and Edward A. Langhans eds, *Biographical Dictionary of Actors, Actresses, Musicians, Dancers, Managers and Other Stage Personnel in London: 1660–1800*, 16 vols. (Carbondale: Southern Illinois University Press, 1973–93).

Hillebrand, Harold Newcomb, *Edmund Kean* (New York: Columbia University Press, 1933).

Hilliard, Nicholas, *A Treatise Concerning the Arte of Limning*, edited by R. K. R. Thornton and T. G. S. Cain (Ashington: Mid Northumberland Arts Group, 1981).

Hirsch, Foster, *Laurence Olivier* (Boston: Twayne, 1979).

Hodgdon, Barbara, *The Shakespeare Trade: Performances and Appropriations* (Philadephia: University of Pennsylvania Press, 1998).

Holden, Anthony, *Laurence Olivier* (New York: Atheneum, 1988).

Holme, Randle, *Academy of Armory*. London, 1688, facs. reprint (Scolar Press: Menston, 1972).

Honigmann, E. A. J., ed., *Othello*, by William Shakespeare, Third Arden Series (London: Arden Shakespeare, 1997).

Hornback, Robert, "Emblems of Folly in the First *Othello*: Renaissance Blackface, Moor's Coat, and 'Muckender,'" *Comparative Drama* 35 (2001): 69–99.

Horstmann, C., ed., *The Lives of Women Saints of our Contrie of England* (London: Early English Text Society, 1886).

The Three Kings of Cologne: An Early English Translation of the Historia Trium Regium (London: Early English Text Society, 1886).

Howard, Jean E., "An English Lass Amid the Moors: Gender, Race, Sexuality, and National Identity in Heywood's *The Fair Maid of the West*," In *Women,*

"Race," and Writing in the Early Modern Period, ed. Margo Hendricks and Patricia Parker (London: Routledge, 1994), pp. 101–17.

Hoy, Cyrus, *The Dramatic Works of Thomas Dekker*, 4 vols. (Cambridge: Cambridge University Press, 1980), vol. IV.

Hughes, Derek, *English Drama, 1660–1700* (Oxford: Clarendon, 1996).

The Theatre of Aphra Behn (London: Palgrave, 2001).

Hughes, Paul L., and James F. Larkin, eds., *Tudor Royal Proclamations*, vol. III (New Haven and London: Yale University Press, 1969).

Hume, Robert D., *The Development of English Drama in the Late Seventeenth Century* (Oxford: Clarendon Press, 1976).

Hunt, Leigh, *Critical Essays on the Performers of the London Theatres* (London, 1807).

Inchbald, Elizabeth, ed., *The British Theatre, or A Collection of Plays*, 25 vols. (London: Longman, ca. 1825), vol. XII.

Ingram, R. W., ed., *Records of Early English Drama, Coventry* (Toronto: University of Toronto Press, 1981).

Iyengar, Sujata, *Shades of Difference: Mythologies of Skin Color in Early Modern England* (Philadelphia: University of Pennsylvania Press, 2004).

Jones, Eldred D., *Othello's Countrymen: The African in English Renaissance Drama* (London: Oxford University Press, 1965).

Jonson, Ben, *The Works of Ben Jonson* (London, 1616).

The Complete Works of Ben Jonson, ed. C. H. Herford and Percy Simpson, 11 vols. (Oxford: Clarendon Press, 1925–52).

The Gypsies Metamorphosed, ed. George Watson Cole (New York: Modern Language Association, 1931).

Jordan, Winthrop D., *White Over Black: American Attitudes Toward the Negro, 1550–1812* (Chapel Hill: University of North Carolina Press), 1968.

Kwei-Armah, Kwame, "My Problem with the Moor," *Guardian*, 7 April 2004, G2.

Kyd, Thomas, *The Spanish Tragedy*, Malone Society Reprint (Oxford: Oxford University Press, 1949).

Langbaine, Gerard, *An Account of the English Dramatick Poets* (London, 1691).

Lawner, Lynne, *Harlequin on the Moon: Commedia dell'Arte and the Visual Arts* (New York: Harry N. Abrams, 1998).

Lea, K. M., *Italian Popular Comedy: A Study in the Commedia dell'Arte, 1560–1620*, 2 vols (Oxford: Clarendon Press, 1934).

Levin, Richard, "The Longleat Manuscript and *Titus Andronicus*," *Shakespeare Quarterly* 53 (2002): 323–40.

Ligon, Richard, *A True and Exact History of the Island of Barbados* (London, 1657).

Linton, Joan Pong, *The Romance of the New World* (Cambridge: Cambridge University Press, 1998).

Little, Arthur L., Jr., *Shakespeare Jungle Fever: National-Imperial Re-Visions of Race, Rape, and Sacrifice* (Stanford: Stanford University Press, 2000).

Lodge, Thomas, *The Wounds of Civil War*, ed. Joseph W. Houppert (Lincoln: University of Nebraska Press, 1969).

Loomba, Ania, "'Delicious Traffick': Racial and Religious Difference on Early Modern Stages," in *Shakespeare and Race*, ed. Catherine M. S. Alexander and Stanley Wells (Cambridge: Cambridge University Press, 2000), pp. 203–24.

Shakespeare, Race, and Colonialism (Oxford: Oxford University Press, 2002).

Lott, Eric, *Love and Theft: Blackface Minstrelsy and the American Working Class* (New York: Oxford University Press, 1993).

Lupton, Thomas, *A Moral and Pitiefvl Comedie, Intituled, All for Money* (London, 1578).

MacDonald, Joyce Green, "'The Force of Imagination': The Subject of Blackness in Shakespeare, Jonson and Ravenscroft," in *Renaissance Papers 1991*, ed. George Walton Williams and Barbara J. Baines (Southeastern Durham, NC: Renaissance Conference, 1992), 53–74.

Women and Race in Early Modern Texts (Cambridge: Cambridge University Press, 2002).

Mahar, William J., *Behind the Cork Mask: Early Blackface Minstrelsy and Antebellum American Popular Culture* (Urbana: University of Illinois Press, 1999).

Mark, Peter, *Africans in European Eyes: The Portrayal of Black Africans in Fourteenth and Fifteenth Century Europe* (Syracuse: Maxwell School of Citizenship and Public Affairs, 1974).

Marks, Elise, "'Othello/Me': Racial Drag and the Pleasures of Boundary-Crossing with Othello," *Comparative Drama* 35 (2001): 101–24.

Marlowe, Christopher, *The Complete Plays of Christopher Marlowe*, ed. Irving Ribner (New York: Odyssey Press, 1963).

Marshall, Herbert, and Mildred Stock, *Ira Aldridge: The Negro Tragedian*, 2nd edn. (Washington, DC: Howard University Press, 1993).

Marston, John, *The Selected Plays of John Marston*, ed. Macdonald P. Jackson and Michael Neill (Cambridge: Cambridge University Press, 1986).

Massinger, Philip, *The Plays and Poems of Philip Massinger*, ed. Philip Edwards and Colin Gibson (Oxford: Clarendon Press, 1976).

Matteo, Gino J., *Shakespeare's "Othello": The Study and the Stage, 1604–1904* (Salzburg: Institut für Sprache und Literatur, 1974).

McDonald, Russ, *The Bedford Companion to Shakespeare*, 2nd edn. (Boston: Bedford Books of St. Martin's Press, 2001).

Middleton, Thomas, *The Triumph of Truth* (London, 1613).

Morris, Clara, *Confidences: Talks about Players and Play Acting* (London, 1902).

Morrison, Toni, *Playing in the Dark* (New York: Vintage Books, 1993).

Munday, Anthony, *Chruso-thriambos: The Triumphs of Gold* (London: Privately Printed, 1962).

Murray, Barbara A., *Restoring Shakespeare: Viewing the Voice* (Madison: Fairleigh Dickinson Press, 2001).

Nadelhaft, Jerome, "The Somersett Case and Slavery: Myth, Reality, and Repercussions," *Journal of Negro History* 51 (1966): 193–208.

Nashe, Thomas, *The Works of Thomas Nashe*, ed. Ronald B. McKerrow, vol. 1. (Oxford: Basil Blackwell, 1958).

Neill, Michael, "'Unproper Beds': Race, Adultery, and the Hideous in *Othello*," in
*Putting History to the Question: Power, Politics, and Society in English Renais-
sance Drama* (New York: Columbia University Press, 2000), pp. 237–68.

Newman, Karen, "'And wash the Ethiop white': Femininity and the Monstrous in
Othello," in *Shakespeare Re-Produced: The Text in History and Ideology*, ed. Jean
E. Howard and Marion F. O'Connor (New York: Methuen, 1987), 141–62.

Nolan, Michael, ed., *The Thracian Wonder, a Comical History* (Salzburg: Institut
für Anglistik und Amerikanistik, 1997).

Nunns, Stephen, "Wilson, Brustein and the Press," *American Theatre* (March 1997).

Orgel, Stephen, *Impersonations: The Performance of Gender in Shakespeare's England*
(Cambridge: Cambridge University Press, 1996).

Orr, Bridget, *The Empire on the English Stage, 1660–1714* (Cambridge: Cambridge
University Press, 2001).

Parker, George D, "The Moor's Progress: A Study of Edward Young's Tragedy, *The
Revenge*," *Theatre Research International* 6, no. 3 (1981): 172–95.

Pechter, Edward, *Othello and Interpretive Traditions* (Iowa City: University of Iowa
Press, 1999).

Peele, George, *King Edward the First*, ed. Horace Hart (Oxford: Oxford University
Press for the Malone Society, 1911).

The Battle of Alcazar, in *The Dramatic Works of George Peele*, ed. John Yoklavich,
vol. II (New Haven: Yale University Press, 1961).

Polemon, John, *The Second Part of the Booke of Battailes, Fought in Our Age* (London,
1587).

Potter, Lois, *Othello*, Shakespeare in Performance Series (Manchester: Manchester
University Press, 2002).

Quarshie, Hugh, *Second Thoughts about Othello*, Occasional Paper no. 7 (Chipping
Camden: International Shakespeare Association, 1999).

Ravenscroft, Edward, *Titus Andronicus, or the Rape of Lavinia* (London, 1686).

Rede, Leman Thomas, *The Road to the Stage* (London: J. Onwhyn, 1836).

Redford, John, *Wit and Science*, (1908), ed. Arthur Brown (Oxford: Oxford
University Press for the Malone Society, 1951).

Richards, Kenneth, and Laura Richards, *The Commedia dell'Arte: A Documentary
History* (Oxford: Basil Blackwell, 1990).

Robertson, Jean, and D. J. Gordon, eds., *A Calendar of Dramatic Records in the
Books of the Livery Companies of London, 1485–1640* (Oxford: Oxford University Press for the Malone Society, 1954).

Rosenberg, Marvin, *The Masks of Othello* (Berkeley: University of California Press,
1971).

Rosenthal, Laura J., "Owning *Oroonoko*: Behn, Southerne, and the Contingencies
of Property," *Renaissance Drama* 23 (1992): 24–58.

Rowley, William, *A Tragedy Called All's Lost by Lust* (London, 1633).

Royster, Francesca T., "The 'End of Race' and the Future of Early Modern Cultural
Studies," *Shakespeare Studies* 26 (1998): 59–69.

"White-limed Walls: Whiteness and Gothic Extremism in Shakespeare's *Titus
Andronicus*," *Shakespeare Quarterly* 51 (2000): 432–55.

Rudlin, John, *Commedia dell'Arte: An Actor's Handbook* (London: Routledge, 1994).

Rutter, Carol Chillington, ed., *Documents of the Rose Playhouse* (Manchester: Manchester University Press, 1984).

Sancho, Ignatius, *The Letters of Ignatius Sancho*, ed. Paul Edwards and Polly Rewt (Edinburgh: Edinburgh University Press, 1994).

Schaer, Frank, ed., *The Three Kings of Cologne* (Heidelberg: C. Winter, 2000).

Schlueter, June, "Rereading the Peacham Drawing," *Shakespeare Quarterly* 50 (1999): 171–84.

Scot, Reginald, *The Discoverie of Witchcraft* (London, 1585).

Serres, Jean de, *A General Inventorie of the History of France*, trans. Edward Grimeston (London, 1607).

Settle, Elkanah, *Love and Revenge: A Tragedy* (London: William Cademan, 1675).

Shakespeare, William, *Titus Andronicus*, ed. John Dover Wilson (Cambridge: Cambridge University Press, 1948).

   A Midsummer Night's Dream, ed. Harold F. Brooks Shakespeare, Second Arden Edition (London: Methuen, 1979).

   The Merchant of Venice, ed. M. M. Mahood (Cambridge: Cambridge University Press, 1987).

   The Norton Shakespeare, ed. Stephen Greenblatt et al. (New York: Norton, 1997).

   The Tempest, ed. Virginia Mason and Alden T. Vaughan, Third Arden Series (London: Thomson Learning, 2000).

Sharpe, Kevin, *The Personal Rule of Charles I* (New Haven: Yale University Press, 1992).

Siemon, James R., "'Nay, That's Not Next': *Othello*, V.ii in Performance, 1760–1900," *Shakespeare Quarterly* 37 (1986): 38–51.

Smith, Ian, "Those 'Slippery Customers': Rethinking Race in *Titus Andronicus*," *Journal of Theatre and Drama* 3 (1997): 45–58.

   "White Skin, Black Masks: Racial Cross-Dressing on the Early Modern Stage," *Renaissance Drama* ns. 32 (2003): 33–67.

Southerne, Thomas, *Oroonoko* (London, 1696).

   Oroonoko, ed. Maximillian E. Novak and David Stuart Rodes, Regents Restoration Drama Series (Lincoln: University of Nebraska Press, 1976).

Spencer, Hazelton, *Shakespeare Improved: The Restoration Versions in Quarto and on the Stage* (Cambridge: Harvard University Press, 1927).

Spencer, M. Lyle, *Corpus Christi Pageants in England* (New York: Baker and Taylor, 1911).

Spenser, Edmund, *The Faerie Queene*, ed. A. C. Hamilton (London: Longman, 1977).

Sponsler, Claire, "Outlaw Masculinities: Drag, Blackface, and Late Medieval Laboring-Class Festivities," in *Becoming Male in the Middle Ages*, ed. Jeffrey Jerome Cohen and Bonnie Wheeler (New York: Garland, 2000), pp. 321–47.

Sprague, Arthur Colby, *Shakespeare and the Actors: The Stage Business in His Plays (1660–1905)* (Cambridge: Harvard University Press, 1944).

The Stage, 2 (1815): 169–70.

Stallybrass, Peter, "Transvestism and the 'Body Beneath': Speculating on the Boy Actor," in *Erotic Politics: Desire on the Renaissance Stage*, ed. Susan Zimmerman (New York: Routledge, 1992), pp. 64–83.

Stone, George Winchester, et al., eds. *The London Stage, 1660–1800* (Carbondale: Southern Illinois University Press, 1962–72).

Streitberger, W. R., *Court Revels, 1485–1559* (Toronto: University of Toronto Press, 1994).

Sturdevant, Winifred, *The Misterio De Los Reyes Magos: Its Position in the Development of the Mediaeval Legend of the Three Kings* (Baltimore: The Johns Hopkins Press, 1927).

"The Sublime," *The Bedford Glossary of Critical and Literary Terms*. 2nd edn., ed. Ross Murfin and Supryia M. Ray (Boston: Bedford, 2003), pp. 467–68.

Sypher, Wylie, *Guinea's Captive Kings: British Anti-Slavery Literature of the Eighteenth Century* (Chapel Hill: University of North Carolina Press, 1942).

Taylor, Gary, *Buying Whiteness: Race, Culture and Identity from Columbus to Hip Hop* (New York: Palgrave, 2005).

Thomas, Susie, "'This Thing of Darkness I Acknowledge Mine': Aphra Behn's *Abdelazer, or The Moor's Revenge*," *Restoration* 22 (1998): 18–39.

Tilley, Morris Palmer, *A Dictionary of the Proverbs in England in the Sixteenth and Seventeenth Centuries* (Ann Arbor: University of Michigan Press, 1951).

Tokson, Elliot, H. *The Popular Image of the Black Man in English Drama, 1550–1688* (Boston: G. K. Hall, 1982).

Tryon, Thomas, *A Discourse in Way of Dialogue, Between an Ethiopean or Negro-Slave and a Christian* (London, 1684).

Tynan, Kenneth, *Othello: The National Theatre Production* (New York: Stein and Day, 1966).

Vaughan, Alden T., and Virginia Mason, "Before Othello: Elizabethan Representations of Sub-Saharan Africans," *William and Mary Quarterly*, 3rd series, 54 (1987): 19–44.

Vaughan, Virginia Mason, *Othello: A Contextual History* (Cambridge: Cambridge University Press, 1994).

"The Construction of Barbarism in *Titus Andronicus*," in *Race, Ethnicity, and Power in the Renaissance*, ed. Joyce Green MacDonald (Madison: Fairleigh Dickinson University Press, 1997), pp. 165–80.

"Race Mattered: *Othello* in Late Eighteenth-Century England," *Shakespeare Survey* 51 (1998): 57–66.

Webster, John, *The White Devil* (London, 1612).

The White Devil, ed. J. R. Mulryne (Lincoln: University of Nebraska Press, 1969).

The Devil's Law-Case, edited by Frances A. Shirley (Lincoln: University of Nebraska Press, 1972).

Webster, Margaret, *Shakespeare Without Tears* (1955, reprint, New York: Capricorn Books, 1975).

Whitney, Geoffrey, *A Choice of Emblems* (Leiden, 1586).

Wickham, Glynne, *Early English Stages, 1300–1660*, vol. III (London: Routledge and Kegan Paul, 1981).

Wilson, August, "The Ground," *American Theatre* (September 1996): 72.

Wood, Anthony à, *Athenae Oxonienses*, ed. Philip Bliss, vol. III (Hildesheim: Georg Olms, 1969).

Wright, Thomas, *The Passions of the Minde in Generall* (London, 1604).

Young, Edward, *The Revenge: A Tragedy* (London, 1721).

FILMS CITED

Burge, Stuart, dir., 1965, *Othello*, Warner Brothers.

Cukor, George, dir., 1948, *A Double Life*, Republic Pictures.

Lee, Spike, dir., 2000, *Bamboozled*, New Line Productions.

Nelson, Tim Blake, dir., 2001, *O*. Lions Gate Films.

Parker, Oliver, dir., 1995, *Othello*, Castle Rock Entertainment.

Sax, Geoffrey, dir., *Othello*, 2001, Granada.

Index